A SEASON OF *Singing*

HBI SERIES ON JEWISH WOMEN

Shulamit Reinharz, General Editor
Sylvia Barack Fishman, Associate Editor

The HBI Series on Jewish Women, created by the Hadassah-Brandeis Institute, publishes a wide range of books by and about Jewish women in diverse contexts and time periods. Of interest to scholars and the educated public, the HBI Series on Jewish Women fills major gaps in Jewish Studies and in Women and Gender Studies as well as their intersection.

The HBI Series on Jewish Women is supported by a generous gift from Dr. Laura S. Schor.

For the complete list of books that are available in this series, please see www.upne.com

Sarah M. Ross, *A Season of Singing: Creating Feminist Jewish Music in the United States*
Margalit Shilo, *Girls of Liberty: The Struggle for Suffrage in Mandatory Palestine*
Sylvia Barack Fishman, editor, *Love, Marriage, and Jewish Families: Paradoxes of a Social Revolution*
Cynthia Kaplan Shamash, *The Strangers We Became: Lessons in Exile from One of Iraq's Last Jews*
Marcia Falk, *The Days Between: Blessings, Poems, and Directions of the Heart for the Jewish High Holiday Season*
Inbar Raveh, *Feminist Rereadings of Rabbinic Literature*
Laura Silver, *The Book of Knish: In Search of the Jewish Soul Food*
Sharon R. Siegel, *A Jewish Ceremony for Newborn Girls: The Torah's Covenant Affirmed*
Laura S. Schor, *The Best School in Jerusalem: Annie Landau's School for Girls, 1900–1960*
Federica K. Clementi, *Holocaust Mothers and Daughters: Family, History, and Trauma*
Elana Maryles Sztokman and Chaya Rosenfeld Gorsetman, *Educating in the Divine Image: Gender Issues in Orthodox Jewish Day Schools*
Ilana Szobel, *A Poetics of Trauma: The Work of Dahlia Ravikovitch*
Susan M. Weiss and Netty C. Gross-Horowitz, *Marriage and Divorce in the Jewish State: Israel's Civil War*
Ronit Irshai, *Fertility and Jewish Law: Feminist Perspectives on Orthodox Responsa Literature*
Elana Maryles Sztokman, *The Men's Section: Orthodox Jewish Men in an Egalitarian World*
Sharon Faye Koren, *Forsaken: The Menstruant in Medieval Jewish Mysticism*

A SEASON OF *Singing*

Creating Feminist Jewish Music in the United States

SARAH M. ROSS

BRANDEIS UNIVERSITY PRESS
Waltham, Massachusetts

Brandeis University Press
An imprint of University Press of New England
www.upne.com

Manufactured in the United States of America
Typeset in Garamond Premier Pro by Westchester Publishing Services

This book was published through the generosity of the Laura S. Schor fund.

Library of Congress Cataloging-in-Publication Data

Names: Ross, Sarah M.
Title: A season of singing: creating feminist Jewish music in the United States / Sarah M. Ross.
Description: Waltham, Massachusetts : Brandeis University Press, [2016] | Series: HBI series on Jewish women | Includes bibliographical references and index.
Identifiers: LCCN 2016008178 (print) | LCCN 2016015771 (ebook) | ISBN 9781611689594 (cloth: alk. paper) | ISBN 9781611689600 (pbk.: alk. paper) | ISBN 9781611689617 (epub, mobi & pdf)
Subjects: LCSH: Jews—United States—Music—History and criticism | Feminist music—United States—History and criticism. | Women in Judaism—United States.
Classification: LCC ML3776 .R67 2016 (print) | LCC ML3776 (ebook) | DDC 782.42082/0973—dc23
LC record available at https://lccn.loc.gov/2016008178

5 4 3 2 1

CONTENTS

FOREWORD

A Season of Singing: Creating Feminist Jewish Music in the United States is the fifty-second volume in the HBI Series on Jewish Women and the first in the series to deal with music. That it is the first suggests that studies of Jews, gender, and music are few and far between, although music—particularly singing—is an important aspect of Jewish life all over the world, ranging from singing in summer camp to singing at the Friday night Shabbat table, and more.

As Sarah Ross informs us, from the 1960s and into the twenty-first century, a feminist Jewish music scene developed in the United States, specifically in the Conservative, Reform, Jewish Renewal, and Reconstructionist communities, but also in some Orthodox venues such as the synagogue Shira Hadasha (literally "a new song") in Jerusalem. She calls the individuals who led this music scene "singer-songwriters," meaning that they both composed and performed/led/taught their songs.

As Ross states correctly, feminist Jewish music is both a musical genre and a sociopolitical phenomenon, a model designed to change conventional ideas and open up new possibilities. We have seen peoples turn to participatory singing in many countries, including Cuba and South Africa, as a way of protesting against the status quo. Folk music promoting peace was an element in the American public's effort to end the Vietnam War. Folk music in Israel has focused on celebrating the land and escaping from the jaws of military defeat. Ross puts it this way: "Immediately accessible and emotionally compelling, music helps people forge a community . . . music has the potential to have a public voice and to imagine alternative ways of thinking."

But music is not only about change. In fact, feminist Jewish singer-songwriters strove to balance the preservation of Jewish tradition while advocating change. Perhaps that is why this music has been accepted enthusiastically in many circles and adopted to such an extent that some Jews think this music was "always there."

In Ross's introductory chapter, she accounts for the emergence of this music by exploring a wide variety of subjects including feminist theology (Judith Plaskow's writings, for example) and feminist writing about Judaism in general; the American counterculture; changes within the denominations; the Six-Day War; relations to African Americans; the havurah movement; the American folk music revival; and the embrace of a range of sexualities. Jewish women did more than challenge and revise Halakhah (religious law); rather, they attempted to make Judaism more spiritually enriching. Music played a large role in this move. Feminist Judaism also embraced ritual innovation, such as putting an orange on the seder plate, ordaining women as rabbis and cantors, tackling the Agunah problem (women's inability to obtain divorce from recalcitrant husbands), open prayer at the *kotel* (the Wailing Wall), and much more. New rituals created a need for new music to accompany them.

Jewish feminist singer-songwriters, according to Sarah Ross, were also inspired by emergent female folk singers such as Joan Baez, Holly Near, Mary Travers (of Peter, Paul and Mary), and others. As singer-songwriter Meg Christian defined women's music of the time, it is "music that honors women, that respects our strength, celebrates our lives, supports and validates us, and teaches us." Although Jewish women could be inspired by secular women's music, Jewish women had a special challenge stemming from the concept of *Kol Isha*, a rabbinic prohibition against women's voices being heard in public prayer. Even if this idea is irrelevant in non-Orthodox Jewish settings, it still creates a damper on women's vocal expression more generally.

Ross makes a special effort to balance the stories of such great individual singer-songwriters as Debbie Friedman and Rabbi Geela Rayzel Raphael with the story of these women as a group. Her work is very inclusive. In addition to the individual giants she analyzes, she discusses the thorny problems of publishing feminist Jewish music (no specifically feminist Jewish songbook has been published) and distributing the materials. She explores the relation between these singer-songwriters and the role of cantors. Ultimately, these singer-songwriters invented new sacred songs that recognized Jewish people such as women, gays, lesbians, and transgender people in order to create an egalitarian, inclusive community.

Given this enormous but underappreciated accomplishment and contribution to Jewish life, it is imperative that a book appear to explain its history and meaning. We are pleased to be able to present this book as a vital component of the HBI Series on Jewish Women and hope it will lead to many more related studies.

Shulamit Reinharz, PhD
Director, Hadassah-Brandeis Institute

PREFACE

Shiru ladonai shir chadash; shiru ladonai kol ha'aretz

("Sing unto the Lord a new song; sing unto the Lord, all the earth!")

—Psalm 96:1

There are passages in the Torah (for example, Psalms 27:6 and 98:4) that tell us to sing songs of praise and joy to the Lord and that also tell us (Psalm 96:1) that the whole earth, meaning all people, shall sing. While the Torah itself does not make any sexual differentiation between men and women who sing, the rabbis who later interpreted the *Tanach* (the Hebrew Bible) did, and so do some Jews today. Among hundreds of mitzvahs regulating Jewish life, the Talmudic dictum of *Kol Isha* (a woman's voice), which was originally a rule that prohibited men from listening to women's voices (as doing so was deemed to be sexually exciting), best indicates how the call for all people to sing unto the Lord has been turned into an injunction for only men to sing. Within Orthodox communities, Kol Isha now refers to women's exclusion from vocal participation in the synagogue or public Jewish worship in general, which profoundly affected Jewish women's religious lives and their possibilities for music making in religious and spiritual contexts.

The first time I fully experienced the effects of Kol Isha was during a stay in Jerusalem in September 2003. On a Friday night, I went to the *kotel* (the Wailing Wall) to attend *Kabbalat Shabbat*, the Friday night prayer service receiving the Sabbath. Some of my male friends had told me that this is one of the most magnificent experiences one can have in Jerusalem. Determined not to miss it, I went to the kotel shortly before sundown, which marks the beginning of the Sabbath. I was surprised by the small number of people that I met there, but suddenly I heard singing from afar. It became louder and louder the nearer it got. By sunset, hundreds of men, most of them yeshiva students, had poured from the stairs to the kotel, singing joyful songs and dancing. I knew that I was expected to stay in the women's section, which is divided from the men's by the *mekhitzah* (a high fence separating the two sections), and to remain quiet. Incredibly impressed by what I saw and heard, I had to force myself not to sing and dance along with the men. After a while, I looked at the other women praying at the kotel. Some of them seemed unimpressed by what was going on right next to us and continued to pray silently, but others seemed to have the same longings as I did. For several days, I kept asking myself where and what are the women singing? Soon afterward, in a small Judaica bookstore on King George Street in Jerusalem, I found the answer in Susan Berrin's *Celebrating the New Moon* (1996), which had some women's music printed in the appendix. My friends had been right: that Friday evening in Jerusalem had been a crucial experience, one that directly led me to the study of Jewish women's feminist music. After I conducted fieldwork in 2003–4 in a Jewish women's *Rosh Hodesh* (a feminist new moon ritual) group in Utrecht, the Netherlands, I realized that more music had been written by American feminist Jews but not yet studied in detail.

The present study must therefore be understood as a continuation of my preliminary examination of Jewish women's songs in the Rosh Hodesh ritual (Ross 2004). While that earlier work was focused on the function and meaning of feminist-informed songs performed in a well-defined ritual context, the present study seeks primarily to give an ethnographic description of the people creating feminist Jewish music in the United States. Throughout my research in 2003 and 2004, it became apparent that the repertoire of feminist Jewish music thematically overreached the concepts of Jewish feminism as presented in the Rosh Hodesh ritual, which I discovered was primarily a product of early Jewish second-wave feminism (which lasted roughly from the 1960s through the 1980s).

This book is framed by the perspective of today's Jewish feminism—whose primary goal, I contend, is to bring about gender equality on every level in Judaism, especially in the realm of Jewish liturgy. In contrast to Jewish second-wave feminists, whose rallying cry was "separate but equal," today's feminist Jews would prefer the slogan "*not* separate *and* equal." They seek to create an inclusive and egalitarian Jewish community in which men and women can have different, but equally meaningful, spiritual experiences.

The advent of feminist Jewish theology in the 1990s marked an important paradigm shift in Jewish feminism. Consequently, this book uses liberal Judaism as its primary research context, and thus focuses on feminist Jewish singer-songwriters related to Reform Judaism, to Reconstructionist

Judaism, the Jewish Renewal movement, and to a lesser degree on Conservative Judaism, as these singer-songwriters are most dissatisfied with the still prevailing attitudes and cultural norms of gender imbalance in American Judaism. In Orthodox Judaism, the sexes are still separated in synagogue worship. However, many of the concepts and themes of Jewish feminism are also relevant here. The difference is that Orthodox singer-songwriters do not exploit the concepts and themes of Jewish feminism to try to change gender imbalances in their communities. This study asks how much have the diverse backgrounds of feminist Jewish singer-songwriters, especially their denominational affiliations (that is, their religious, cultural, and political socialization), influenced not only their brands of Jewish feminism (theological, social, or politically motivated) but also their musical choices and the structure of their songs.

After I finished my fieldwork and completed my research on American feminist Jewish music, one of the most important American Jewish singer-songwriters and pioneers of feminist Jewish music, Debbie Friedman, z"l, suddenly died in 2011. Friedman was the first American Jewish woman to have a major impact on Jewish liturgy. Through her feminist-inspired, religious popular music, as well as in her role as a highly charismatic song leader, she fostered Jewish egalitarianism and thus encouraged women to take ownership of synagogue worship. In the course of time, not only did Friedman's songs become an integral part of synagogue services across the Jewish denominations, but she also inspired young female musicians and songwriters to continue her heritage. These young women are now entering the feminist Jewish music scene, and their musical contributions will soon be published—among others—in an anthology of feminist Jewish music titled *Adding Our Voices* (G. Raphael, Ross, and Milgram forthcoming). Thus, this book is also dedicated to Debbie Friedman, in the hope that no one will ever forget the historical origins of her music—as this is, after all, how traditions are established.

The study of the emergence of feminist Jewish songwriting at the turn of the millennium in America, and thus of Jewish women's music making in today's Jewish communities, is not finished, and this work can be seen as an introduction to future research.

ACKNOWLEDGMENTS

The present publication, based on my dissertation, "Performing the Political in American Jewish-Feminist Music" (Ross 2009b), would not have been possible without the support of many people to whom I would like to express my gratitude. First of all, my thanks for their outstanding support go to my dissertation supervisors, Ellen Koskoff, professor of ethnomusicology at the Eastman School of Music, University of Rochester, in New York; and Hartmut Möller, professor of musicology at the University of Music and Theatre Rostock, in Germany.

Furthermore, the research and fieldwork I conducted in the United States would not have been possible without the financial support of the German Research Council, which awarded me a PhD scholarship in the Graduate School of Cultural Encounter and the Discourses of Scholarship (Graduiertenkolleg "Kulturkontakt und Wissenschaftsdiskurs") at the University of Rostock and the University of Music and Theatre Rostock. My thanks also go to the Hadassah-Brandeis Institute at Brandeis University, in Waltham, Massachusetts, for its financial support. The Hadassah-Brandeis Institute was the first academic institution to honor my project with a research award. Finally, I would like to express my thanks to the Mariann Steegmann Foundation, which provided financial support for publication of this book.

My special thanks go to all the feminist Jewish singer-songwriters who over many years answered my questions; gave me important information, contacts, and research material; and, last but not least, provided me with accommodation during my fieldwork in the United States. Above all, I would like to thank Rabbi Shefa Gold, Linda Hirschhorn, Rabbi Geela Rayzel Raphael, Juliet Spitzer, Rabbi Margot Stein, and all the other singers, songwriters, scholars, and feminist Jews who agreed to share their knowledge and thoughts with me in countless interviews and conversations. My several stays in the United States also would not have been possible without the support of friends such as Christoph and Chiho Bangert, Rhea Bertelli, Rose Jick, Eric Nelson, Siren Polat, and others who selflessly gave me their assistance when I asked for a place to stay, technical support, or anything else that I needed while doing research far away from home. My thanks also go to Rochelle Rowe for her assistance in text editing and to Cantor Ronald Fishman, z"l, who edited some of the musical transcriptions.

Last but not least, my thanks go to my partner, Avi Epstein, and my family, who gave me more support than anyone could ever ask for. I would like to express very special and heartfelt thanks to my mother, Rita Ross.

INTRODUCTION

WHAT THIS BOOK IS ABOUT

This book concerns the music and musical practices of a select group of Jewish singer-songwriters in the United States, who consider themselves and their music to be feminist and Jewish. Because of this and for practical reasons, the purpose of this book is not to provide hard representative data about each feminist Jewish singer-songwriter in the United States. Rather, it seeks to impart their and my understanding of and reflections on the flavor of the interrelationships of some singer-songwriters who collectively constituted the feminist Jewish music scene in the United States between the 1960s and the 2000s, and who are discussed in this study as examples.

That is why the book is based on fieldwork among female and male feminist Jewish musicians, singer-songwriters, and rabbis and cantors related to Conservative, Reform, and Jewish Renewal and Reconstructionist communities in the United States. I believe that fieldwork has special resources and materials to offer and is the only method that can delineate the various threads of music, feminism, spiritual feeling, and religious experience that are interwoven into a complex pattern for the members of the feminist Jewish music scene. The viewpoints of feminist Jewish singer-songwriters in the United States are essential to an adequate understanding of the research topic (see, for example, Smith 2012). The importance of fieldwork in this context is indicated by my interactions with the people I studied. In those interactions there was a real dialogue between us, and my interviewees had some agency in what is written about them.[1]

As both a sociopolitical phenomenon and a musical genre, feminist Jewish music—which addresses the diverse inequalities between the genders and women's subordinated status in Judaism—emerged from the renewal processes of American Judaism. Its rise was supported by greater political and cultural movements in the American mainstream, such as the American counterculture of the 1960s and 1970s and the contemporaneous advent of the women's liberation movement. This book is thus a study of the many facets of countercultural and feminist views and beliefs and their cultural expression through music. This study offers an alternative perspective on the established history of late twentieth-century American Jewish music, which lacks an adequate discussion of Jewish women and their music making. In this regard, the history of so-called American new Jewish music (which is an egalitarian form of Jewish sacred music) will be integrated into the history of contemporary Jewish feminism.

While acknowledging the fact that feminist Jewish music reflects and represents all shades of Jewish feminism, the book addresses two major issues. First is the significance of music as an effective political tool in the context of contemporary Jewish feminism. Immediately accessible and emotionally compelling, music helps people forge a community, while allowing its members to assert their individuality. Even more important, music has the potential to have a public voice and to imagine alternative ways of thinking (see, for example, Klein 1997; Raimist 2006, 175). Second is the way feminist Jewish singer-songwriters try to keep the balance between preserving Jewish tradition on the one hand and promoting religiopolitical change in American Judaism on the other hand, thereby seeking a kind of spiritual self-assurance in the context of an accelerated change in the mainstream culture. In addressing these two issues, the book reveals the forgotten story of contemporary feminist Jewish music making and identifies new research material to be used for future research on Jewish feminist music.

My focus is on the musical repertoire of a relatively small but active network of feminist Jewish singer-songwriters located on the East and West Coasts of the United States. Some members of this network compiled their work in a collection titled the "Jewish Feminist Songbook" (Elwell et al. 1992), which for many reasons—both personal and related to music publishing—was never published. This selection of feminist Jewish songs is a compilation of liturgical, paraliturgical, folk, and popular melodies. Based on my examination of the songs in this collection and other songs I collected in my fieldwork, as well as the sociocultural circumstances in which they emerged, the questions that I believe should guide the study on feminist Jewish music are: How are feminist politics performed in Jewish music? How are issues of identity politics and of Jewish women's (and men's) perspectives on Judaism and Jewish traditions represented and negotiated in these newly invented songs, both the liturgical and nonliturgical ones? What have the core values and concepts of contemporary Jewish feminism been since the 1980s, and how are those performed through music? And can feminist Jewish music be considered sound and also the sounded embodiment of core values and ideas of contemporary Jewish feminism?

The variety of new feminist Jewish concepts—particularly marked by the emergence of feminist Jewish theology, as introduced by Judith Plaskow (1992)—and identities (including those of a new generation of feminist Jews, born after the end of the Baby Boom in 1965) is reflected in the music, whose styles are embedded in diverse cultures even as they are molded by cross-cultural contacts. This complexity of feminist politics and musical genealogies seems to keep the contradictoriness of personal and Jewish histories real (see, for example, Drake 2006, 226). That is why the present study is based on the hypothesis that the feminist reconceptualization of Jewish liturgical texts and feminist understandings of community structures and, most important, of the concept of God emerge in feminist Jewish music.

Music is one of the central sites for the exploration of key feminist Jewish concepts, especially those not adequately discussed in academic literature. There are a number of excellent studies dedicated to various aspects of American Judaism and American Jewish culture in general, and to Jewish feminism in the United States in particular, but they contain few or no detailed references to music, either recorded or transcribed. As a consequence, there has been little comprehensive discussion or analysis of feminist Jewish music. Why is this?

FEMINIST JEWISH MUSIC: DEFINING THE GAP IN SCHOLARSHIP

The study of feminist Jewish music in the United States lies at the intersection of contemporary feminist Jewish scholarship and ethnomusicological, gender, and Jewish music studies—fields that collectively reveal a significant lacuna in scholarship. As this book seeks to close this gap, the following explanations are relevant for an understanding of the study of feminist Jewish songwriting. Despite the advance of women's studies, ethnic studies, and Jewish studies since the late 1960s and the 1970s, and despite the recent interest in Jewish culture and arts in particular, Jewish music has been relatively little examined in comparison to Jewish literature or fine arts. The field of Jewish music studies in the United States constantly negotiates "the lines between the scholar and the practitioner; between the seminary, the conservatory, and the university" (Judah Cohen 2008, 29; see also Bohlman 2002a). With regard to scholarly works on feminist and gender studies in Jewish music, it is important to note that—at the time of writing—hardly any research on contemporary American Jewish women's music in general, and on feminist Jewish songwriting in particular, has been done. Only Ellen Koskoff (1993, 2001a) combined ethnomusicological feminist and gender studies with American Jewish music studies.[2] Koskoff is now also the only scholar who has examined—in her recent book, *A Feminist Ethnomusicology* (2014)—how the sometimes paradoxical interdisciplinary nature of feminist ethnomusicology has developed over the past four decades.

However, it is ironic not only that gender is not considered central in Jewish music studies, but also that feminism as a global movement, in which music plays a key role, has attracted little attention in ethnomusicological studies. In music scholarship, feminist theory has become simply one of many equally valid forms of interpreting music, especially with respect to identity politics (see, for example, Koskoff 2002, 743). After a short heyday in the 1980s and 1990s, ethnomusicological feminist and gender studies seem to have declined—in the same way that mainstream and Jewish feminism have experienced a backlash as their next waves emerged.[3] The only difference is that in comparison to the larger feminist movements, this decline in scholarship does not appear to be provoking another distinct wave of general ethnomusicological works applying feminist and gender theories, let alone Jewish musical studies considering the relevance of gender as a central research category. Two primary reasons for this difference can be identified.

First, the so-called new musicology, which emerged in the 1970s and 1980s and basically addresses the intersection of the former fields of ethnomusicology and historical musicology, now also focuses on the examination of non-Western music in the context of Orientalism, Western popular music, and issues of globalization in music. In doing so, adherents of new musicology draw on research models taken from such fields as literary criticism, cultural studies, and feminist and queer theory (Koskoff 2005a, 92; see also 97–98). This means that the study of non-Western and popular music against the background of theories of feminist and gender studies—which were until then reserved to the field of ethnomusicology—is now identified with and ascribed to the field of new musicology. In addition, historical musicology and ethnomusicology are also distinguished on the basis of methods (work with texts versus fieldwork), which implicates ethnomusicologists' relative level of interest in postmodern feminist and gender theory, an approach that is first of all based on text critique rather than on participant observation and the collection of empirical data through personal interviews, as Koskoff demonstrates (2005a, 92, 97–98).

Second, the same problems that affect ethnomusicological feminist and gender studies also affect Jewish music studies, as Jewish music is primarily studied in ethnomusicology. Furthermore, Jewish music is largely seen as marginal to the principal concerns of American musicology or ethnomusicology, which is why Jewish music studies and programs are often housed in seminaries. This explains the facts that there was a complete lack of doctoral students interested in Jewish music before the 1970s, and that there are still not many students today. These are some of the reasons why only a few scholarly works on gender and Jewish music exist (Judah Cohen 2008, 46).

This book combines these two fields of music research—that is, the application of gender and feminist studies in ethnomusicological research and Jewish music studies—and thus fills the lacuna in scholarship. I believe recent feminist Jewish thought has informed and provoked the emergence of a new kind of Jewish music, called feminist Jewish music. Acknowledging that there is a crucial lack of research on feminist Jewish music in both Jewish women's studies and ethnomusicology, this book seeks to make the genre of feminist Jewish music attractive for further research and to integrate this music into scholarly discourses.

HISTORICAL, SOCIOPOLITICAL, AND CULTURAL CONTEXTS

To understand the historical, sociopolitical, and cultural conditions that spurred the emergence of feminist Jewish songwriting in the United States in the late twentieth century, one must take into consideration the larger context of the American religious life—more precisely, the context of the American counterculture and its impact on the renewal of American Judaism since the 1970s. In this context, so-called new Jewish music is considered as not just a political and musical model for the advent of feminist

Jewish music. For the first time, young Jews combined American popular music, such as folk-rock, with Jewish liturgical texts, thus contributing to the reformation of synagogue worship. This reformation was also fostered by the advent of Jewish feminism in the early 1970s.

Religious Life in America

In the middle of the twentieth century, religious life in the United States was fueled by social and political activism that turned in the late 1960s and early 1970s from universalistic to particularistic concerns. During this time religion moved into the center of countercultural interest, and American youth (who had previously protested about social issues) turned to new religions and "unorthodox spiritual disciplines" (Kent 2001, 1). But the ways in which people in the American mainstream and traditional denominations—like the Roman Catholic Church or various Protestant denominations—worshiped God also changed significantly: religious membership in a denomination was no longer seen as obligatory but as a matter of individual and voluntary choice (see, for example, Oppenheimer 2003; Summit 2000, 153).

The influence of both American Protestantism and the American counterculture on mainline streams of Judaism and Catholicism appeared, from a political perspective, to lead to an increasingly tolerant attitude on the part of church and synagogue communities toward feminism, homosexuality, premarital sex, and interracial marriages. From a personal perspective—following an aesthetic rather than theological and doctrinal change that affected, for example, the style of liturgical music and décor—it appeared to mean that people increasingly identified themselves with their religion. Consequently, worship services became more informal and permissible and allowed women to become more involved in preaching, leading services, and participating in the planning of the liturgy (prayer and song; see, for example, Oppenheimer 2003, 1–28). The "expectation that worshippers can find or create the kind of service they need, the role of the empowered individual in creating new structures and institutions, and the ready tendency to form communal associations are all themes common to American religious life" that grew out of Protestant worship and were reinforced by the countercultural movements in America (Summit 2000, 152).

Thus, the increasing American focus on religious individualism (manifested in the idea that the self must be the source of all religious meaning as well as in the search for spiritual, cultural, and historic authenticity) pervaded American religious life in the late twentieth century and also resulted in a revitalization of American Judaism (see below). The revitalization began at a time when American Jewish life was also experiencing a general changing of the guard, from one generation to another. Simultaneously Jewish identity and culture in the United States became defined instead as American Jewish (see Picard 2004; Summit 2000, 152–54). As a consequence, American Jewish society became more flexible and started to value religious improvisation, even schism. Breaking with traditions (in terms of the use of liturgical music, for example) became and remains normal, with the recognition that even standard synagogue ritual and music is itself a product of often unorthodox inventions in earlier generations.

However, to better understand the context in which feminist Jewish songwriting emerged, and thus the ways that music is used strategically in prayer by women and men as they define, present, and maintain their religious and cultural identity, it is necessary to take a closer look at the making of a particular Jewish counterculture and Jewish feminist movement.

The Making of a Jewish Counterculture

The Jewish counterculture was a product of rapid social changes, influenced by the interaction of economic, demographic, and political transformations and by landmark events that included the rise of movements seeking racial and sexual equality. Moreover, the Jewish counterculture was driven by a generation of young adults searching for a new American Jewish identity outside the established Jewish organizations and institutions (see, for example, Adams 2000, 94–210; Gair 2007, 122; Glanz 1977, 125). The oppositions between modernity and tradition and between Judaism as an integrated culture and its timeless essence—manifested within its canonical textual tradition, which Jewish college students addressed in their political activities—became particularly obvious in the wake of two key sociopolitical events that set off the establishment of the Jewish counterculture: the rise of the Black Power Movement in 1966 and the Six-Day War in Israel one year later. Each of these had an intense effect on Jewish young people in the United States (see, for example, Novak 2004, 283).

JEWS AND AFRICAN AMERICANS

After World War II, when antisemitism and legal discrimination against Jews decreased in the United States, American Jews made social, economic, and political gains, and their religion was accepted as one of the three great American religions—together with Catholicism and Protestantism (see Biale, Galchinsk, and Heschel 1998, 4). However, despite their success and absorption into mainstream U.S. society, they felt that their insecure historical status was unchanged, and they considered themselves a minority group with a separate culture and set of beliefs (Biale 1998, 27). These deeply felt contradictions in Jewish self-consciousness eventually motivated young Jews to put the issue of civil rights for African Americans at the top of their social agenda. Jews equated their historical narrative with that of African Americans in the rhetoric of the early civil rights movement and compared their own story of persecution and their persistent and vexing minority status in Europe with the conditions of African Americans (Biale 1998, 28; C. Greenberg 1998, 62–63; Sarna 2004, 308). Thus, Jewish students and scholars became involved in social action projects associated with the civil rights movement. Social activism was not only a general political question, but also a central religious issue: the Talmudic concept of "mip'nei tikkun ha'olam" (found in Mishna Gittin; in English, "for the sake of repairing the world") became shorthand for social action in the Jewish counterculture and in Jewish feminism and its music. Since the 1950s, a more holistic understanding of *tikkun ha'olam* (or simply *tikkun olam*) that embraced the protection of people who were on the margins of society gained traction in liberal American Jewish communities (see, for example, Jacobs 2007; Rosenthal 2005).

The Jewish counterculturalists' involvement in the civil rights movement broke off when the formerly nonviolent civil rights movement led by Martin Luther King Jr. took up arms under his successors (see Adams 2000, 102), and when members of the new separatist Black Power Movement repudiated the vision of an integrated society.[4] Jewish activists were told to leave the civil rights movement. In the wake of the Israeli-Arab conflict, some African American separatists allied themselves with the Arab cause and held derogatory views of Jews. The African American separatist critique was sometimes hard to distinguish from antisemitism, and it exacerbated the Jewish leadership's vexed relationship with African American activists. Accordingly, many Jewish activists abandoned the civil rights movement and started to focus their efforts on the rights of their own people. The Six-Day War in 1967 further accelerated this process (see, for example, C. Greenberg 1998, 57–71; Novak 2004, 282–83).

THE SIX-DAY WAR

When Israel declared itself to be an independent state in May 1948 and celebrated its rebirth as the homeland of the Jewish people—where their religious, spiritual, and political identity had been shaped—the long-lasting conflict with Arabs burst into renewed violence. Israel was attacked and succeeded in warding off the assault, a process that was repeated in 1967 in the Six-Day War (see Sarna 2004, 315). Later, the war caused mixed feelings among Jews worldwide: on the one hand, they recognized the danger of losing Israel as their spiritual and religious homeland; on the other hand, the unexpected victory of Israel caused an unfamiliar feeling of superiority among world Jewry (Porath 1972). Thus, American Jews who did not really identify with Israel before the war became much more aware of the shared fate of all Jews and thus of their people's distinctiveness bound up with the state of Israel (see, for example, Sarna 2004, 316). The emergence of a new Jewish self-consciousness intensified the formation of the Jewish counterculture and thus the renewal of American Judaism. The Six-Day War in Israel engendered Jewish pride and inspired young Jews to look more closely into their Jewish traditions, and thus into traditional Jewish and Israeli music.

Developments in Jewish musical cultures have always responded to political events and social changes. After 1967 American Jews started to embrace Israeli musical culture as a vehicle for expressing their identity and included the singing of Israeli songs in American synagogues and at camps and social gatherings. In this context, Naomi Shemer's popular song "Jerusalem of Gold" (1967) became the hymn of the Six-Day War—inside and outside of Israel—and was sung to the text of the Adon Olam ("master of the universe") prayer in the Shabbat morning services across American synagogues. This metaphorical switch in the melodies of Jewish liturgy as well as the so-called *kum sitz*—musical jam sessions of countercultural Jewish youth similar to the *shira betzibur* (public singings) in Israel at that time—reflects "the American Jewish support and solidarity with Israel" during the war (Summit 2000, 174, note 5). Female Israeli singer-songwriters—including Chava Alberstein, Shoshana Damari, Naomi Shemer, and Yaffa

Yarkoni, who contributed to *Shirei Erez Israel (Songs of the Land of Israel)* in general and to Israeli song in particular (see Shahar 2009)—may have served as role models for future feminist Jewish singer-songwriters in the United States. They were both female performers and songwriters of "original songs in trendy pop styles . . . and of translations of foreign songs in the same vein" (Regev and Seroussi 2004, 41).

NURTURING JEWISH AMERICAN PRIDE

In response to sociopolitical events such as the civil rights movement and the Six-Day War, a wave of new ethnicity captured American society. Minority groups started to claim that their cultural heritage was equal to that of white Anglo-Saxon Protestants (see, for example, Adams 2000, 118). Consequently, Americans began to concentrate on the politics of identity, especially focusing on their roots, ethnicity, and gender. Jewish youth who now consciously emphasized their Jewish identity and ethnic background reacted to these recent events, which set off a new and wide-ranging process of Jewish identity construction (see, for example, Glanz 1977, 126; Sarna 2004, 318).

A small minority of Jewish students—who felt a sense of Jewish pride analogous to African Americans who held that, in the common expression, "Black is beautiful"—merged their political views with their newly discovered Jewishness and formed a Jewish student movement whose members would work only for their own political causes (see, for example, Oppenheimer 2003, 105; Sarna 2004, 319; Novak 2004, 282–83). They consecrated themselves to a new progressive Zionism, Jewish education, cultural and social action, the peace movement, and feminism.[5]

The Jewish counterculture could not have been defined as such were it not for its members' antiorganizational tendencies and built-in distrust of the American synagogue in general. Driven by the same mainstream antiestablishment restiveness and expressions of minority group liberation and pride that other counterculturalists displayed, Jewish Baby Boomers[6] directed their rebelliousness and alienation into Jewish programs, which spurred the renewal of American Judaism. Jewish young people had long lost their interest in organized communities that failed to communicate what Jewish life and Judaism really meant. They began to take ownership of their Judaism, to break down the long-established divisions between the religious and secular spheres of American Jewish life and thus between tradition and modernity (Sarna 2004, 318–19). In this context, Jewish summer camps (like the popular conservative Ramah camps) became very important (see, for example, Zola 2006).

This generation of American Jews expressed their new sense of being Jewish by experimenting with different forms of articulation. Politically, they participated in civil rights and antiwar activism and in feminism. Artistically, they embraced fiction, drama, music, and print media. And religiously, they adopted New Age spirituality and invented new forms of Jewish worship, such as the *havurah* (friendship, fellowship; plural, *havurot*) (Glanz 1977, 127). Feminist Jewish ritual and music making emerged.

THE HAVURAH MOVEMENT IN AMERICA

At the end of the 1960s and in the early 1970s, the Jewish Baby Boomers, also referred to as New American Jews, became more secure in their Jewish identity and their sense of self in America than their parents had been. This resulted in distinctive demands on synagogue life (see, for example, Staub 2004, xviii), which led to an extensive transformation in the structure of the American Jewish community. From the Jewish Baby Boomers' point of view, established synagogue communities lacked spirituality and thus did not give the individual's life a sense of larger purpose and meaning (see, for example, Schwarz 2003, 19–22).

Young Jewish people addressed this problem by creating alternative and parallel organizations and forms of worship, attempting to bridge the separation of Jewish life from Jewish values and culture. The community—the havurah—was core. Those intentional communities developed both on and off campuses and offered a creative environment for experimenting with non-Western forms of liturgy and worship such as New Age spiritual alternatives (Glanz 1977, 118–120). In their search for an authentic faith rooted in Jewish history and modernity, some Baby Boomers returned to Jewish mysticism and Hasidism (see, for example, Prell 2006, 161; Schwarz 2003, 22–23; Sarna 2004, 319; Staub 2004, xviii–xxi).

Against this background, the havurot were founded without a common ideology, with no rabbis or buildings, and with only loose structures. Their members gathered on a regular basis for devout Jewish study, discussion, and prayer and experimented with ritual making and voluntary social work. The Havurotniks added ethnic flavor to Judaism and invoked a "strong sense of community, high levels of participation, an egalitarian [nonsexist] and democratic ethic, and a renewed sense of spirituality" (Schwarz 2003, 43; see also Oppenheimer 2003, 97).

The Havurotniks preference for Hasidism and their evocation of previous times offered them an idealized vision for a new Judaism and a potent model of community that rejected the large suburban synagogues and isolation of American Judaism. Their turn to a romanticized past also rejected the notion of a hyphenated Jewish life in the United States. Identity politics became central to the havurah movement, its reimagination of Judaism and Jewish identity as a revolutionary force was not mere theory (Prell 2006, 167). With the publication of *The First Jewish Catalogue* (Siegel, Strassfield, and Strassfield 1973)—a three-volume Jewish do-it-yourself kit including Jewish laws and teachings, essays and reflections, and instructions for kosher cooking and ritual making—the ideals and values of the Jewish counterculture and the havurah movement moved from the margins to the mainstream, and the movement became an influential mass movement. Jewish worshipers practicing a havurah-style worship now sat in circles wearing casual clothing; celebrated together by candlelight while people alternately led the worship and study groups; and above all turned to group singing and the singing of *niggunim*, the wordless melodies borrowed from Hasidic chants, to punctuate their prayers.[7]

In subsequent years, egalitarianism, informality, cohesive community, participatory prayer and group discussions, and unconventional forms of governance had an impact on American Judaism (see, for example, Oppenheimer 2003, 6–7) as Reform and Conservative synagogues adopted the havurah idea. Normative Jewish denominations integrated some of the havurah movement's essential elements into their own institutions to promote the humanization and personalization of worship and the democratization of synagogue life. The havurah movement's countercultural ideals and counteraesthetic values became, in a moderate form, part of the American Jewish mainstream.

On the whole, the American synagogue of the late twentieth century became less performance oriented and more participatory. Associated with the more intimate, informal, and cozier religious settings, the hierarchical choreographed synagogue services (with a rabbi and/or cantor standing in front of the passive congregants) were replaced by a form of service that called for new synagogue music (see Sarna 2004, 321–24). Since the 1950s, the cantor as a musical virtuoso, quite often famous, became a synagogue professional. The former operatic style of Jewish liturgical music gradually was complemented and occasionally replaced by folk tunes, sung at paraliturgical song sessions in idiomatic vocal harmonies, accompanied by guitar. Those tunes "referenced what young people found to be 'timeless' Jewish values of social justice and activism" (Judah Cohen 2006a, 102). Emerging from Reform summer camps since the 1960s, this music found its way into the cantorial curriculum of Reform Judaism that is now split between self-styled traditional and reform repertoires (see, for example, ibid., 97). Song leading and communal singing became a new ideal of worship performance.

MAKING A NEW JEWISH MUSIC

The same countercultural spirit and creativity that sparked the renewal of American Jewish forms of worship also contributed to the development of new American Jewish music as an element in the emergence of feminist Jewish music in the United States. The redefinition, which was partially a reinvention, of American synagogue music was greatly influenced by the folk music revival of the 1940s through the 1960s, led by singer-songwriters like Woody Guthrie and Pete Seeger.

Folk music was conventionally defined at that time as anonymous and orally transmitted compositions that were transformed into various versions by folk musicians and sung by folk singers to and with their own communities.[8] Since the 1960s, the term "folk song" became increasingly associated with an American usage, meaning the work of singer-songwriters (for example, Bob Dylan; Tom Paxton; Joni Mitchell; Peter, Paul, and Mary; and Joan Baez). Singer-songwriters had a more flexible stance toward issues of repertory and not as much concern about authentic tradition. They used songs in their own political activism, accompanied themselves on acoustic guitar, and usually sang to large audiences of strangers but nevertheless created a feeling of shared intimacy through their music (see, for example, Laing 2001; Pegg 2001, 9:63–65; Rodnitzky 1999, 55). It was this understanding of music and performance that was brought into synagogue worship. Furthermore, it was group singing in particular that foregrounded a sense of solidarity and collective identity, as the singing of oral traditions connected the imagined community of counterculturalists not only to their successors in the future but also to a shared historical past, thus functioning as a fundamental and powerful instrument for communicating political ideas (see, for example, Eyerman 2002, 3:445–46 and 450). It was the practice of group singing that linked Jewish countercultural visionaries (participating in Reform and Conservative summer camps) with the sound of their surroundings and the messages conveyed through their music. Rabbi Zalman Schachter Shalomi (1924–2014)—a member of the havurah movement, teacher at the famous Conservative Ramah camp, and later charismatic leader of the Jewish Renewal movement (a spiritual, neo-Hasidic movement in American Judaism)—was among the first to use American folk tunes and group singing to revive traditional Jewish texts and hymns. For example, he sang the Adon Olam prayer to the popular tune of "Amazing Grace" (Aleph 2015).

Thus, the folk-music revival affected American Judaism in different ways. Within neo-Orthodox communities, including those in the havurah movement, Rabbi Shlomo Carlebach (1925–94)[9] created a new genre of neo-Hasidic Orthodox folk music that later became mainstream.[10] American Jews recognized that songs in popular and folk styles that were based on Jewish sources (that is, liturgical texts) could convey an authentic Jewish message. The first recordings of noncantorial Jewish music that came into the market at this time sold well. More important, this music's combination of the participatory character of folk music with the energy of newly created Israeli music and the religious passion of real Hasidic niggunim made it popular. This is what finally moved liturgical music out of the synagogue and into a wide range of other performance settings, including the concert hall. Given the countercultural idea of renewing American Judaism, this music functioned well as a medium to educate Jews and inspire them to renew their Jewish life and identity (see, for example, Kligman 2001b, 95–96, 98–99). As Mark Kligman states, Carlebach understood Jewish music as an effective vehicle for connecting Jews to Judaism (a goal that Jewish Baby Boomers were generally aiming for), and later served as a model for the new liturgical music of younger feminist Jewish musicians in all denominations (ibid., 103).

Thus, Jewish Baby Boomers, mainly through Conservative and Reform camps and synagogues, developed another new folk-rock based genre in American Jewish liturgical music—new Jewish music (see, for example, Dreyfus 2001, 33). Impressed by the popular folk singers of the 1960s and 1970s and Pete Seeger's belief in the democratic nature of collective singing (see, for example, Kligman 2001b, 115–17), young musical innovators in the Reform movement such as Debbie Friedman—"the Joan Baez of Jewish song" (Sarna 2004, 353)—and Jeff Klepper were looking for new Jewish music that reflected their Jewish identity, balancing between Jewish traditional values and the modern American mainstream. They turned away from the well-known musical paradigms of their home synagogues (like the "classical" cantorial repertoire, organ, and choir), and composed new Jewish music for group singing and with acoustic guitar accompaniment (Dreyfus 2001, 33). The most evident innovation here was the use of English lyrics, sometimes in combination with Hebrew.

Reenergized by their Jewish camp experience, those young people brought camp music to their home synagogues, as this was the primary setting for traditional Jewish expression and the place where young musicians had to direct their efforts to revitalize Reform synagogue practices. Despite resistance, Reform popular music eventually displaced the traditional repertoire to a significant degree and set off a revolution not only in liturgical music, but also in American Judaism as a whole. During the late 1970s Hebrew-infused, folk-rock-style camp music had begun to influence synagogue liturgy throughout various denominations, and in the 1980s it was already commonly used in Reform worship (see Kligman 2001b, 119). Young singer-songwriters like Debbie Friedman also discovered feminist Jewish issues and began to write folk-rock songs with an undeniable feminist message. Those young people's music communicated their religious beliefs and a political message that attempted to renew American Judaism by making it not only more contemporary and participatory but also egalitarian. Thus, American Jews were not only ideologically and aesthetically influenced by the American counterculture. Instead, they turned the musical culture of America into an American Jewish musical culture. One can argue that the folky American Jewish music style sounded anything but Jewish, but for the young Jewish people of the countercultural era, it sounded Jewish enough. It was how they best expressed who they were and what they believed. Like women's music (discussed below), the genre of new Jewish music was an important model for feminist Jewish music.

THE BIRTH OF FEMINIST JEWISH MUSIC IN THE UNITED STATES

The advent of the Jewish women's spirituality movement, as well as the emergence of women's music as a new musical genre paved the way for feminist Jewish music making in the United States. Feminist Jewish music was also fostered by the paradigm shift in feminist scholarship around the year 1990, which in turn was highly influenced by Judith Plaskow's feminist Jewish theology and its redefinition of the central concepts of Judaism—the Torah, Israel, and God (see Plaskow 1992). Her theology served to legitimize feminist Jewish singer-songwriters' adapting the tradition of Jewish liturgical music to the new social, political, and cultural American Judaism and its communities.

The Jewish Women's Spirituality Movement (Late 1960s to 1970s)

Americans were rebelling against the empty religious conventions of their day and seeking new forms of spiritual self-expression. The American Jewish community also began to feel the influences of the Jewish women's spirituality movement, which posed a great challenge to the institutions of American Jewry as well as to its social and religious norms (Lefkovitz and Shapiro 2005, 102). Jewish women in the (secular) American feminist movement were already attempting to shed the consciousness of being the other and of redefining themselves in relation to the mainstream society. But feminist Jews first had to become aware of the possibility that their newly gained feeling of power could also be expressed religiously and spiritually. Thus, a grass-roots movement of Jewish women's spirituality preceded an all-out Jewish women's or feminist movement. The original intent of the Jewish women's spirituality movement was to address the absence of women in the public domain of Judaism, especially women's exclusion from ordination and halakhic codetermination (that is, the right to have a say in the interpretation of the Jewish law), and to demand more opportunities for women to participate in Jewish organizations and synagogue life—for example, as rabbis and cantors (ibid.). This intent was based on feminist challenges to the Jewish women's role and religious status in traditional Judaism, which is briefly outlined in the following section and which is relevant for an understanding of the political ideas behind feminist Jewish music as discussed in this book.

THE HALAKHIC VIEW OF JEWISH WOMEN

In traditional Judaism, women are mostly seen as separate from but equal to men, and their duties and responsibilities are no less important than those of men. However, women are easily defined according to their biological qualities, such as their role as mothers. This is why rabbis traditionally viewed women with ambivalence and discomfort and why they were finally excluded from the public and political spheres of the Jewish society. Although Judaism has great respect for the responsibility that a woman has for her family—and her spiritual influence on that family—the notion of separateness diminishes her role and active participation in the synagogue, and that is what feminist Jews criticized. There are several reasons for the separation of women, such as *niddah* (a woman's impurity caused by her menstrual period), which is discussed in the Talmudic tractates on *taharat ha'mishpakhah* (Jewish laws on family purity) and becomes apparent in the mikvah ritual—the woman's immersion in the ritual bath after menstruation (see Fonrobert 2001, 2:88; Wasserfall 1992, 309 and 323, note 3).[11] A women's impurity has social and religious implications beyond the mere observance of the laws: it also has to do with female sexuality and fertility (see, for example, Schwer 1995, 148–49).

Thus, a wide range of reasons can be given for excluding women from central modes of religious practice and expression. Traditionally, women's relationship to the official religious aspect of Judaism, the synagogue worship, is characterized by a double exclusion: both exclusion from the study of the Torah and Talmud and exemption from the mitzvahs that have to be performed at certain times a day (see, for example, Plaskow 1992, 90). As all religious obligations in Judaism are, by definition, characterized by the possibility of nonperformance (otherwise there would not be commandments to perform them), someone who is not bound to fulfill a religious practice does not have the same status in the community as someone who is obligated to perform all mitzvahs (Wasserfall 1992, 315). Thus, women are not counted in the minyan (literally, a gathering; the quorum of ten) that is required to say a public prayer (see Lipstadt 2001, 294; Plaskow 1992, 90). Women's exemption from the observance of the time-bounded mitzvahs and exclusion from the central modes of religious expression further leads to their exclusion from studying and reading the Torah in the presence of the community, which is a religious obligation only for men (5 Moses 11:19; see also Fonrobert 2001, 2:81). As a result, women's access to Jewish knowledge and education is systematically obstructed (see, for example, Sered 1992, 16). On this basis, they are also excluded from the performance of religious rituals and from holding leading positions in an

Orthodox synagogue community such as rabbi, cantor, or reader (see, for example, B. Greenberg 1998, 8). Moreover, as normative Judaism is mainly referred to as male,[12] most of the rituals in Judaism—such as the brit milah (circumcision) and the bar mitzvah (literally, "son of the commandment," the coming of age at thirteen) are rituals of and for men, in which female bodily experiences are ignored. Thus, the question arises as to what role can women play in traditional Judaism, if its primary symbols and rituals are related only to men (Plaskow 1992, 112; Sered 1992, 16).

In Judaism, the community is the primary vehicle and place for religious experience. Exclusion from the Jewish community consequently means exclusion from Jewish intellectual and spiritual life. Therefore, women's otherness is not only a matter of social and religious marginalization, but also one of intellectual and spiritual exclusion that further hinders the construction of a communal Jewish identity—one that includes women. This leads women to develop alternative strategies to enable them to experience Jewish religion as subjects and agents and to create the subject identity of a Jewish woman (see Plaskow 1992, 116).

RE-CREATING FEMINIST RITUALS AND SPIRITUAL VIEWS IN JUDAISM

The Jewish women's spirituality movement focused on the reclamation of women's religiousness and the right of individual spiritual self-expression by encouraging women to reexamine Jewish and non-Jewish traditions and customs in ways that would give them more cultural authority, and thus more power (see, for example, Alpert 1991, 66; Plaskow 1992, 260). Although Jewish women could consult a collection of spiritual texts such as prayers, sermons, and poems from the sixteenth century onward, Jewish women's spiritual consciousness-raising emerged mainly with the revival of the ancient women's holiday Rosh Hodesh,[13] the monthly festival of the new moon, and the innovation of Rosh Hodesh groups in the early 1970s (Lefkovitz and Shapiro 2005, 102). In these groups, which met in synagogues as well as in more private settings, the newly rediscovered holiday was celebrated in different ways. Once women realized their own invisibility in Jewish liturgy and ritual (Jewish practices as grounded in the Halakhah), they used the intimacy of these women-only meetings to study sacred texts like the Talmud and Torah and to experiment with new, gender-sensitive rituals that filled in the gaps in existing Jewish worship and forged a connection between the women's religious faith and the realities of their everyday life (see, for example, Alpert 1991, 69–70; Umansky and Ashton 1992, 21).

The American Catholic philosopher Mary Daly was among the first to see the inherent connection between religion and gender, and she referred to religion's part in defining gender roles as depending on the construction and maintenance of the core belief in the fundamental connection between womanhood and nature (see, for example, Daly 1968, 1973, and 1978). Jewish feminists began to exploit this connection for their own benefit (see, for example, Porterfield 2001, 165–201). Thus, since the early 1970s, both religion and nature became important dimensions in Jewish feminism, and there was a growing interest in nature-friendly or nature-based forms of spirituality. Nature-based religions allowed feminists to link nature's and women's fertility and to define womanhood in terms of nature, but in a way that gave a positive and liberating meaning to both women and nature. This new approach challenged traditionally negative identifications of women and nature in Christianity and Judaism (see Porterfield 2001, 177). Women started to search for nonpatriarchal models and images that demonstrated respect for women and nature (such as in the Rosh Hodesh ritual) and moreover affirmed their sense of women's connectedness to the earth. In addition, New Age models of spirituality acted as a counterbalance to the Western mind-body split.[14]

Another important dimension of the Jewish women's spirituality movement was the issue of the gendered God, even though Judaism does not envision God as only male or female, since Jewish theology insists that God is without body (Lefkovitz and Shapiro 2005, 104). Thus, the resurgent interest in the study of goddesses was put at the center of feminist thinking, and adherents of the countercultural goddess movement, such as the feminist Jewish writer Starhawk,[15] were convinced that the core Jewish and Christian traditions were hopelessly sexist. The only way to free women from those traditions was to reject the biblical past and to focus on the history of goddess worship and goddess symbols (Christ and Plaskow 1992, 4 and 10–11). It was Starhawk, as Christ and Plaskow write, who encouraged her followers to exploit the prebiblical past to construct new feminist spiritual visions and ceremonies that were also reflected in spiritual songs (ibid., 11; see also Porterfield 2001, 180).

THE CRITERIA OF FEMINIST JEWISH RITUAL MAKING AND CREATIVITY

Although feminist proponents of New Age religions tended to romanticize women's roles in premodern tribal societies and idealized ancient, non-Western cultures as egalitarian, utopian societies (see Porterfield 2001, 180), the influence of New Age spirituality clearly functioned as a catalyst in the invention of feminist Jewish rituals, music, and visions of theology and community. American Jewish women turned from being objects, the suppressed, and the others and became subjects and (ritual) agents (Sered 1992, 10). Thus, with the development of Jewish women's spirituality and its entry into academic discourse, central criteria that help identify and categorize feminist Jewish rituals became clear.

For example, what characterizes a Jewish ritual (or any other custom or form of art) as feminist is its distinction from the male (official) form of Judaism. Nevertheless, some feminists still referred back to the traditions of normative Judaism to enhance their Jewish identity rather than totally ignoring their religious backgrounds (see, for example, Adelman 1990, 1; Sered 1992, 26–27). Lori Lefkovitz and Rona Shapiro define feminist rituals as those that include "women, men, and children, their voices, and the range of their experiences—biological, communal, and personal" that previously have been excluded or ignored by Jewish tradition. "Protecting the earth, working for peace, fighting against racism, striving toward economic justice, and fighting for human rights are feminist causes," too (2005, 112). As Mary Collins (1993) has observed, the principles of feminist Jewish liturgy and ritual are the ritualization of relationships between women and nature (for example, in Rosh Hodesh) and between women and the *Shekhinah* (literally, settling or dwelling; the feminine aspect of God), as well as the relationship of modern women to their foremothers Sarah, Rebecca, Leah, and Rachel and other biblical women, especially the prophetess Miriam. Emphasizing these connections symbolically rejects patriarchal culture. It also implies a feminist critique of male-dominated Jewish liturgy. In terms of community building and leadership skills, women developed alternative, symbolic forms of gatherings, most often egalitarian meetings that enabled all participants of feminist ritual groups to learn how to lead services and become more proficient in doing so.

FROM SPIRITUALITY TO THEOLOGY: THE DEVELOPMENT OF JEWISH FEMINISM SINCE THE 1980S

Although the Jewish women's spirituality movement failed to acknowledge individual religious ideals and backgrounds (such as differences between liberal and Orthodox Judaism) and paid little attention to the concerns of lesbians, it did provide many women with a sense that Judaism is a living and adaptable tradition. This motivated them to make significant contributions to political and social change in American Judaism in the decades to come (Alpert 1991, 67–70). How far Jewish feminism has really come, and how easy or hard it was to strongly influence women's status in American Judaism, did not become obvious until the late 1980s and early 1990s, when the Jewish women's spirituality movement evolved into a feminist Jewish movement driven by scholarship. Women's position in Judaism changed significantly: their former status of being separate and formally equal gradually shifted to the status of being not separate and formally (but still not actually) equal. The problem of pluralism instead of the question of egalitarianism alone came to dominate contemporary Jewish feminism and its scholarship.

Feminist Jews began to focus their attention on the question of how women's sensibility and experiences can be reflected in Jewish life, and the realm of theology (and its impact on liturgy and ritual) became the staging ground of feminist innovation. The question of whether or not women can be counted in the minyan was replaced in the center of feminist Jewish thinking and activism by the question of how women pray, and that change reveals the ambiguity of feminism in American Judaism at the end of the twentieth century and the beginning of the twenty-first.

Judith Plaskow's Feminist Jewish Theology

In the 1980s a new generation of feminist theologians in the United States, influenced by the postmodern climate in philosophy, began to reshape Jewish theological discourses. Judith Plaskow, a feminist Jewish scholar who identified herself as a reconstructionist, published an article titled "The Right Question Is Theological" (1983), which was the first critique of women's subordinated status in Judaism from a theological perspective. Plaskow (1994, 68) argues that women's subordination in Judaism is not only a sociological issue, but a matter of theology. In 1990, she published the groundbreaking *Standing Again at Sinai*, which signaled the entry of feminist Jewish theology into academic discourses.[16] In the book, she not only reviews American Jewish feminism from the 1960s to the 1980s but also discusses the recent call for honoring differences among Jews in general and Jewish women in particular. Contemporary feminist Jewish scholarship now acknowledges that the experiences of Jewish women and their complex ethnic and religious identities cannot be understood by looking only through a heteronormative gendered lens (T. Cohen, Hammer, and Shapiro 2005, 68). Concepts like multiculturalism, pluralism, and individualism—as well as the ideas of inclusiveness, choice, and thus the multidimensionality of identity (including the notion of the fluidity of gender and sexual identities)—entered feminist Jewish discourses, setting the agenda for the future of feminist Jewish theology and leading the feminist Jewish movement into the next stage, which not only sought to reframe the outer shell of Judaism but also to delve into its fundamental conceptual beliefs (see ibid., 7; Litman 2009, 253–4; Millen 2007, 28). As noted above, Plaskow's feminist Jewish theology redefined the central concepts of Judaism—the Torah, Israel, and God (see Plaskow 1992). Plaskow (1994, 68 and 73) argued that the normative character of maleness in the Bible, the Halakhah, and other sacred texts not only causes the subordination of women in Judaism but also makes it impossible for feminist Jewish theologians to root themselves in the Jewish tradition without simultaneously questioning its most essential beliefs.

Plaskow's (1996, 105) critique of the Torah focuses on how the complex content of Jewish religious reflection is represented and how women are thus excluded not only from the pivotal events and moments in Jewish history, as recorded in the Torah but also from the content of Jewish memory. The Torah is not just the history but also the living memory of the Jewish people that continues to shape Jewish identity and self-conception—but not for women. That is why the content of memory itself has to be transformed (Plaskow 1992, 52 and 55; see also Millen 2007, 30). However, despite the anger Jewish feminists feel at their subordination in the Jewish tradition and its sources, they never fully turn their back on it. Non-Orthodox feminists tend to characterize the Torah as partial and incomplete, arguing that only half "of the record of the Jewish encounter with God has been passed down through the generations" (Plaskow 1996, 105). This view of the Torah allows feminist Jews to define the discovery of Jewish women's history and spirituality as "a process of continuing revelation" (ibid.). By employing feminist historiography, midrash (interpretation of Jewish sacred texts), and liturgy, it is possible to make visible women's religious experiences and practices, as well as their interaction with accepted Jewish sources and one another. At the same time, the patriarchal nature of Jewish history and its sources is revealed. Thus, Jewish women receive new understandings not only of Jewish stories, practices, and concepts but also of themselves and become able to formulate a feminist vision of the past (Plaskow 1992, 54, and 1996, 105). This process of reconstructing and rewriting the history of the Jewish people from a feminist perspective is further understood as the reclamation of the so-called women's Torah, (Plaskow 1992, 54). Plaskow also criticizes the common (male) understanding of the Halakhah and how it constructs women's otherness. She states that Jewish feminism is about emancipation from deeply embedded preconceptions about gender roles and their implications for women's religiousness, making the point that it is Jewish law that mainly causes the subordination of women in Judaism and their inferior legal status, as that law provides the structure and content of Jewish life and shapes the individual's religious and social vision of Judaism, according to Rochelle Millen's summary (2007, 31) of Plaskow's explanations.

The central concept of Israel is placed between those of Torah and God. The reason for this is that Plaskow considers Israel, symbolizing the Jewish community, as a vehicle for the creation and continuation of a Jewish (feminist) memory, as well as a place for experiencing God. She argues that the reclaimed Torah is the basis for the modern Jewish community, in which women are considered to be full members, and that the Jewish memory, as it is shaped through Torah, defines the structure of that community. Thus, if we reclaim the women's Torah, we also need a community that lives and remembers it (see Plaskow 1992, 118–21). She further considers the conceptualization of difference in the community as most important and calls for a Jewish community that honors and respects the distinctiveness of Jewish identities, beliefs, and practices that are not invidious or hierarchical. She calls for "equality in our particularity" (quoted in D. Berman 2009, 16).

The third central concept in Plaskow's analysis is God. She demonstrates the effect that male and androcentric images of God have on the individual's and the community's religious experience. In Judaism, God has never been viewed as exclusively male or female. But this is not true in the context of actual religious life. In traditional Judaism, the divine is usually addressed in the second-person masculine and otherwise is exclusively referred to in male terms such as the Lord, the *Avinu Malkenu* ("Our Father, Our King"), and the *Adon Olam* ("Master of the Universe") (Plaskow 1992, 155–60). Consequently, the traditional way of talking about God, as well as the entirely patriarchal perception of the divine, not only excludes the points of view of women and reinforces their marginalization in the dominant spheres of Jewish religious praxis, but it also indicates the social structure of a community (ibid., 166–69; Plaskow 1994, 69).[17] That is why new linguistic and conceptual alternatives were needed. The use of a wide range of new metaphors for God—from concepts of the female (Shekhinah, Mother, and Queen) or of the abstract (flow of life, the Great One) to gender-neutral and nonhierarchical (lover, friend) ones—indicated a shift toward a concept of God informed by feminism that speaks to men and women alike. The traditional image and gender of God, as well as the concept of God's nature and power, have been profoundly transformed (Plaskow 1996).

To implement these feminist theological thoughts in the Jewish liturgy, the traditional language of prayer and the way of performing prayer, ritual, and liturgical music had to be changed as well. Feminist Jews responded to what they considered to be inappropriate language of prayer by translating the sacred texts from the masculine Hebrew into so-called feminist Hebrew or a gender-neutral language, such as English. Hebrew does not have a neuter gender. Thus, instead of *baruch ata adonai* (Blessed are you Lord our God), which marks the beginning of traditional Jewish blessings, feminists suggested using the term *eyn hahayim* (source of life), a grammatically feminine term; or saying *n'vareykh et eyn hahayim* (Let us bless the source of life), which uses the first-person plural instead of the common second-person masculine (see Falk 1999, 18–23; Plaskow 1994, 73–75, and 2007, 212).[18] Plaskow is well aware of the need for feminist terms for God that allow women to experience God in their own new sense of empowerment and experience their presence and selfhood in the context of the Jewish tradition and the larger Jewish community. Nonetheless, Plaskow objects to such terms. She points to a certain naivety "in the assumption that the insertion of female pronouns or images into traditional prayer provides a solution to women's invisibility" (Plaskow 1994, 75). She argues that using merely female images or terms for God is as exclusionary as the traditional images and terms are, and it is as much a part of a larger pattern of hierarchical dualism (ibid.).

Sexual Diversity and Jewish Theology

In addition to the reconceptualization of the Torah, Israel, and God, Plaskow (2007) stresses the importance of sexual diversity as another crucial aspect in feminist Jewish theology. Not only does a formal and explicit theology raise valuable overarching questions, such as those concerning gender models in Judaism that inform Jewish feminist theory and organization (Plaskow 2009, 8–9). But a feminist theology that acknowledges the problem of sexual diversity is also an important element in creating an inclusive and egalitarian, and thus feminist community (see Levitt 1997, 94).

Thus, Plaskow (2009, 9) criticizes feminists' efforts to transform the Jewish community by drawing on only the female concept of gender, while ignoring the existence of more than two sexes and of people who have changed their gender. She demands a wider understanding of the categories of male and female to extend the social and physical spectrum of human diversity and to include intersexual categories such as *tum tum* (a Talmudic term for androgyny). She also notes that feminism is not only about gender and certainly not only about or for women (ibid.). In contrast to the rather women-centered second wave of Jewish feminism, the third wave focuses on the diversity and inclusion of both men and women, regardless of their sexuality (ibid. 10).[19]

THE BIRTH OF WOMEN'S MUSIC: 1970S TO 1980S

The emergence of the Jewish women's spirituality movement and of a feminist Jewish theology provided the framework for the evolution of feminist Jewish music, which was modeled on women's music but seen as a new and independent musical genre. The following sections thus examine the birth of a new women's music and feminist Jewish music in America during the course of the feminist Jewish movement. In doing so, the sections show where feminist Jewish singer-songwriters came from musically, politically, and professionally.

The Making of a New Women's Music

During the folk revival of the 1960s, the names of popular women folk singers, such as Judy Collins, Joan Baez, and Joni Mitchell became inseparable from the great protest songs of the antiwar and civil rights movements, but those songs were all written by men. Although female folk singers may have been no more than mouthpieces for male musical activists such as Bob Dylan, Phil Ochs, and Paul Simon, they nevertheless benefited from the folk music boom of the middle 1960s. As Jerry Rodnitzky (1999, 72) puts it, the image of female folk singers turned from cute and sexy to saintly and outspoken.

Although it was not typical for prominent female vocalists to play instruments as well as sing before the 1960s, folk music's new instrumentation helped establish new conventions and inspire confidence in women as instrumentalists (see, for example, Perone 2004, 84; Rodnitzky 1999, 58 and 72–73). Folk songs and the acoustic guitar became the trademark of female singer-songwriters, and later on also of feminist Jewish singer-songwriters. They also became the new countercultural tools in the women's liberation movement, when feminism started to accept new types of female singers in the 1970s (Rodnitzky 1999; 73). As a result, the general exclusion of women from certain realms of musical expressions, such as rock music, and the never-ending stream of antifeminist songs (such as Raymond A. Smith's "Here's to the Women's Liberation" and Lana Roush's "Don't Liberate Me") in popular music became more and more obvious. Feminist critics and female, mainly lesbian, musicians (such as Alix Dobkin, Meg Christian, and Toni Armstrong Jr.) and audiences began to respond negatively to the sexist lyrics of pop and rock music as well as to the exclusive, oppressive, and alienating male musical culture and business (see, for example, Morris 1999, 3; Petersen 1987, 206).

Between 1970 and 1980, women active in the mainstream women's liberation movement created a vibrant, independent, and self-supporting female musical community and production network that was centered on a new genre of popular music that expressed and reflected women's experiences, self-worth, and points of view—a genre called women's music or women-identified music (see, for example, Kok 2002; Morris 1999, 3; Petersen 1987, 206). However, as a result of negative and sexist experiences, and the fact that even feminist music was either managed and distributed by men or inaccessible to masses of women, lesbians and feminist separatists stressed the need to create a separate space for women to write, perform, and distribute their alternative music (Rodnitzky 1999, 59–62). In 1973 the first women's music festival was held at Sacramento State University, in California. Since then, women's music festivals have taken place all over the United States and have provided a safe space not only for showcasing women's music and culture, but also for supporting many other aspects of feminist and lesbian culture. The transformative power of movement music as a countercultural tool to raise consciousness was discovered—a tool that allowed feminist musicians and activists to communicate issues central to the women's liberation movement (see, for example, Love 2002, 74–94).

But in a time when music meant so much for a generation that it became an ideological battlefield, and records and tapes became the real alternative media, women went farther than mere consciousness-raising (see, for example, Rodnitzky 1999, 57). Most feminist musical energy was centered on the establishment of small alternative record companies such as Olivia Records (founded in 1973) and Ladyslipper, which later became the center of women's music publishing (see, for example, Lont 1992, 242–44; Petersen 1987, 208–9). Professional experiences in the context of this new musical entrepreneurship helped feminist Jewish songwriters distribute and sell their own music later on (see chapter 2).

However, women's music as an independent genre began to develop when feminist and especially lesbian lyrics were accompanied by melodies in the popular musical styles of the time (see Perone 2004, 85). As Toni Amstrong first defined women's music, it is "music by women, for women, about women, and financially controlled by women" (quoted in Love 2002, 75). This rather open definition later became more specialized with the works of different women musicians and the categorization of music by record labels. Thus, Meg Christian, who—along with Chris Williams, Margie Adam, and Holly Near—was one of the original performers of women's music, extended the definition by describing it as "music that honors women, that respects our special strength, celebrates our lives, supports and validates us and teaches us" (quoted in ibid.). Women working at Olivia Records defined women's music as music that "speaks honestly and realistically about women's lives" (Rodnitzky 1999, 62) while stressing women's needs, anger, fears, dreams, and relationships with other women, and the Ladyslipper catalogue defined women's music as taking women seriously (Dobkin n.d.). This understanding of women's music emerges from a feminist awareness, recognizing and taking women's talent, intellect and spirit into account (see Rodnitzky 1999, 62 and 69).

Through the contributions mainly of lesbian feminist musicians, such as the musical trio Lavender Jane (Alix Dobkin, Kay Gardner, and Patches Attom), women-identified music was divided into two subgenres: feminist music and lesbian music. Whereas the former focused on the political and social freedom of women, the latter emphasized women's personal space and freedom (Petersen 1987, 207). The common denominator of the songs of the 1960s and 1970s women's liberation movement, however, was the rich variety in styles, ranging from folk songs using acoustic guitar to hard rock, "from worker's songs to ballads of cultural pride and psychological independence" (Rodnitzky 1999, 59), from organizing songs (songs calling for collective action and thus presenting it as the solution to a perceived problem) to love ballads characterized by a harsh spirit and with a fundamental goal in mind (ibid., 59 and 65). Nonetheless, the music of the early women's movement largely followed women's traditional musical forms, whose sound was characterized at that time by accessibility and intimacy in musical groups, as well as by musical eclecticism and the integrity that comes from not trying to reach a mass audience (see, for example, Kok 2002, 2:675). By the late 1970s, when women's liberation music had hit its first peak, feminists began to understand culture in general as an indirect form of power that could shape ideas. They created their own images in their own music, while those in the field of pop music did not care about who wrote the song, but only what it sounded like. Feminist music continued to cherish music that came from personal experience and was sung by the songwriter.

The Making of Feminist Jewish Music

> *We sang ourselves into life.*
> *—Rabbi Sue Levi Elwell*[20]

The birth of feminist Jewish songwriting and music in the United States coincided with and was highly influenced by the advent of mainstream women's music but pursued another object. As the quote from Elwell shows, feminist Jews did not primarily seek separate spheres to perform their music—to live in a Jewish women's musical culture—but to sing themselves back into Jewish religious life. In the context of the feminist Jewish movement of the late twentieth century, music became one of the most crucial and important political tools for realizing the goals of feminist Jewish theology—discussed above—and achieve women's full integration into the synagogue and Jewish worship in general.

When I examined the large variety of feminist Jewish literature, pamphlets, and ritual sheets produced since the 1970s and in the 1980s in particular, I realized that music—although only marginal—was always mentioned not only as an important part of the feminist experience, but also as a crucial factor in the process of community building. But as natural as the existence and performance of contemporary Jewish women's music might seem today, many religious obstacles were associated with the entrance of women into Jewish liturgical music making. Thus, women's voices were not only underrepresented in Jewish texts, prayers, rituals, and the repertoire of synagogue music, but their singing and speaking voices were unheard in Jewish worship. To sing themselves back into public Jewish life—that is, to take part in the central rituals of synagogue worship (such as the public reading from the Torah), and thus to enter Jewish liturgical music from a feminist perspective—women had to criticize Jewish musical traditions by challenging the Talmudic dictum of Kol Isha, which identifies a woman's voice as a source of sexual stimulation.

THE PROBLEM OF KOL ISHA

The rationale for women's exclusion from participating vocally in synagogue worship (for example, reading from the Torah and singing in the presence of men besides their husbands, as in a mixed synagogue choir)[21] is the Talmudic declaration in Berakhot 24a "Kol be'ishah 'ervah" (the voice of a woman is nakedness; see, for example, S. Berman 1980, 45; Schreiber 1984–85, 27), which in turn is based on the Song of Songs 2:14: "My dove in the clefts of the rock, in the hiding places on the mountainside, show me your face, let me hear your voice; for your voice is sweet, and your face is lovely." The connection between the Talmudic dictum and the biblical passage lies in the homophonic analogy of the verbs *'ervah* (literally nakedness, meaning genitalia and, in Talmudic terms, forbidden) and *'arev* (to be pleasant). The former is based on an *al-tiqre-midrash* (a purposely false reading) of the biblical passage and in which the sensuality of a woman's voice is given a negative connotation and thus associated with her sexual and feminine charms, which might distract men from prayer and religious duty (see, for example, Zimmerman 2000, 183). Because of the equation of a woman's singing (and speaking) voice with her exterior—her uncovered body—Talmudic authorities decided that it was forbidden for men to recite any prayer or benediction while listening to a woman's singing, if she is present (see, for example, S. Berman 1980, 46–48; Schreiber 1984–85, 27).

Later rabbinical discourses extended the prohibition to musical performances in which a woman, because of her inherent sexuality, could take control of the performance and thus of men attending it. The argument here is that in a musical performance, a man does not merely listen to a woman's singing but also pays attention to her and the music, which are both considered as "being sexually loaded entities" (Koskoff 2001, 132–33). Thus, even today most Orthodox communities consider singing in mixed groups unthinkable. Some rabbis today apply the prohibition of Kol Isha only in contexts where a man could see a singing woman or is able to imagine her exterior because he knows her. Nonetheless, scholars are now concerned with the question of hearing a woman's singing, as on the radio. Also Orthodox men are traditionally prohibited from listening to recordings of women singing (see, for example, S. Berman 1980, 45; Schreiber 1984–85, 27).[22]

The concept of Kol Isha has had serious consequences for women. Although, according to the Talmud, it is not explicitly forbidden for a woman to read the Torah aloud, she is expected not to do so, out of respect to the community[23] (see, for example, Schreiber 1984–85, 28). The most important point here is that the original commandment given to men—not to expose themselves to a singing woman while praying—was turned into a ban on women singing in synagogue worship. The inescapable consequence of Kol Isha is that in Orthodox contexts today women's bodies and voices, which are considered secondary sex characteristics, have to be banned from men's field of vision. This was an unquestioned norm prior to the reformation of Judaism in the nineteenth and early twentieth centuries (see, for example, Schreiber 1984–85, 29). Consequently, men and women have to separate during worship, which led to segregating women behind the mekhitzah or on the balcony. Baruch Schreiber points out that "since the women are not visible, the seductive powers of the voice are minimized" (ibid.).

This interpretation of Kol Isha finally made it impossible for women to meaningfully follow synagogue services, as they are not allowed to participate actively. Today, the Talmudic dictum of Kol Isha is fully observed only in Orthodox communities. The Conservative and Reform synagogues do not ban women's singing, and members of those communities interpret the dictum as the expression of an individual opinion or as not applicable to modern times. Nonetheless, against the background of Jewish feminism, the concept of Kol Isha and women's performance context gain a different meaning. Whereas in Orthodox contexts separate spheres for men's and women's musical activities are unavoidable, in the context of Jewish feminism, women in single-sex communities choose to be there. Similar to the general concept of women's voice in mainstream feminism, in Judaism the dictum of Kol Isha became a feminist symbol of women's taking an active and creative role—usually as rabbis, cantors, or ritual makers, and too often ignored as composers, who developed a new genre of Jewish music (Rischar 2002, 679). Thus, Debbie Friedman stated:

> It was *kol isha* (the voice of women) for *col isha* (every woman) that inspired me to write inclusive music. It is beneficial not only for women, but for men and children as well. Singing helps us learn how to be vocal. Ultimately, the voices of women, their sense of empowerment, can be born from song, which can form the core of political, spiritual, and economic transformation. The more our voices are heard in song, the more we become our lyrics, our prayers, and our convictions. Then every woman will be heard, and every voice will be heard: *kol isha* for *col isha*. (quoted in Jewish Women's Archive n.d.)

MUSIC AND FEMINIST JEWISH CRITIQUE

Feminist critique and creativity have been communicated not only through the works of Jewish scholars, but also through the arts, offering a critical and feminist perspective on Judaism and Jewishness as a cultural, ethnic, and religious identity. Art about women moreover emphasized their absence from certain forms of religious or cultural production (Levitt 2001, 8013). Women rediscovered their voices. Some of them understood that process not only in terms of speaking out on behalf of themselves but also musically—most often in terms of singing, which is considered "the most common form of musical expression for women" (Rischar 2002, 2:678–79). Moreover, it is a very effective vehicle of empowerment.

Feminism and the cultural and religious freedom of the American and Jewish counterculture can be regarded as the ideological and aesthetic foundations of feminist Jewish music, and Rosh Hodesh groups[24] (as well as any other feminist Jewish group) can be regarded as its laboratory. Although the separation of men and women has largely been abolished in liberal Jewish communities, and women are now able to participate in synagogue worship (even as rabbis and cantors), the rediscovery of the feminist Rosh Hodesh ritual can be seen as a reaction to women's exclusion from synagogue worship. Accordingly, it can be stated that Jewish women to some degree, and as in the women's music festivals mentioned above, created their own isolation that maintains the character of the private arena, as they feel more secure in discussing personal and intimate concerns apart from men (see, for example, Post 1994, 37). In the context of feminist rituals, then, women's new songs are no longer geared to the women's traditional and domestic duties, but to their religious needs and experiences. Inspired by the wide variety and quality of new Jewish music and women's music, more and more Jewish women began to express their religion by music, and through it they also expressed their newly awakened identity as female Jewish subjects.

Once some feminist songwriters started to play at feminist gatherings and rituals for the first time, their songs inspired more Jewish women to play music in feminist contexts or even write feminist Jewish music. However, the presence of female cantors and rabbis, who were now allowed to go up to the bimah (to make an *aliyah*) only marginally led to their wanting new music to sing. As Rachel Adelstein discusses in her dissertation (2013), the appearance of female cantors did not have an immediate impact on the acceptance of female singing within their communities.

The intentions with which songs are integrated into Jewish feminist rituals and gatherings are diverse. One of the most obvious and important reasons is to connect the participants with one another and to demonstrate the togetherness of the group, beyond their loyalty to Jewish tradition—which is only one of the characteristics that these women have in common. As Martha Ackelsberg puts it, "the fact that the community can generate the energy and inspiration for beautiful music is empowering itself; but the feeling in the room when all of us sing together cannot be described. Our spirituality, as a group, is not only political; it is, I have come to understand, intensely musical. And that has served as yet another strong bond among us" (1986, 119).

A large collection of feminist Jewish songs emerged throughout the 1970s and 1980s that took up different topics celebrated and discussed in the context of feminist rituals (see chapters 3 and 4). Instrumental music and dance, but principally collective singing, functioned to create a sacred time and space, as well as an atmosphere of spirituality and *kavannah*.[25] The music was meant to connect the women with the divine, especially with Shekhinah (see S. Ross 2004, 54). Against the background of Kol Isha, the act of singing within a feminist ritual gains special meaning. Whereas some women share the view that Kol Isha is no longer important in all-female communities, others consider feminist rituals such as Rosh Hodesh to be a space and opportunity to tap the full potential and function of sacred singing that makes the real essence of prayer transparent (see ibid., 55, Heskes 1994, 56). Through the creation of and experimentation with feminist Jewish songs in the context of feminist rituals and communities, women also have the opportunity to experience leading prayer and song. Sue Levi Elwell writes: "The rituals that most deeply touched the participants were led by women with a charismatic, but not overpowering, presence, and a strong, clear voice. Music is the most immediate means for moving people into sacred space, for it moves beyond potentially leaden words and directly addresses the hunger of the seeker" (1993, 118).

As shown above, the birth of feminist Jewish music in the United States is not only closely related to the political and especially to musical developments in the Jewish counterculture and the women's liberation movement. In addition, it has to be understood as a result of the feminist critique of the traditional allocation of roles by gender in normative Judaism and its impact on the musical behavior and activity of Jewish women. Feminist Jewish music is thus a paradigmatic case study of Jewish feminism. Consequently, the emergence of feminist ritual and study groups unified women as Jews for the first time and enabled them to experience and experiment with different forms of religious expressions, including music. Women's inability to participate in the music of synagogue worship and influence its style is reversed in feminist communities, since in those communities societal restrictions concerning Jewish communal life, and particularly the prohibition to sing, are no longer valid. Rosh Hodesh groups in particular offered women the opportunity for unlimited musical activity. The most important result of the impact of the traditional Jewish patriarchal ideology on Jewish women's music making is that Jewish women in general, and feminist Jewish singer-songwriters in particular, sought to transfer the experiences of communal singing and music making they had in the separate sphere of Rosh Hodesh groups to the larger context of synagogue services. Feminist Jewish songwriters to some extent fell back on the traditional liturgical music repertoires, but they also composed music that expresses the religious needs of women. Thus, they had an influence on the transformation of Jewish musical customs in synagogue worship (see, for example, S. Ross 2004, 63).

With the emergence of feminist Jewish music as one of many feminist ways of articulation, American Judaism had to accept Jewish music written in folk-rock style (which was created during the countercultural years) as liturgical music in Jewish communities, and to accept the presence of Jewish women not only as rabbis and cantors but also as singer-songwriters, who "appeal to women, not only as [women themselves] but also as writer[s] and performer[s] of songs that mirror their feelings and concerns" (Kligman 2001b, 123). Feminist Jews started using music as a vehicle to connect not only men but also women to Jewish communities and to Judaism as whole. In this way they transformed Jewish liturgy by reconceptualizing the meaning and structure of Jewish liturgical music. Thus, feminist Jewish singer-songwriters in the 1970s and the 1980s created a very powerful medium, challenging the system of cultural and religious prestige by celebrating aspects of Jewish women's culture through their songs, and sanctifying experiences of both women and men that had been ignored by tradition (see, for example, Lefkovitz and Shapiro 2005, 111–13).

Whereas the music of feminist Jews of the 1970s and 1980s had the function of reaffirming their lifestyles and experiences, the music of today's feminist Jews has become an experimental ground for young women's understandings of recent gender expectations and roles that affect their lifestyles and demonstrates the fluidity and practicality of feminist Jewish theory in everyday life (see, for example, Munford 2004). Until the mid-1990s, various feminisms (both secular and Jewish) have most often been described by political type, such as liberal or radical. As a result of increasing diversity, however, young feminist Jews of today have more or less blurred the boundaries between common forms of feminism. Popular culture, especially music, became the most productive site for activism by Jewish feminists (particularly those outside the academic world) who sought alternative ways to make their ideas accessible to a large number of people (Heywood and Drake 1997, 17). Feminist Jewish music always gives insights into the current concerns and experiences of the present generation of American feminist Jews—no matter what they believe in (see, for example, ibid., 2 and 10). But in contrast to the popular culture of the 1960s, 1970s, and 1980s, that of today in general,[26] particularly its music, has played a central role in the production and propagation of Jewish feminism, mostly because of the opportunities offered by new information technologies as well as new media and the Internet (see, for example, Drake 2006, 1:225).

THE ORGANIZATION OF THIS BOOK

Each chapter of this book is based on my study of previous scholarship on related subjects and on my field notes, interviews, and analyses of documents and music. For further notes on my fieldwork and source materials, see appendix A and B.

Thus, the book is chiefly based on data collected during fieldwork among female and male feminist Jewish musicians, singer-songwriters, and rabbis and cantors affiliated with Conservative, Reform, Jewish Renewal, and Reconstructionist communities in the United States. I am less interested in concert performances of feminist Jewish music than I am in the question how the core values of contemporary Jewish feminism are materialized in, or are performed through, feminist Jewish music. Thus, the following parts of the book will not give detailed descriptions of concerts or ritual performances. Rather, I believe that the performance of feminist politics is as much laid out in the biographical backgrounds of feminist Jewish songwriters (chapter 1) and the diverse local and translocal networks supporting them and their work (chapter 2) as it is in the themes and sounds of their songs (chapters 3 and 4). Chapters 3 and 4 take up the core beliefs of contemporary Jewish feminism as outlined above. I will show that feminist Jewish songwriters respond in their lyrics and musical choices to feminist theological concepts. This response reveals the religiopolitical intentions behind the music. Chapter 4 closes with a final definition of feminist Jewish music based on the previous explanations. The book concludes with a discussion of feminist Jewish music as a discursive tradition and answers the question of how feminist Jewish music balances between Jewish tradition and feminist innovation.

The book avoids any attempt to provide an all-encompassing description and discussion of contemporary feminist Jewish music in the United States. Rather, it should be understood as a survey of major theoretical issues of Jewish feminism and their manifestation in particular examples of feminist Jewish songs. Thus, the book covers only part of the spectrum of feminist music in American Judaism, a topic that is still far from being fully studied, analyzed, and understood. The book seeks to present the beginning of the study of feminist Jewish music, a study that I hope will be continued in future research projects focusing on Jewish communities in other cultures.

PART ONE

The phenomenon of feminist Jewish music in the United States is less well known and understood than are the stories of individual feminist Jewish musicians who formed collectives. Thus, first, I take a close look at the constantly growing feminist Jewish music scene in the United States, looking first at the lives of a selected group of singer-songwriters working toward a new understanding of liturgical Jewish music that values religious improvisation and innovation. This biographical approach helps the reader understand who these self-styled feminist Jewish protagonists are, where they come from, and what motivates them to write feminist music for Jewish rituals and synagogue services.

Second, I demonstrate how these women choose local and transnational forms to express their connection to the broader musical, cultural, social, and political environment of American Judaism. The women belong to local Jewish women's groups, organize feminist rituals and concerts, try to get their music published by well-known Jewish music and women's music labels, and network with like-minded musicians in the United States and Canada. For them, singing is not just entertainment but prayer, a point that will be discussed in more detail in the second part of the book.

Thus, the songwriters presented in this part of the book perform in diverse cultural and religious contexts, and their music can be analyzed and discussed in more than just one way. They are presented here both because they can be regarded as the pioneers of feminist Jewish songwriting in the United States and because they seek—through the power of their music—to unite men and women in synagogue worship, which is the main point of interest in this book. Consequently, chapter 1 focuses on songwriters related to the more liberal and progressive streams of American Judaism, and not on Orthodox feminist songwriters, who perform only in all-female contexts.

1

Who Sings unto God?

Pioneer Feminist Jewish Singer-Songwriters in the United States

This chapter will present biographical background information on some feminist Jewish songwriters and will discuss their musical signature styles, to show the diversity within the genre of feminist Jewish music and its content. It is important to note that there exist differing musical conventions as well as understandings and forms of Jewish feminism that influence each songwriter's individual style of composition.[1] Consequently, the success of each songwriter cannot be defined by a uniform criterion of excellence; instead differing sets of criteria and values must be used to measure their individual achievements.

DEBBIE FRIEDMAN (1951–2011)

FIGURE 1.1: Debbie Friedman. Courtesy Cheryl Friedman

Who and what Debbie Friedman is, is the person who has become the sweet singer in Israel. And she is that voice that touches the heart of Jews everywhere, and people of faith everywhere, and people who care about each other everywhere. —(Gerard Kaye, my transcription of Ann Coppel, A Journey of Spirit)

With her first album *Sing unto God* (1972), the Reform singer-songwriter Debbie Friedman, z"l, paved the way for many in the American Jewish community to integrate contemporary songs of prayer into Jewish worship. Friedman described this album, which includes songs in the folk-rock style that are easy to sing and that use Hebrew sacred texts or a combination of Hebrew and English lyrics, as "a new experience in worship that emphasizes through song the importance of community involvement in worship" (quoted in Kligman 2001b, 122). The album and its title song are clearly in the tradition of new Jewish music, but Friedman broke new ground with regard to content—at least within the Jewish Reform movement. According to Benjamin Dreyfus (2001, 35), at her Carnegie Hall performance in 1996, Friedman changed the masculine language of the original English lyrics in her title song "Sing unto God," adapted from the Friday night Kabbalat Shabbat service, into a gender-neutral language, a point that will further be discussed below. By that time, female songwriters related to the Jewish Renewal and Reconstructionist movements had already developed a new genre of Jewish liturgical music that boasted an explicit feminist character. Although at the beginning of the 1990s, Friedman was already one of the most influential and best-selling musicians in American Judaism, she had not largely been recognized as a feminist songwriter either in the academy or by feminist Jewish songwriters related to the Reconstructionist and Jewish Renewal movement and other movements, such as the Orthodox movement. However, in changing the lyrics not only in "Sing unto God" but also in most of the rest of her repertoire, Friedman aligned herself with other feminist Jewish songwriters in the United States.

Deborah Lynn Friedman (1951–2011) was born in Utica, New York, and raised in a Reform family in Minneapolis. During her early childhood, she and her parents lived with Friedman's grandparents, who taught her to love the Jewish tradition. But when her parents decided to move to St. Paul, Minneapolis, they left all the tradition behind, as Friedman later recalled (Josephs 1996, 47). Mark Kligman (2001b, 121) argues that Friedman's interest in motivating other Jews to achieve a closer connection to Judaism originates from her own need and desire to reconnect to the Jewish practices she had lost during her childhood. Inspired by a cantor (a friend of her father) who had written rock music for prayer services, Friedman first transformed her longing to get more involved with Jewish liturgy into music. She realized how easy and almost natural it was for her to set Hebrew prayers to contemporary melodies that she felt very strongly about, and she found inspiration in texts from the Hebrew Bible and in midrashic literature (Josephs 1996, 47). At the age of seventeen, Friedman became a song leader at a Reform youth camp and at various educators' conferences, as well as other adult programs that were run by the Reform and Conservative movements (Kligman 2001b, 121).

Friedman's first recording, "Sing unto God" (1972), which draws on a Jewish youth service, was a demo she produced to promote herself. It sold out in two weeks. After she recorded six further albums on her own, Sounds Write Productions signed a contract with her. Although Friedman was self-taught instead of being a classically trained musician, she had great influence on the music of American Judaism in general, and the music of the Reform movement in particular (see Musleah 1995, 22).

Friedman's aim to make Judaism relevant to modern life is reflected in the style of her music, which might be described as original American folk-rock pervaded with Jewish spirituality. Since she was a young adult in the American counterculture era, Friedman's early work was highly influenced by the social-action songs of the 1960s and 1970s and bears a striking similarity to the popular music of the time, such as that of Peter, Paul, and Mary; Joan Baez; Judy Collins; and Melissa Manchester. Susan Josephs wrote that Friedman's "more recent compositions retain a folky quality but have become increasingly reflective of Friedman's effort to create an authentic Jewish music sound" (1996, 46; see also Kligman 2001b, 121). The combination of Hebrew sacred texts mostly accompanied by explanatory or interpretative lyrics written in English and popular folk-rock tunes has also been called American *nusach* (Jewish prayer modes; see Dreyfus 2001).

Friedman's song "Birkat HaLevana—Season of the Moon" (released on her 1998 album *It's You*) will be discussed as an example of her work, to show her style of composition. As is the case with all common popular, folk-rock, and contemporary spiritual songs—in part because of marketing—here Friedman sticks to the ideal of a singable song, as standardized by the

FIGURE 1.2: Introductory section (bars 1–15) of Debbie Friedman's "Birkat HaLevana—Season of the Moon"

American popular music industry (Pickow and Appleby 1988). Thus, the song consists of two clearly demarcated sections: a repeated verse and chorus section of thirty-two bars. The song, which is written in E minor, opens with an introductory section (see figure 1.2) presenting not only the melodic pattern of the verse, but also the transcribed Hebrew blessing of the new moon, the Birkat HaLevana that is traditionally recited when seeing the moon at the beginning of a Jewish month.

This section sets up the verse and finally leads to the refrain (see figure 1.3.).

Along with the basic song structure and the simple rhythm in ¾ time, the melody of Friedman's song is simple. The range of the melodic development is also limited (floating around G above middle C), which makes the song singable for each community member. However, this lack of compositional complexity enables the singer to reveal his or her personal vocal style and to improvise. It also provides the opportunity for instrumentational experimentation and, most important, puts the focus on the lyrics—which together with the music communicate the songwriter's political and femi-

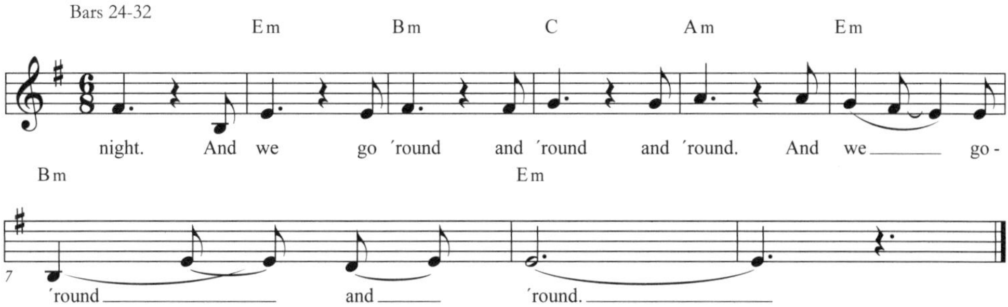

FIGURE 1.3: Refrain (bars 24–32) of Debbie Friedman's "Birkat HaLevana—Season of the Moon"

nist message. In terms of harmony, the song uses an extended conventional chord progression—I–VI–II–V–I—which lets the melody become sweeter in sound. An overused harmonic progression would instead restrict the melodic development. The song closes with a plagal cadence (V–I), which creates the feeling of more movement and adds an interesting and pulsating touch. Because of this rather conventional folk-rock style, the song can sound different each time it is sung by Debbie Friedman and/or her audience. The song thus becomes for the moment of performance an audible representation of a particular community, which can create a sense of unity.

Friedman's music, classified as American nusach, is by now widely seen as one aligned with the movement of Reform Judaism and thus has entered the movement's core repertoire, which consists of participatory songs that can be accompanied on the guitar.[2] Later on, the music was also adopted by Conservative and other Jewish congregations. Reform Judaism on the whole aims to integrate American culture into Jewish culture, because American ideals communicate a sense of progress. Similarly the movement's music emerges from the junction of Judaism and American life and culture, on the one hand, and, on the other hand, the Reform musician's intention to revitalize the traditional musical repertoire, which is considered as too formal and outdated (Kligman 2001b, 115–16; Zaidman 1996, 48–50).

Nevertheless, Friedman faced criticism (see Kligman 2001b, 123). Reform and Conservative cantors in particular criticized her music for being written not in a modal tradition (nusach) but in a very different style—namely, a popular folk idiom (see ibid., 122; Mark Kligman in Coppel, 2006). A dialogue between Debbie Friedman and Jacob Ben-Zion Mendelson, cantor at Temple Israel Center, in White Plains, New York, in the documentary *A Journey of Spirit*, highlights this conflict:

> FRIEDMAN: "The problem is, if you don't have people coming to temple, to synagogue, because they are totally disconnected from their tradition, because they are totally alienated, because they don't know Hebrew, because the nusach, [. . .] the traditional mode is a totally foreign sound to them . . ."
>
> MENDELSON: "The prayer modes are sacred, and I'm a nusach policeman. I mean, that's my job!"
>
> FRIEDMAN: "If they [the worshipers] don't know these sounds, and they can't relate to these sounds, they're not gonna show up to services, and there ain't gonna be a future, and any one to carry on traditional modes. So, it's ludicrous! [. . .] And I agree with him [Mendelson]. We have to preserve traditional music, traditional prayer, but first we gotta get them in the door." (my transcription of Coppel 2003)

In a roundabout way, critics say that Friedman's music lacks the power to connect the Jewish people to Jews from other places and times. It lacks what tradition is all about—namely, shared cultural, historical, and religious memory. This, in fact, can be said of the whole repertoire of feminist Jewish songs in the United States. But while nusach policemen like Mendelson preserve tradition, they ignore one crucial fact in the history of Jewish music: musical innovators now considered traditional were once the challengers. For example, Salomon Sulzer and Louis Lewandowsky revolutionized synagogue music in German-speaking countries in the nineteenth century by following the example of European church music. In fact, Friedman's music is now considered traditional. In spite of the criticism, she knew how to connect Jews to each other. Her remarkable stage presence and her ability to integrate and encourage her audience, as well as the power of her music to create a transcendental experience among the listeners, can also be seen in how people talk about her music: "Singing prayers together was like being cleansed inside," as Marci Erlebacher stated (quoted in D. Cohen 1996, 50); "that music has the ability to rock the soul," "the music helps develop kavannah . . . it helps to open up" the soul, and "we didn't understand a word, but the music conveys the sentiment as much as the words" (Cabot 2000). Also the dynamic relationship between Friedman and her audience in concerts often entered the realm of liturgy, so the concerts came close to a synagogue worship experience (see Dreyfus 2001, 43). Friedman describes that relationship this way: "[The concert experience] is circular. I don't separate myself from the community. I can only be as good as they are. I want them to be with me, and I want to be with them" (quoted in Rogat 1998). Friedman's music bursts the boundaries between prayer and song (Kligman 2001b, 122–23). Not only does her music make prayer singable and songs prayerful, but she also seeks to educate her audience and engage them in a positive Jewish life—one that addresses women's issues (ibid.).

Although Friedman does not have a cantorial diploma, she served as a cantor in Los Angeles for many years, working with young Jews on the conception of new prayer services (Kligman 2001b, 121). During those years, she also served as a leader in prayer and song at the local Feminist Jewish Center, established by Rabbi Sue Levi Elwell (interview March 2008). In Reform Judaism the commitment to Jewish feminism becomes apparent in the absolute equality of women in all areas of Jewish life and in the fact that religious participation no longer depends on gender. Women in Reform Judaism have responsibilities that are similar to those of men (Zaidman 1996, 49–59), although the discrepancy between the rhetoric and the reality of gender equality, particularly in male-dominated central institutional and leadership structures remains blatant (Goldman 2007, 121). Consequently, Reform feminists are concerned about reformulating gender relations and changing the "formal position of women in the synagogue" (ibid., 124), and less concerned with the profound transformation of texts and rituals per se—which differentiates them from feminists of the Reconstructionist and Renewal movement, for example (Zaidman 1996, 48 and 52).

Friedman originally objected to making Jewish liturgy accessible to all people. In the early 1990s, she was invited by Elwell and Rabbi Laura Geller to participate in the American Jewish Congress feminist seder in Los Angeles. She remembers her initial distraction and worry about saying the *b'rachot* (blessings) in the feminine: "The first time it sounded so strange, but as the seder went on and as the years went on, the feminization of the liturgy became more and more natural to me" (quoted in Cohen, Friedman, and Elwell 1997). As Elwell told me, Friedman and some other feminists did not think much about traditional god language in those days, but that issue became particularly prominent in academic feminist Jewish discourses later. However, the issue of changing traditional, masculine prayer language into the feminine marks a crucial turning point in Friedman's career and repertoire. It is not clear when exactly Friedman started to use gender-neutral language in her songs, but it was before the 1990s. Benjamin Dreyfus (2001, 36) points to the liner notes of her album *In the Beginning* (1994), where she states that the impact of feminism would have been reflected in her songs had she recorded them today. In addition, Josephs mentions another crucial occasion, Friedman's performance at the Coalition for the Advancement of Jewish Education "some twenty years ago" (that is, about 1976) (quoted in Josephs 1996, 47).[3] This date seems reasonable, as the performance in question is that of Friedman's song "Not by Might, Not by Power," which contains the phrase "shall all men live in peace" and which was recorded on the eponymous album in 1974. Friedman discusses the same occasion in *A Journey of Spirit*:

> I was doing a sound check and I was singing "Not by Might, Not by Power," and I was singing, "but by the spirit alone shall all men live in peace." And some woman, I can't remember who it was, gave a *geshrei* [clamor] from the back of the room and said, "it's all people, you can't sing all men anymore because we're men and women, and we're all people. You have to sing all people!" So I realized at that point that she was right. I had to start changing the language, at which point I changed it that night when I did the performance, and I said we're going to change the lyric and I sang "shall we all live in peace," and it caught on and we did it. (my transcription of Coppel 2003)

Although the exact date of this performance, and thus the first moment when Friedman changed her language, cannot be absolutely determined, the impact of Jewish feminism on her work is undeniable. Thus, Friedman stated: "That was the day I started to have more consciousness about feminism. I thought about how hurt someone could be who felt excluded. I started to write differently" (quoted in Josephs 1996, 47).

After that, Friedman was closely associated with feminist circles and continued writing feminist songs and invented rituals. In particular, her

"Miriam's Song" has been widely used. *The Journey Continues* combines liturgical integrity with a consciousness-raising message (Cohen, Friedman, and Elwell, 1997). Thus, and as Kligman states (2001b, 123), her appeal to women as both a writer and a performer of women's music is one crucial factor that propelled her career.

Another factor, which is closely related to Jewish feminism, is Friedman's association with the phenomenon of healing services (ibid.). She struggled with illness for many years and devoted much of her attention and music to the issue of healing and to the renewal of mind and body. She considered involvement with healing not only as the natural province of women, but also as a part of tikkun olam, and thus of social justice: "My music is about engaging anyone willing to be a partner in tikkun olam, repairing the world" (quoted in Musleah 1995, 22). Especially popular is Friedman's "Mi Shebeirach," a version of the traditional prayer of healing, which was written for the Simkhat Chokhmah ritual (a ritual for celebrating wisdom as well as for reclaiming respect and honor for elders) of Marcia Cohen Spiegel (a prominent figure in the Jewish feminist movement) and led the way for all other feminist healing songs. In fact, "Mi Shebeirach" is the most often requested song in the Reform movement, and it has become a hallmark of the Jewish healing movement (Kligman 2001b, 123).

In contrast to feminist Jewish singer-songwriters related to the Jewish Renewal and Reconstructionist movements, Friedman does not primarily focus on feminist interpretations of Jewish sacred texts, nor does she address particular women's issues (often of a biological nature). Accordingly, it would be an exaggeration to describe her feminism as theological or woman centered. Rather, Friedman represents a socialist approach to Jewish feminism or a gender-centered feminism. From this perspective, it is not coincidental but "natural"—as Friedman explains in the booklet of her recording *One People* (2006)—that she writes her music in the folk genre, as folk music is all but inseparable from the philosophy of Reform Judaism and the social justice movement of the 1960s and 1970s, an era that formed Friedman personally and musically. Thus, her interest in and perspective on Jewish feminism in general emerged from her belief in and activism related to social consciousness, and her songs reflect this. At the same time, she combines issues of social justice, women's topics, and feminist Hebrew in a given song or album. In the titles of her recordings and songs, as well as in the style of her music, Friedman makes a statement: her music "enables those who are willing to join together as a community in contemporary songs of prayer" (Friedman on her album *In the Beginning*; see also Dreyfus 2001, 33).

RABBI GEELA RAYZEL RAPHAEL AND THE WOMEN OF MIRAJ

> *Rabbi Rayzel Raphael brings a rich background in spirituality, ritual, feminism, and music to Judaism. She hails from Tennessee and sings the song of the south in her soul.—(CDBaby 2015a)*

Rabbi Geela Rayzel Raphael could not be better characterized than she is by CD Baby, a small online record store selling albums of independent musicians. Raphael is one of the most important figures in the feminist Jewish music scene and was my main informant during my fieldwork in the United States. Her goal is to "bring a vision of a feminist Judaism, which, through the discipline of the arts, can be healing, transformative and joyous" (quoted in Targan 1995). In Philadelphia, Pennsylvania, on February 27, 2007, I met Raphael for the first time. During a car ride from the city

FIGURE 1.4: Rabbi Geela Rayzel Raphael. Courtesy Rabbi Raphael

center to Melrose Park, the suburb where she lives, and between stopping at a costume store to buy a fancy dress for Purim and picking up her daughter from school, Raphael told me about her life.

She grew up in a Conservative family in Tennessee. Her journey with music began when she was a child in the synagogue choir at Heska Amuna Congregation, in Knoxville, where she learned to love the singing by Rabbi Max Zucker, z"l. In 1966, she had a bat mitzvah (which was already common for girls). However, while boys were given the honor of reading the Torah in the Shabbat morning service, girls were only allowed to read the haftorah on a Friday night. While this ceremony marked the end of her public service leading for a decade, she kept on singing with a group called "The SWEJS,"[4] whose other members were the well-known Conservative Rabbi David Golinkin; his brother, Cantor Abe Golinkin; and Raphael's high school friend, Merryl Ross. Together, they sang "Down by the Riverside" on the Jerry Lewis Labor Day telethon (an annual event to raise money for the Muscular Dystrophy Association), which was a foreshadowing of things to come.

As a young woman in the late 1970s and early 1980s, Raphael first encountered the Jewish Renewal movement and Jewish feminism. Between 1975 and 1988 she studied religion with a focus on Jewish studies at York University, in Toronto, Ontario, and at the Graduate School of Contemporary Jewish Studies at Brandeis University. At these universities, she explored the women's minyan for the first time: "This was a group of all women who took turns leading Shabbat and other services. We were trying to find our voices as strong women. In that feminist context, ten years after my bat mitzvah, I rediscovered my service leading and embroidered my first tallit. Exposed to many different tunes than what were available to me in Tennessee, I began to learn to collect niggunim to expand my repertoire" (personal correspondence October 2013). In 1984, after working as director of the Jewish Student Federation of York University, Raphael spent a sabbatical year at Pardes Yeshiva, in Jerusalem. She became increasingly involved with Jewish feminism while reading Susannah Heschel's edited volume, *On Being a Jewish Feminist* (1983). The book's negative tone, rather than its radical content, caught her attention. Raphael felt an urge to respond to the volume, but in a positive manner. Her music should be understood against this background.

During Raphael's year in Israel, she also attended her first meeting of a Rosh Hodesh group. After she returned to Toronto, greatly inspired by feminist Jewish arguments and the spiritual practice of Rosh Hodesh, she decided to found her own Rosh Hodesh group and to start writing feminist Jewish songs:

> My first song had tumbled out when I was filled with emotion. This time I was driving in rush hour traffic on the way to the gym. My Rosh Hodesh group had been studying about Miriam, the prophetess. I had been thinking of the sentence in Exodus, "*Va-tikach Miriam Hanivea et ha-tof b'yadah* . . . and Miriam took her timbrel out and all the women danced . . ." Suddenly words and music rolled off my tongue, I had to pull over and write them down. . . . My song "By the Shores / Miriam and Her Timbrels" was written. From that point onward I was hooked on trying to repeat that experience and make more music. (personal correspondence October 2013)[5]

Raphael then started to become involved in feminist Jewish activism and began to attend feminist retreats and explore Jewish women's spirituality. Around this time, she came into contact with the feminist Jewish network B'not Esh (Daughters of Fire), led by Rabbi Sue Levi Elwell and Judith Plaskow, and with another Jewish sisterhood called Achyot Or (Sisters of Light) (interview with G. Raphael February 2007). These two groups have met together for twenty-five years on Memorial Day weekend to explore what it means to be a feminist Jew, and they became Raphael's "psychic pillars" in her journey to transform Judaism according to feminist principles. It is in the context of these two Jewish women's groups that feminist Jewish music exists and is developed (personal correspondence October 2013).

Raphael's feminism and music were both influenced by the time she spent living and studying in Israel, and particularly by the annual meetings of B'not Esh, where a great deal of music is played. Raphael was awarded a scholarship in 1988–89 to attend the Melton Senior Educators' Program at Hebrew University, in Jerusalem. During her second stay in Israel, she became a member of the Jewish women's prayer group Women of the Wall. Once a month, on Rosh Hodesh, members of the group go to the Western Wall in Jerusalem to claim their right to worship, as well as read from the Torah and wear phylacteries. However, particularly the women's reading from the Torah at the Western Wall was forbidden by the local rabbinate. At the kotel in 1988, Raphael wrote the lyrics for her well-known song "Holy Mother, Shechinah Soul," which was released on *Friday Night Revived* (G. Raphael 2005), an album that represents a completely transformed musical Shabbat service. This song is characteristic for Raphael in terms of both its content and its eclectic musical style. It can be described as cross-genre, as it shows musical characteristics of both blues and swing and thus gives a bluesy swing impression. The song is written in C minor and in 12⁄8 time, and draws on the common twelve-bar blues structure. In contrast to popular folk songs, such as those of Debbie Friedman, Raphael's song consists only of verses (no chorus) characterized by a three-line lyrical pattern that is used in blues. Consequently, each verse opens with the same statement ("Holy Mother, Shechina Soul"; see bars 5 and 6 in figure 1.5) and is followed by different additions (such as "Rachamena," in bar 7). This same process is repeated until the song ends.

The chord progression is almost reminiscent of typical blues progressions, such as I–IV–V (bars 9–12) and I–V–I–I (bars 5–7). As in common blues songs, Raphael uses only three chords: the tonic (I), subdominant (IV), and dominant (V). The rhythmic structure of the song is reminiscent of swing: a lilting rhythm based on ternary phrasing (two eighth notes are to be considered eight-note triplets, whose first two parts are tied to a quarter) and offbeat accents. Like other feminist Jewish songs, Raphael's song has a simple melody and is easy to learn.

The use of repetition, the musical parameters of blues and swing, and the combination of several musical genres are characteristic of Raphael's songwriting. Her aim is not to meet certain standardized ideals for composition but to express her Jewish spirituality through music. In doing so, she seeks to revitalize traditional Jewish religious music and to advance her or the worshiper's relationship to the divine.

While in Israel, Raphael also began to study the women of the Hebrew Bible. Highly influenced by B'not Esh, Raphael started to write feminist Jewish music with the aim of transforming Judaism by music. She told me that she wanted to be a "feminist Jewish rock 'n' roll star" (interview February 2007). During her studies in Jerusalem, Raphael also began to write music and a study guide on women of the Bible (1998). The related album, *Bible Babes A-Beltin'* (1997) features songs about women of the Bible written between 1988 and 1995 with a contemporary sound.

FIGURE 1.5: "Holy Mother, Shechinah Soul" (2005) by Rabbi Geela Rayzel Raphael. Courtesy Rabbi Rayzel Raphael.

In her unpublished study guide (which includes sheet music), Raphael writes that the purpose of her project was to provide an in-depth study of the stories of biblical women. Furthermore, she wanted to add her voice "to the wealth of Jewish women's literature, art and culture that is emerging at the turn of the millennium" (1998, 1). In the late 1980s or early 1990s, Raphael also founded the Shechinah Soul Sisters, an all-female choir. During this time, she wrote various Shechinah songs that have been recorded on audiotape. Some of them were released on her albums years later. A secular influence on Raphael's music making was the music and culture she experienced in the 1980s at the Womyn's Michigan Music Festival (interview February 2007), when women's, or feminist, music was established as a genre for the first time (see chapter 2).

During the nine years Raphael needed to finish the *Bible Babes A-Beltin'* project and release the album of the same name, she went to rabbinical school and raised her first child (interview February 2007).[6] The years she spent at the Reconstructionist Rabbinical College were important to her future career as a rabbi and feminist Jewish musician. Her first contact with the Jewish Renewal and Reconstructionist movements was made through her husband, Rabbi Simcha Raphael, in 1986. At that time, the Jewish Renewal movement was still a part of the Reconstructionist movement (ibid.). Before she received her rabbinical ordination from Reconstructionist Rabbinical College in 1997, Raphael was involved in many important religious developments. Although she is a trained Reconstructionist rabbi, her heart is Renewal, which makes her a "Reconewal Jew," as she described herself to me (ibid.). Finally, she helped to set up the Jewish Renewal movement in the greater Philadelphia area: "Renewal was also a support lab for Jewish feminist music. I had found my Shechinah Soul Sisters. I remember Rabbi Shefa Gold, at that time Sheri Pelicrow, singing her song 'Behind the Mehitza' at Aleph Kallah, a bi-annual gathering for Jewish Renewal. I connected with Hanna Tiferet Siegel as well through ritual and song at an early retreat" (personal correspondence October 2013).

While the Reconstructionist movement was rather rational in nature, the Renewal movement established itself as the center for creativity and spirituality. This is also reflected in Raphael's work as a freelance teacher and ritual maker. She teaches courses on biblical women; new rituals; angels; Rosh Hodesh; and Jewish women's sexuality, spirituality, and power. In addition to composing music, Raphael served as rabbinic director of the

Interfaith Family Support Network of Greater Philadelphia. Since 2005, she has served as the rabbi of Beth Israel in Woodbury, New Jersey, a Conservative congregation. She also served at Leyv-Ha-Ir, in Philadelphia, and Temple Israel, in Lehighton, Pennsylvania (ibid.).

Given the background of Raphael's self-description, training, and strong affiliation to the Jewish Renewal movement, and particularly her songs, Raphael's feminism can be described as a women-centered- and theologically oriented feminism. The latter term is justified by her focus on creating a new feminist Jewish liturgy and by her long-standing examination of Shekhinah, feminist god language, and the feminist interpretation of the Torah and Talmud. All these are the basis for many of her songs and explain why she describes her songs as midrash (interview February 2007). In sum, Raphael's goal is to "make music for the revolution" (personal correspondence, October 2013)—to write songs about women of the Bible, songs of empowerment, and ritual songs to express the needs of women; songs that help Jewish women fit their feminist consciousness into a Jewish life. With the formation of MiRaJ (the name is based on the ensemble members' names, Margot, Rayzel, and Juliet), discussed in the next section. Raphael's musical journey has deepened both musically as well as spiritually, and she has refined her goal of creating songs for the feminist Jewish revolution (personal correspondence October 2013).

The Story of MiRaJ

During her years at rabbinical school, Raphael helped found Shabbat Unplugged/Havdallah Live (and later also the band Tof b'Yadah), which is a musical troupe performing rock 'n' roll Shabbat service, as she describes it (for more about Shabbat Unplugged, see chapter 2). She and the other members also organized women's Shabbat services, for which she began to create a new Friday night liturgy and feminist music. At that time, she met Rabbi Margot Stein and Juliet Irene Spitzer in the Hebrew grammar class at the Reconstructionist Rabbinical College. What started as a study group to help reduce the monotony of the class resulted in the founding of the a cappella trio MiRaJ, which is a creative collaboration between the three Jewish leaders and educators. Stein, Raphael, and Spitzer had all been singers and songwriters before they first met, and they realized how well their voices blended together in harmony (Shechinah 2012a). When the songwriter Linda Hirschhorn asked them to open for her at a local concert, the trio was born. Since then, MiRaJ has performed at retreats, women's seders, and synagogue services (CDBaby.com 2015b).[7] Each member of the ensemble writes music; some of the songs are sung individually, and some are sung by the whole trio.

Spitzer is "an international award-winning singer/songwriter and recording artist, interpreting the world through a uniquely Jewish and feminist lens," according to her website (Spitzer n.d.). This message is clearly reflected in her two albums *Full Glory* (1998) and *Shifting Edge* (2005). In addition to singing with MiRaJ, Spitzer serves as guest cantor at Congregation Beth Israel in Media, Pennsylvania, and performs nationally with the non-Jewish vocal ensemble SheWho and the musical troupes Shabbat Unplugged/Havdallah Live and Tof b'Yadah (discussed in chapter 2). She also composes music for and performs with Theatre Ariel, a professional Jewish theater company in Pennsylvania. Spitzer leads music and healing workshops in the Philadelphia area and teaches various topics in Judaism in the Florence Melton Adult Mini-School (interview March 2008). When I asked Spitzer about her denominational affiliation, she answered that she sees herself as "postdenominational," which means that she is a committed Jew who avoids a conventional denominational label (interview February 2007).

Spitzer became involved with feminism in her college years, when she worked at the college women's center and learned about the great (non-Jewish) feminists of those days in classes. She and her friend and MiRaJ colleague Margot Stein were greatly influenced by the songs of Chris Williams and Holly Near. Like Raphael, Spitzer states that she has been strongly influenced by the several women's music festivals she attended (interview March 2008). When I asked her how she would describe her feminism, she said that she was a "socialist feminist" whose primary interest is to free Judaism from its sexism (interview March 2008).

Margot Stein (formerly called Margot Stein Azen) is also a Reconstructionist trained rabbi and an award-winning singer-songwriter. She has produced or coproduced five albums of original Jewish music, including *Create Out of Nothing* (Azen 1991), and her musical play, entitled *Guarding the Garden* (Azen 1993), which toured North America for four seasons. It was seen by some 20,000 people and was featured on the cover of *Lilith*. The song "Eden Once Again" (words based on "Merger" by Judy Chicago, music by Margot Stein, 1991) from *Guarding the Garden* has been well received and interpreted by other performers and choirs.[8] The song has been called the anthem of the Reconstructionist movement: it calls for an update of Judaism to reflect not just the socially constructed gender dichotomy between male and female, but now also transgender and other fluid gender roles. Like Raphael and Spitzer, Stein also composes music for and sings with Shabbat Unplugged/Havdallah Live and Tof B'Yadah. She was formerly the director of communications for the Jewish Reconstructionist Federation. Today she teaches Jewish ethics at Gratz College's Melton Adult Mini-School and uses the performing arts to teach the Torah to teens (Shechinah 2009).

Stein was first exposed to Jewish feminism at college (between 1979 and 1983), where in addition to her official courses, she got interested in themes such as witchcraft and goddess religions, interests that finally resulted in a paper on goddess worship in Judaism. As she told me in a conversation, her family is deeply rooted in the Jewish religion, but her parents expected her to make a career in secular life. At her bat mitzvah her strong interest in Judaism finally awakened. By then, she was already a feminist, she said.[9] Just like Raphael, Stein (who is affiliated with the Reconstructionist movement) describes her feminism as a theological feminism, which includes social and communal aspects of Jewish feminism (interview March 2008). When I asked how she would describe the nature and character of feminist Jewish songwriters, she answered: "Debbie Friedman thinks social, Linda Hirschhorn thinks political, and MiRaJ thinks theological" (interview February 2007).

For the past twenty years, the members of MiRaJ have met every Tuesday at Spitzer's house for rehearsal, and I attended three of those rehearsals during my fieldwork. As Spitzer explained, the meetings are not only for making music but also to have lunch together, to talk, and to cultivate their long-standing friendship (interview February 2007). All three group members regard this friendship time, or the social component of their meetings, as a feminist act, she said. It is the group's "exquisite good fortune to have this sacred, weekly time together [and that we] sustain each other in ways that defy simple description" (CDBaby.com 2015b). As Spitzer and the others told me when I interviewed the trio, their lives have changed over the years (interview February 2007). All three of them became mothers, experienced the deaths of family members, changed their jobs, and had to deal with other life changes, which are reflected in the trio's songs.

The trio consciously uses music as an educational tool and a tool for "cultural change, empowerment and healing" (interview with MiRaJ, February 2007), through which Judaism is understood and can be changed. That is why the music of MiRaJ, and Jewish women's music in general, is often used in combination with education and discussion groups following a performance (ibid.; CDBaby 2015b). The trio's music can first and foremost be characterized by the renouncement of the full use of musical instruments, as the women prefer the sounds of a capella music and like how their voices blend. That is why they focus on rich harmonic vocal compositions for Jewish feminist life rituals, Shabbat, and holidays. The song "She Is a Tree of Life" (words and music by MiRaJ, arrangement by B. Lowe, 2004) demonstrates quite well the trio's preference for rich harmonies and arrangements. Written in A minor and 4/4 time, there are no clearly demarcated sections in the song, which relies instead on the layering of voices and of six different melodic phrases—and thus the layered arrangement of a chorus-like verse ("She is a Tree, is a Tree of Life, she is a Tree of Life / Etz chayyim hi lamachazikim bah"; see bars 3–8 in figure 1.6) and lyrical patterns in stanzaic form (see bar 29–34 in figure 1.7).

The voice-over technique and layering of melodic patterns, from which rich harmonization emerges, creates a spherical sound. In addition, as the trio wants to really hear Kol Isha, it emphasizes the individuality of each single voice as well as the strength and beauty of the united voices. At the heart of MiRaJ is the music, which also means the writing of their own interpretations and arrangements of traditional Jewish religious music and sacred texts ("She Is a Tree of Life" is based on Proverbs 3:18).

Singing a capella also comes in handy when the trio sings at Conservative congregations. Its repertoire includes songs about biblical heroines, Rosh Hodesh songs, and new interpretations of traditional liturgy. The women of MiRaJ seek to develop songs that "make a service more powerful and inclusive of women's experience"—what Raphael calls a "feminist transformation of Judaism through songs, ritual writing and prayer" (CDBaby.com 2015a). Accordingly, the trio's music has been described as "a toe-tapping, finger-snapping, hand-clapping, melodic tour de force through the feminist Jewish experience" (Targan 1995). MiRaJ has recorded three albums: *A Moon Note* (1995), *Counting Angels in the Wilderness* (1999), and *Healing Chants for the Souls* (2007).

FIGURE 1.6: Bars 3–8 of "She Is a Tree of Life" (2004) by MiRaJ, showing the first two melodic patterns and the chorus-like verse. Courtesy Rabbi Geela Rayzel Raphael, Rabbi Margot Stein, Juliet Irene Spitzer

In sum, Raphael and the other two women of MiRaJ seek to communicate their feminist message mainly through the lyrics of their songs. Those songs unmistakably talk about Jewish women's roles—ranging from graceful preservers of tradition and spiritual leaders in prayer and song to nurturers of their children and forceful agents for theological change—experiences, and needs. Thus, the form of Jewish feminism that is communicated in the music of the trio can be compared to the "essentialist" Jewish Renewal feminism that Chava Weissler talks about (2007, 57). Raphael in particular seeks to transform women's position in Judaism through music. While her intention is "to honor women, create cultural and theological change in the Jewish community [by] teach[ing] about Jewish women's heritage and traditions" (e-mail interview June 2005), other feminist Jewish songwriters pursue a more "social constructivist" or "egalitarian" feminism, as Weissler would put it (2013, 4).

FIGURE 1.7: Bars 29–34 of "She Is a Tree of Life" (2004) by MiRaJ showing one lyrical pattern in stanzaic form and three melodic patterns used in the song. Courtesy Rabbi Geela Rayzel Raphael, Rabbi Margot Stein, Juliet Irene Spitzer

RABBI HANNA TIFERET SIEGEL

> *Hanna Tiferet [Siegel] is a poet and a mystic through whom song and inspiration flow. She weaves together prayerful melodies and thoughtful teachings in a web of spirit and celebration. Hanna plants seeds of Jewish renewal wherever she goes and inspires people to experience peace and healing within and with each other.—(ZoomInfo 2015)*

Rabbi Hanna Tiferet Siegel is another very popular liturgical artist and a spiritual guide of the Jewish Renewal movement. She is also an important singer-songwriter who I believe furthered the development of feminist Jewish music as a genre. Tiferet Siegel received her ordination as a rabbinic pastor in 1992 and her rabbinical ordination in 2003 from Jewish Renewal rabbi Zalman Schachter-Shalomi, z"l. Before Tiferet Siegel became a rabbi, she attended the Melton Senior Educators' Program at Hebrew University in Jerusalem (1996–97)—the same program Raphael attended in 1988–89—and earned a master's in Jewish studies from the Hebrew College in Boston in 2003. Tiferet Siegel served as cospiritual leader at Congregation B'nai Or of Boston (1999–2006) and, together with other feminist

FIGURE 1.8: Hanna Tiferet Siegel. www.HannaTiferet.com

songwriters and leading feminist Jews, was a member of the advisory board of Kohenet: The Hebrew Priestess Institute (Hannatiferet n.d.; ZoomInfo 2015).

However, Tiferet Siegel's spiritual and musical career was already under way in the 1970s and shows the influence of the American Jewish counterculture. Tiferet Siegel, who had had musical training in her early years (she studied the flute), started to become a professional singer-songwriter when she met the charismatic singing rabbi Shlomo Carlebach at a Shabbat retreat in college. Tiferet Siegel had already been a song leader at a Jewish youth camp. As Tiferet Siegel told me, she only knew that she loved the music of the countercultural years, loved to lead songs, and particularly loved Jewish prayers (telephone interview February 2007). But she did not know how to effectively use her skills and preferences in worship. Carlebach, "who brought the new melodies in the world," as Tiferet Siegel put it, opened up this whole world of Jewish music to her. He inspired her to write her own music, and "to renew the old" liturgical music, as she said to me (ibid.).

In addition to Carlebach, Rabbi Zalman Schachter-Shalomi, z"l, taught her the basic structures of Hasidic niggunim that later on became the basis for and most characteristic element of her compositions (Musleah 1995, 26). Another role model was Debbie Friedman, who was by then already known for her song leading in Jewish Reform youth and summer camps. Through her music, Friedman communicated to Tiferet Siegel how to re-create and renew Jewish practices (telephone interview February 2007).

Tiferet Siegel and her husband, Rabbi Daniel Siegel, are among the pioneers of the Jewish Renewal movement. Tiferet Siegel, who was already active in the havurah movement in Philadelphia and Boston, moved with her husband to Vancouver, British Columbia, where together they founded the havurah Or Shalom, which was not yet an established synagogue community. In doing this, as well as undertaking basic teaching (on the midrashic tradition, the voice of women, and ecology), they brought Jewish Renewal to Canada, and thus the idea of making Judaism and Jewish worship intimate and empowering for everybody (telephone interview February 2007). Together with Myrna Rabinowitz and Harvey Rothstein, both members of Or Shalom, Tiferet Siegel founded the group Shir Hadash (New Light), which recorded two albums (Musleah 1995, 26). In 1987, when Daniel Siegel accepted a new pulpit in Hanover, New Hampshire, Tiferet Siegel—already the mother of three children—began her solo career as a singer-songwriter and recording artist (ibid.). She primarily focused on composing new melodies for traditional Hebrew sacred texts, which she elaborated on in English, and she combined her singing with teaching the audience, with the goal of making Jewish prayer and synagogue worship more accessible. In so doing, she sought to bring men and women closer to God. She explained that singing in the full congregation—that is, communal singing—can "express the sweetness of Judaism" and "transmit the joy of prayer" and can unify worshipers so that they "become one people" (telephone interview February 2007). She describes her music as "Jewish soul music—acoustic, folk-style tunes that are heartfelt and meditative" (quoted in ibid.).

Thus, her popular song "And You Shall Teach Your Children" (recorded on the album *Shir Hadash*; Tiferet Siegel 1990) exemplifies her personal style of composition. Laid out in a common ABA (verse-chorus-verse) structure and opening with the chorus, Tiferet Siegel follows the basic composition of folk songs. The song's moral is presented in the chorus, giving the first lines of the Ve'ahavta prayer ("You shall love Adonai your God with all your heart, with all your soul, and with all your might"), which is a continuation of the Shma Yisrael. The verses then tell the story of Tiferet Siegel's song, which is an interpretation of the Shma Yisrael. The song is written in B-flat major and in a moderate 4/4 time rhythm, and its harmonic structure is also very common in folk songs: oscillating between I and IV in the chorus (bars 1–8 in figure 1.9), following a I–IV–V–IV chord progression in the verse (bars 10–19 in figure 1.9) and ending with a plagal cadence (V–I). The melody of Tiferet Siegel's song is quite simple—and thus very accessible and easy to learn—as well as spiritual. The tone set does not extend the range above treble C.

Tiferet Siegel's music is explicitly feminist as well. As the first woman to receive the titles of *eshet hazon* (woman of vision) and *miyoledet neshama* (midwife of the soul), both in 1982, at informal feminist rituals, she also sees herself as a teacher of women. However, Tiferet Siegel is not only honored as a female rabbi and spiritual midwife, which means that she is respected by the community, she had also received special acknowledgment for her musical creativity (telephone interview February 2007). Through her music, she seeks to give voice to femaleness in general, and the feminine spirit in particular. Her aim is to value the voices of women and to claim a place equal to that of men in the Jewish tradition. As she told me, music

FIGURE 1.9: "And You Shall Teach Your Children" (1990) by Hanna Tiferet Siegel. www.HannaTiferet.com

written by and for Jewish women is a good way for mothers and daughters to connect with the Jewish tradition, as it "makes a huge difference to hear women's voices" in synagogue services (ibid.).

Her song "The Ways of a Woman," released on *A Voice Calls* (1998), reflects her feminist standpoint. The song elaborates on the Jewish Renewal understanding of Shekhinah as an expression of women's power in the movement, and the affirmation of the holiness of qualities identified with the feminine. In the song's lyrics, Tiferet Siegel told me, she talks about women's deep connection with the earth and with prophetesses (telephone interview February 2007). Or, as Weissler puts it, she links "Shekhinah with a view of women that connects them with natural cycles and the earth" and communicates the message that a woman's ways are mysterious to men (Weissler 2007, 67).

One of Tiferet Siegel's most popular, and most feminist, recordings—which has been well received in feminist Jewish and Renewal circles—is *Olamama* (1995), which she recorded together with the feminist Jewish songwriter Fran Avni. The title song is a fusion of *olam* (which means "world" in Hebrew) and mama, the almost-universal word for mother. Thus, the crucial message of this recording is that the song "invites us all to live with the wonder of a child, appreciating the beauty of our Mother Earth and dedicating our lives to live in harmony with Her" (CDBaby.com, 2015c). In the lyrics of her songs on *Olamama*, Tiferet Siegel also makes extensive use of so-called feminist Hebrew, as well as of other alternative translations of traditional prayer texts and names for God, while the styles of the songs range from folk ballads to calypso, Hasidic niggunim, jazz, and sacred chants.

Tiferet Siegel's songs, such as the Oriental-sounding "Or Hadash," are also widely used in healing services, which emerged from the Jewish feminist movement as well. Her music has also been well received in contexts other than those of feminist rituals and the Jewish Renewal movement, and her songs have been sung in mainstream synagogues, havurot, and homes and at spiritual gatherings all over the world. This might result from her years of teaching at the Elat Chayim Jewish Retreat Center in rural New England and from her extensive travels throughout the United States and Canada as an artist in residence leading workshops and Jewish educational programs and events held on Shabbat. Tiferet Siegel told me that some of her songs are already considered traditional (telephone interview February 2007).

In contrast to the women of MiRaJ, Tiferet Siegel did not specifically define her feminism to me. But based on her repertoire, specifically her feminist Jewish repertoire, her views might be described as women centered or ecofeminist.

RABBI SHEFA GOLD

The characteristic repetition of musical phrases that can be found throughout the repertoire of feminist Jewish songwriters related to the Jewish Renewal movement has been perfected by Rabbi Shefa Gold, who lives in Jemez Springs, New Mexico. She has turned this compositional practice into her own practice of chanting, which she considers a feminist act (interview March 2008; for a further discussion of chanting, see chapter 4). Gold is one of the most successful and best-selling artists in the Renewal movement, as well as among feminist Renewal Jewish musicians.

Gold is also an important spiritual leader in the Jewish Renewal movement. She was ordained both by the Reconstructionist Rabbinical College (in 1996) and Shalomi. According to Rodger Kamenetz, her first contact with the Jewish Renewal movement seems to have occurred around the

FIGURE 1.10: Shefa Gold. www.RabbiShefaGold.com

mid-1980s. Gold earned a master's degree in the philosophy of creativity and wrote a play on Martin Buber, which she later performed throughout the United States. In 1985, Shalomi heard about the play and invited her to the first P'nai Or *kallah* (convention or gathering), which is a Jewish Renewal community located in the West Mount Airy neighborhood of Philadelphia (Kamenetz 1997, 41).

Gold grew up in a traditional Jewish environment. She told Kamenetz, who interviewed her for *Stalking Elijah*: "I had a big fight growing up, . . . I wanted to participate Jewishly and was excluded. I wanted to read from the Torah, to be at the center of prayer. At this synagogue [of her childhood] they still don't count women in the minyan. They said there wasn't really any oppression of women in Judaism. . . . Yet I saw before my eyes something very different. It just made me feel crazy" (quoted in Kamenetz 1997, 41). Thus, the egalitarian and progressive environment she found in Renewal Judaism not only taught her that it could be fun to be Jewish, an experience she had never had before, but also seems to have influenced her future career as a spiritual leader and feminist Jewish singer-songwriter. Thus, she moved from writing plays to composing songs (ibid.). She told me she realized that "music is the key that opens hearts to the flow of the Divine, even when that flow comes in unexpected ways." She also commented on the special quality of music: "Jews have a pattern of arguing with innovation . . . but music transcends argument and opens us to pure experience. My role as a rabbi is to facilitate those experiences of heart opening surprise and then reflect on those experiences so that our rigid models of reality are challenged and expanded. My training as a Reconstructionist teaches me to stay rooted in the depths of history and tradition while reaching into the truth of this moment" (e-mail interview June 8, 2005). Gold believes that Judaism must evolve if it is to survive. Her work as a rabbi and as a singer-songwriter has always been strongly influenced by the women's movement and ecofeminism. The experiences she had in the women's movement and her interest in ecofeminism led to a deeper preoccupation with and connection to Judaism and furthermore spurred her interest in other movements and spiritualties, such as social activism, Buddhism, Native American spiritual traditions, and Christian and Islamic traditions, which she synthesizes in her music (ibid.; see also Kligman 2001b, 128).

Gold clearly articulates her feminism:

> I have found my power and depth as a woman in this world and now I shall live from that place, from this truth. There is a place for women's only ritual . . . but I am more concerned with effecting change in the world and since men still hold much of the power it feels important that my message reaches them. It seems that women are more willing to risk opening their hearts right now, so more women than men come to my workshops and teachings. I believe that the deep message of feminism has to do with inclusivity and connectedness. (e-mail interview June 8, 2005).

Gold intended "to transform how we worship, study, and practice Judaism" (ibid.), and during a stay in Israel in 1990 she developed a unique Jewish chanting service that, as Kligman writes (2001b, 128), has influenced many other contemporary Jewish songwriters. From other traditions, including Hindu mantras and Sufi *dhikr*,[10] Gold learned the technique of hypnotically repeating Hebrew key phrases (Kamenetz 1997, 42). This practice integrates melodic and meditative chants in synagogue service (see Kligman

2001b, 128). Gold's practice of chanting consists of the musical repetition of a sacred phrase, such as one taken from traditional prayer texts, and is meant as a holistic approach that "engages the body, emotions, intellect and spirit and study"; it is thus often used in conjunction with yoga and Buddhist meditation practices (e-mail interview June 8, 2005). The chanting practice that Gold developed makes it possible to explore the deeper levels of meaning of sacred texts. To reach this level of consciousness in worship, especially of praying with kavannah, Gold created a simple, yet multilayered, music. The practice of multilayered chant is meant to empower everyone, to spiritually open the mind, to connect the individual with the community, and to embody the liturgy and scripture (Gold 2006, 228; interview March 2008 and e-mail interview June 8, 2005).

Her song "Under the Wings" (n.d.) exemplifies Gold's personal style of composing—particularly of creating Hebrew chants (see figure 1.11). This chant is a rather minimalistic musical piece written for three voices, in A-sharp minor and 4/4 time. It consists of one basic and short melodic pattern that is repeated by each voice over and over again, while the accompanying voices follow in a third interval the voice of the lead singer. The blending of voices and the constant repetition of a single melodic phrase creates a chant like reciting a mantra, and thus a meditative atmosphere that is characteristic of Gold's performances.

Today, Gold is director of the Center for Devotional, Energy and Ecstatic Practice, in Jemez Springs, where she offers a training course—called Kol Zimra (voice of joy)—in chant leadership for rabbis, cantors, and lay leaders. The center offers a new feminist form of communal worship and model of leadership (e-mail interview June 8, 2005). Gold became a well-known composer and performer of Jewish spiritual music, and she has recorded ten albums. Among her best-known recordings are *Chants Encounter* (1994), *Chanscendence* (1997), and *Tzuri* (1993) (Kligman 2001b, 128–29). Those recordings were also listed on a feminist Jewish resources website (Jewish Feminist Resources 2009). In addition, her music and liturgies are published in several new prayer books. Her music is nationally and internationally, as well as cross-denominationally, known, and she teaches workshops and gives retreats on the theory and art of chanting, devotional healing, spiritual community building, and meditation (see Gold n.d.). She also travels to Europe to teach Jewish and other religious communities prayer, song, and community building. For example, she visits the Netherlands once

FIGURE 1.11: "Under the Wings" (2014) by Shefa Gold. From *Chantsformations* © 2014. www.RabbiShefaGold.com

a year "to teach the Sufis who are hungry for Jewish wisdom" (e-mail interview June 8, 2005).

Gold's feminism can be described as holistic—influenced by Jewish mysticism, non-Western philosophies, the search for Judaism's roots, and ecofeminism. In her view, feminism is accessible to women and men alike, since it is meant to invigorate the relationship between men and women, as well as among Jews, the earth, and the divine (interview Rabbi Gold, March 2008). These views are reflected in her latest New Age–style recording, *The Majesty of Nurture* (2008). She told me: "Feminism has been one of my largest influences . . . although my teaching doesn't talk about it directly but rather embodies its values. The music I write is meant to connect people with each other, themselves and the Divine as Beloved" (e-mail interview June 8, 2005). Raphael, Stein, Spitzer, and Tiferet Siegel communicate their feminist message through the lyrics of their songs. In contrast, Gold communicates it via the musical practice of chanting.

LINDA HIRSCHHORN

Of the feminist Jewish songwriters featured in this chapter, Linda Hirschhorn—based in Berkeley, California—is the most professionally trained songwriter. Hirschhorn grew up in a traditional but progressive Jewish environment in New York City, where she had the chance to fully unfold—musically as well as politically. She says: "While we did indeed attend an orthodox synagogue and I did attend an orthodox school when I was young, my family was not orthodox. It was typical of Jewish refugees of that generation to want to ensure that their children got a thorough Jewish background, but their interest had to do with the preservation of tradition and ritual and less to do with religious belief. So, I felt the complete freedom to enjoy the beauty of the rituals and songs without feeling the constraints of orthodox practice" (e-mail interview July 2005).[11] Although Hirschhorn did not have to struggle with the issue of Kol Isha while singing in synagogue, she nevertheless experienced the disadvantages of being a Jewish girl in her childhood. For example, she did not have a bat mitzvah or get the same Jewish education her brother did. However, as her parents did not expect from her what they expected from their son, Hirschhorn had the freedom to follow her own inclinations, which ultimately led her back to her first love—singing (ibid.). Her musical career started at the age of six at a Manhattan yeshiva choir (see Musleah 1995, 24).

FIGURE 1.12: Linda Hirschhorn. Courtesy L. Hirschhorn

Hirschhorn was always the soloist in school choirs. She was admitted to the very prestigious public High School of Music and Art in New York City. During her high school years, she also continued to sing with different choirs, such as Jewish choirs and symphony choirs, before she began to develop a solo career as a political folk singer. Her political life and her music were greatly influenced by her involvement in the Zionist labor movement and in other sociopolitical movements of the time. She had her first contact with the idea of Zionism when, as a child in the 1950s, she attended the movement's camps. This had a lasting impact on her life. Hirschhorn remembers: "It taught me about the American labor movement, and about socialist Zionism. We studied Marxism and it gave me a strong intellectual foundation for my radicalism in later life. It took my Judaism out of old world Shtetl Poland and brought it into contemporary America and Israel" (e-mail interview July 2005). "The prophets," as Hirschhorn labels political role models such as Karl Marx who she had studied as a child and teenager, became relevant to her in the 1970s, when their voices inspired her own social activism and those of her fellow campers in the era of the civil rights and antiwar movements. When she moved to California and decided to write her own songs, form various bands, and perform in coffeehouses, she put these ideas to work (ibid.). By then, her Jewish and social consciousness, as she calls it, had been greatly influenced not only by American countercultural political activism, but also by the music of the American working class and by early Israeli pioneers' songs: "The songs taught me about people coming together to make their dreams come true and about fighting injustice. It taught me about working together in community and how to overcome differences" (ibid.). In the following years, her songs became increasingly political, especially as she became involved in the antinuclear movement and Central American struggles.

While Hirschhorn did not experience much resistance against her singing in Orthodox synagogues and choirs in her childhood in New York City's Washington Heights neighborhood, she struggled with acceptance on the part of both Jewish audiences and progressive left-wing audiences (both Jewish and non-Jewish) when she began to express her politics through music. According to her, Jewish people attending her performances were not always open to her ideas about achieving peace in the Middle East by means of cooperation between Israel and Palestine, while the "lefties" were not generally open to her Hebrew songs: "It was hard convincing people on the left that I could be a proud Jew and Zionist, and yet at the same time be critical of Israel and advocate for a two-state solution" (e-mail interview July 2005). However, the lesson she learned was that music is the strongest way to express oneself and to get involved in political activity: "I wrote many songs dealing with anti-nuclear issues and the liberation struggle in Central America. I taught my songs on picket lines and at protest rallies, went to jail a couple of times, and taught my songs there. Every movement needs its poets and artists and musicians, and I have been proud of my role as one of them" (ibid.). In the 1980s, Hirschhorn's career as a singer-songwriter took a slight turn. She was asked to lead services and provide music for the first Jewish women's conference. She recalled that it was then that she "realized how totally inappropriate traditional liturgy would be in this context" (e-mail interview July 2005). God language was a particular concern for her, as it represented the patriarchal nature of Jewish prayers: "So what I did was to take traditional liturgy that did not use the name of God—there is much beautiful poetry in prayer that evokes our sense of what is sacred in our lives without god-language—and set that to music" (e-mail interview July 2005). Hirschhorn composed one of her earliest rounds for the Jewish women's conference (ibid.)—the well-known "Ilu Finu," which was later recorded on her album *Gather Round* (Hirschhorn and Vocolot 1989).

It was then that Jewish feminism inspired her to speak out on behalf of women, and she started to compose feminist Jewish music, using egalitarian language that was not male-god-centered, and that she began writing songs that tell Jewish women's stories. Jewish feminism offered her a space where she could integrate her political views and Jewish roots with no fear of sanction (e-mail interview July 2005). Since then, Hirschhorn has focused on writing Hebrew and English women's songs and rounds in four- and five-part harmony with distinctly feminist themes.

Velvel Pasternak of Tara Publications, who is known to be very supportive of Jewish women's music, offered Hirschhorn a chance to publish her songs and rounds in a songbook that Hirschhorn called *Gather Round* (1989). She told me that it then became clear to her that she needed to have an accompanying recording, so she gathered some women to help her make the album *Gather Round* (e-mail interview July 2005). The women continued to sing together, and this finally led, in 1988, to the formation of an all-female a cappella ensemble called Vocolot—which is a bilingual play on the Hebrew word *kolot* (voice) and the English word "vocal" (Musleah

FIGURE 1.13–14: "Women Gathering Round" (1989) © Linda Hirschhorn

1995, 24). Hirschhorn said: "I couldn't be a solo singer with a back up band anymore. I was also far more interested in just the pure human voice and didn't want to perform with instruments" (e-mail interview July 2005). Over the past twenty-one years, the cast of female singers has changed several times, but Vocolot's music still "reflects not only a feminist approach to Judaism but also carries universal messages of peace—much of it based on the wisdom of the prophets and on modern poets (e.g., Marcia Falk, my [Hirschhorn's] own poetry etc.)" (ibid.).

One of the songs released on *Gather Round* is "Women Gathering Round" (1989; see figures 1.13–14), which Hirschhorn recorded with Tay

FIGURE 1.13–14: (continued)

Holden, Rosalind Glazer, Max Ventura, and Judith-Kate Friedman (who were then members of Vocolot) and with Sky Pelicrow playing the *dumbek* (a goblet drum from Persia). Like the music of MiRaJ, Hirschhorn's music in general, and her song "Women Gathering Round" in particular, is characterized by a capella singing, that is the blending of voices, as well as by the harmonies that are created in multi vocal singing. The song is written in A-minor and in 4/4 time, and it has a clearly demarcated structure of verse-chorus-verse. The song consists of four verses, each of which sung in a slightly different way. Thus, one distinctive feature of the song is the alternation of short (verses 1 and 3) and long verses (verses 2 and 4), while the melodic pattern of the long verses is a variation of the melodic phrase of the short verses. Also the chorus at the end of the song is a variation of the opening chorus, which results in the following overall song structure: A–B–C–B1–C1–A1. Figure 1.13 shows the chorus (A, bars 1–6), verse one (B, bars 7–19) and verse two (C, bars 11–18). Hirschhorn uses simple but dramatic musical effects to jazz up the arrangement's texture. In addition to the variations in the melody, the harmonic composition of the song is also enriched by layering not only the voices but also verses and chorus. Hirschhorn (the lead singer) sings the verses (for example, verse one mainly stays on the tonic), and the rest of the vocal ensemble simultaneously keeps on singing the chorus (the chord progression of the chorus is I–III–V–I). After each verse, Hirschhorn and the ensemble sing the chorus in unison. Another musical effect that is often used by Hirschhorn is the call-and-response formula.

When I asked Hirschhorn about the feminist message in her music, she first explained that the label "feminist" is often problematic but is nevertheless very important for her. Thus, she pays attention to Jewish women's subjects and uses a gender-neutral god language in her lyrics. The use of such a language leaves open the question of the nature of one's relationship to the divine, she explained to me. In general, she sets a high value on the relationship between music and text, as the music emphasizes the "feeling and understanding" of the single word and the whole phrase (interview February 2008). Moreover, she wants to sing about general sociopolitical themes, as these affect both women and men. When I asked her to describe her music, she said: "I think my music combines all my influences. It's folky, its harmonies are classical, and it has its distinct Jewish and cantorial twists and turns, and it's accessible and complex at the same time" (e-mail interview July 2005).

Hirschhorn is particularly interested in writing songs and harmonizing them for women's voices. She is affiliated with the Jewish Renewal movement, and thus to some degree also with the movement's musical conventions. But she pointed out that the personal background of each singer-songwriter chiefly shapes his or her respective style of music. The music of Raphael, who grew up in Tennessee, sounds very much like country music, and Hirschhorn's Orthodox background shows through in her preference for niggunim. Beyond this, she noted the influence of globalization. The world is becoming more interconnected, and that is why more and more musical cultures from around the world are becoming integrated into feminist Jewish music (interview February 2008).

In contrast with the other feminist Jewish singer-songwriters presented in this study, Hirschhorn primarily writes music for the stage, not for synagogue service. Today, she works not only as a performer but also as a cantor,[12] choral conductor, bar and bat mitzvah teacher, and life-cycle events manager. Especially through Vocolot's program called Concerts Starring You, in which she integrates a Jewish community's own choir into a Vocolot performance, her music has become well known and widely enjoyed and has entered synagogue worship as well (Musleah 1995, 24; interview February 2008).

In sum, Hirschhorn defines herself, as well her feminism, as political. While Raphael focuses on the feminist theological interpretation of Jewish sacred texts, set to rather simplistic compositions, and Gold concentrates on spirituality and the feminist practice of chanting, Hirschhorn's focus is on the interrelationship between musical and liturgical text. Thus, her "intention is to draw people in, to make them want to sing along and make them want to understand the poetry" (e-mail interview July 2005). She describes her compositions as "music that spans the breadth of the personal and the political, the Jewish and the feminine" (Hirschhorn n.d.b), which is something she expresses musically by composing rounds. From her perspective, rounds are the best expression of the blending of diverse experiences of Jewish women. Singing in Western harmony also has a major impact on how people experience themselves in relation to others and helps deepen people's understanding of texts (ibid.). Thus, "political" in this case can be interpreted as linking the personal lives of women and men with a feminist understanding of Judaism. Hirschhorn stressed to me that the songwriters related to the Reconstructionist and Jewish Renewal movement were far more feminist than those related to other streams of Judaism, such as the Reform and Conservative Judaism (interview February 2008). It is therefore not surprising that Hirschhorn finds Friedman's music "not very feminist" (ibid.). This perception can be explained by the fact that the lyrics of feminist-inspired songs of songwriters in the Renewal and Reconstructionist movement communicate feminist political messages much more directly than the lyrics of songwriters related to other denominations.

As this chapter has shown, not only is each songwriter's style of writing music distinct, the women's stance regarding Jewish feminism and their understanding of it are also quite diverse. However, they are similar in their handling of Jewish traditions, which Gold explained as follows: "The theology of . . . Renewal Judaism offer[s] the permission to take traditions of the liturgy and to reshape and transform them without any restrictions by the Halakhah. You are able to take some tools of the tradition and turn them into something contemporary, something that works. Jews received the traditions and are now responsible to pass them down to other generations in forms that are more relevant and more useful" (interview March 2008). This chapter has also shown how much influence the political and cultural environment in America since the 1960s, and feminism in particular, has had on each songwriter's understanding of Jewish feminism and thus on her style of writing music. Although the feminist Jewish singer-songwriters presented in this chapter are spread across the United States, they are closely connected to each other.

This chapter has provided the historical, cultural, and political context for feminist Jewish music. The following chapter seeks to give an ethnographic description of the feminist Jewish music scene that spans the United States.

2 The Feminist Jewish Music Scene

Since the 1990s, the concept of music scene gained higher importance within music scholarship, although the term is not easy to define. However, in the context of this study, a music scene is when people (such as producers, performers, and recipients) voluntarily cluster around a certain cultural phenomenon—like feminist Jewish music—whether it is local, translocal, or virtual. Furthermore, the concept of music scene directs the attention to the comprehensive interactions among the music, its producers, audiences, and locations of production and thus provides insight into a safe space in which identities can be constructed, stretched, and shared (see Irwin 1977; Peterson and Bennett 2004, 12; Vallee 2006, 468).

The common academic definition of a local music scene considers the relationship between local music-making processes and the everyday life and social activity of a specific community. Thus, the forms of music in question are embedded in long-standing local cultures, and producers, musicians, and fans share not only a specific musical taste, but also the use of selected cultural signs and a certain way of living (Peterson and Bennett 2004, 7–8). The aim of this chapter is not to give a dense description of one local community, but to paint a broader picture of the network of feminist Jewish singer-songwriters in the United States. Nevertheless, the category of local is important in many different ways. First, and most obvious, it refers to the geographical distribution of feminist Jewish songwriters throughout the United States; second, it concerns the self-location of individuals on the religious spectrum of American Judaism; and third, it also refers to the impact of the local culture on the style and structure of feminist Jewish music. Moreover, the following discussion of the feminist Jewish music scene reveals some of the contexts in which this music is performed and received, and thus it provides an impression of how widely the music is accepted: some synagogue communities refuse to integrate feminist Jewish music into their synagogue liturgy at all, others allow feminist

Jewish singer-songwriters to perform their music on special occasions (such as particular musical Shabbat services taking place once a month), while still other communities or informal ritual groups fully embrace this new tradition of Jewish liturgical music. Feminist Jewish music is also sometimes rejected and sometimes accepted in the music publishing industry, as will be discussed in this chapter, too.

THE LOCAL COMMUNITY

Concerning the geographical distribution of feminist Jewish singer-songwriters, it is no coincidence that my fieldwork took me in 2007 to the East Coast of the United States—more precisely to Philadelphia, New York, and the Boston area. In 2008, I moved westward to New Mexico and California, in particular to the San Francisco area. Those places are the centers not only of feminist Jewish music making, but also of Jewish life in the United States. According to a study of the Jewish population in the United States, there are an estimated 6.7 million Jews in the country, making up 2.2 percent of the U.S. population (Sheskin and Dashefsky 2013). The majority of American Jews lives on the East and West Coasts. Jews account for 3.2 percent of the population of California and 9.0 percent of the population of New York State, which has the largest percentage of Jewish population of any state. Also on the East Coast, Jews make up 2.3–5.5. percent of the populations of the District of Columbia, Florida, Massachusetts, New Jersey, and Pennsylvania (ibid.). Jews account for smaller percentages of the population of other states. For example, New Mexico's population is only 0.6 percent Jewish.[1] I conducted only one interview in New Mexico, with Rabbi Shefa Gold—one of the leading figures in the feminist Jewish music scene.

My findings on the central locations of feminist Jewish music making correspond to the general distribution of the Jewish population in the United States. However, in terms of denominational affiliation, the other crucial factor in the study of feminist Jewish music, my informants are not representative of American Jews. According to the same study on Jewish population, the majority of the members of Jewish communities in the areas mentioned above identify themselves as Reform or just Jewish (Sheskin, and Dashefsky 2013). The latter term means the person indicated no particular denominational affiliation. Only 2–4 percent of those who considered themselves Jewish said they were Orthodox or Reconstructionist Jews, with the exception of New York State—where about 19 percent of the Jewish population is Orthodox. About 20–30 percent of the Jews in New York said they were Conservative Jews (ibid.).

In comparison with my data, the largest numbers of musicians who define themselves as feminist Jews, are not affiliated with Reform or Conservative Judaism, as one might presume, but with the Jewish Renewal and Reconstructionist movements. However, the Jewish Renewal movement is not mentioned in the study of the Jewish population. One reason for this is that Jewish Renewal is not a denomination but a cross-denominational movement that transcends the boundaries of Orthodox, Conservative, Reform, and Reconstructionist Judaism. Another reason might be that people who identify themselves as Renewal Jews are presumably included in the study's category of Reconstructionist. According to Rabbi Geela Rayzel Raphael, the Jewish Renewal movement emerged from Jewish Reconstructionism, which is why Renewal and Reconstructionist Jews share some ideas about community and spirituality (interview February 2007). Although the Jewish Renewal movement has not appeared in the official statistics to date, it is of importance with regard to the aspect of the local in the feminist Jewish music scene, and it helps us better understand the interrelatedness of Renewal Judaism, feminism, and music.

It is worth considering the Jewish Renewal community in the greater Philadelphia, a network of both Jewish Renewal musicians and feminist Jewish musicians in that area. I gained this insight mainly through Raphael and her husband, Rabbi Simcha Raphael, with whom I stayed during my fieldwork in Philadelphia.

According to Rabbi Simcha Raphael, Philadelphia is the center of Jewish Renewal. Especially in the neighborhood of Mount Airy, in the northwest of the city, where most of my informants live, one can find a lively Jewish Renewal community and a tight-knit group of rabbis and cantors and other Jewish musicians. Besides serving as the main organizers of the movement, they are also some of the most important spiritual leaders in Philadelphia—for example, Arthur Waskow and Rabbi Marcia Prager and her husband, Hazzan Jack Kessler, who both serve the P'nai Or Jewish Renewal Community in Philadelphia (interview with Simcha Raphael, March 2008).

During my fieldwork in the Philadelphia community, I had the chance to meet and interview a comparatively large number of feminist singer-songwriters, whose lives and professions as Reconstructionist-trained rabbis or cantors center on their music and its incorporation into Judaism. They included Rabbi Geela Rayzel Raphael, Rabbi Margot Stein, Juliet Spitzer, Yofiyah (a part-time cantor also known as Susan Deikam), and Rabbi Sigal Brier,[2] to mention just a few. Living in this area, I was able to observe that these Philadelphia-based feminist Jewish singer-songwriters were integrated into a loosely associated collective of Jewish Renewal musicians, in which there was much collaboration between the musicians. Like the women in the feminist trio MiRaJ, most of the Renewal musicians, such as Rabbi Shawn Zevit,[3] know one another from their studies at the Reconstructionist Rabbinical College in Wyncote, Pennsylvania, part of the greater Philadelphia area. The college is thus not only an important religious and scholarly institution in this area but also, as became clear to me through interviews, informal meetings and conversations, a central meeting place for creative musicians. The singer-songwriters Leila Gal Berner, Tamara Cohen, Shefa Gold, and Judy Kummer are dropouts from the Reconstructionist Rabbinical College who are known for their feminist Jewish music.

Thus, Rabbi Geela Rayzel Raphael is very closely connected to other Jewish Renewal and feminist singer-songwriters in Philadelphia. As noted in chapter 1, she was instrumental in the foundation of Shabbat Unplugged/Havdalah Live, a musical troupe once consisting of herself, Stein, Spitzer, Rabbi Myriam Klotz,[4] Zevit, and Rabbi Micah Becker-Klein.[5] Shabbat Unplugged/Havdalah Live was founded in 1995 in Philadelphia. For seven years, the group toured throughout the United States, using music to draw Jewish college students to Shabbat services.[6] Although not all of the original members are still playing in the band Shabbat Unplugged/Havdalah Live, Raphael, Zevit, and Spitzer still perform under the group's name, playing songs from their individual repertoires at synagogue services.

The members of MiRaJ are also very much engaged not only in the Jewish Renewal music scene in Philadelphia, but also in the local and translocal feminist Jewish music scene. For occasions such as women's seders, retreats, and conferences, MiRaJ will also perform together with Klotz and Yofiyah as an all-female band called Tof B'Yadah, whose intention is to honor "in name and in spirit . . . Miriam the Prophetess, who led the women dancing with timbrel in her hand ('tof b'yadah')" (Shechinah 2012c).

I was able to experience how much feminist Jewish music depends on and is characterized by the interaction of everyday life experiences and the social as well as religious activity of the local community when I attended a Friday night Kabbalat Shabbat service in June 2008 at the Beth Israel Conservative synagogue of Woodbury, New Jersey. Rabbi Geela Rayzel Raphael led the service. As a "Reconewal" rabbi (see chapter 1) serving a Conservative community, Raphael has had some difficulties regarding the integration of her music into the Conservative-style synagogue service: she collected her feminist songs (with other liturgical songs in pop style) on song sheets and taught the songs to the congregants. During her first years as a rabbi at Beth Israel, the community rebelled against the rabbi's modern, New Age tunes and way of performing. In an attempt to revitalize synagogue service and make it more participatory for Beth Israel's worshipers, Raphael relied on her song-leading skills, drawing on hand clapping, finger snapping, singing canons, and integrating bodily movements into congregational singing.

The night that I attended the service, the worshipers showed little enthusiasm for the integration of bodily movements especially. Although Raphael's community has gradually accepted some of her songs and her way of performing Jewish sacred music, especially her popular and widely recognized songs "Moving into Shabbos Time" (1984) and "Rock to the Rock" (1995), it was still clear to me that the community, full of vim and vigor, showed more enthusiasm for traditional congregational singing whenever Raphael struck up a more traditional tune. Raphael explained to me that it is sometimes easier for her, as the leader in prayer and song, to sing traditional sacred songs, as she does not have to argue with the community. In addition, when singing traditional songs, the community carries her musically, and she does not have to focus to such an extent on leading songs (interview June 2008). This example, however, gives an impression of the resistance to feminist Jewish music and shows that not all synagogue communities are immediately (if ever) open to the integration of new music into their traditional liturgy.

A considerably different picture was presented when I attended a meeting of the Wild Women Wisdom Group in Philadelphia in March 2008. This interdenominational group usually meets once a month in private homes. There are about thirty women on the mailing list of the group, whose members are in their mid-thirties or older. Nine women took part at the meeting I attended, which lasted from 10:00 a.m. to 4:00 p.m. Among the attendees were the host of the day, Brier, and Yofiyah, both of whom perform with Raphael on occasion. The meetings of the Wild Women Wisdom Group are generally meant to give women a chance to share and exchange experiences, special skills, and knowledge. Thus, the March meeting was centered on a workshop on feng shui in the morning, followed by lunch and a workshop on medicinal herbs in the afternoon. However, blessings, meditation, and—more important—group singing, drumming, and dancing were also part of the meeting. In comparison to the synagogue service mentioned above, the women at the meeting especially welcomed the popular tunes sung by Raphael and Brier.

Performance contexts like these describe the various supporting networks into which feminist Jewish singer-songwriters are integrated. Some of the feminist Jewish musicians I interviewed in Philadelphia are, as professional rabbis or cantors, integrated into their respective denominations, which shape the everyday experiences of their communities in Reconstructionist Judaism and more significantly, the Jewish Renewal movement. As musicians, feminist Jewish singer-songwriters interact continuously with the members of the local Jewish Renewal or Reconstructionist music scene that surrounds the Reconstructionist Rabbinical College and are part of, as well as supported by, the Philadelphia-based organization Harmoniyah. The organization's mission "is to nurture, facilitate, and energize the evolving musical culture of Jewish civilization in accordance with the values and principles of Reconstructionist Judaism. Harmoniyah will serve to connect all who are involved in the musical transmission of our religious civilization by providing a central place for philosophical, educational, material, and logistical knowledge to be disseminated and shared by all of its members" (Jewish Reconstructionist Communities n.d.).[7] As Raphael explained to me, the support of Harmoniyah is also important to the publishing and distribution of Reconstructionist/Renewal music (interview March 2008). It can thus be regarded as a counterbalance to the music programming of the Union of Reform Judaism and its Transcontinental Music Publications, directed by cantor Alane Katzew (who is also director of music programming at the Union for Reform Judaism), which is the biggest supporter and publisher of the so-called Reform Repertoire, including the music of artists such as Debbie Friedman and Jeff Klepper (interview with Katzew, February 2007). More details about the publishing of feminist Jewish music appear below.

As feminists, however, female Jewish singer-songwriters are above all part of the larger local network of feminist Jews and feminist scholars in Philadelphia, and they are also connected with feminist Jews throughout the United States. A unique phenomenon is that most of feminist Jewish singer-songwriters are either trained as rabbis or cantors, or hold another academic degree, such as in Jewish studies. Thus, they contribute to the Jewish women's movement and feminist Jewish discourses not only by creating new liturgical music, but also by scholarly work, including teaching at academic institutions.

The Reconstructionist Rabbinical College is not only an important and central meeting point for musicians, as indicated above; it also houses Kolot: Center for Jewish Women's and Gender Studies. As a feminist center in a rabbinical college, Kolot can be regarded as the heart of the scholarly network of feminist Jews in the Philadelphia area. Lori Lefkovitz, who holds the Gottesman Kolot Chair of Gender and Judaism—so far the only endowed senior professorship in this field—has directed the center since 2001. Kolot is characterized by a unique combination of academic studies—namely, of gender, Judaism, and community work in the broadest sense. The center trains rabbis and Jewish leaders and offers programs and materials that make the traditions of Judaism meaningful and relevant for contemporary Jews, by supporting innovation in Jewish living and thought, and thus help them build inclusive Jewish communities (Kolot 2015).

Thus, local feminist Jewish scholars, such as Rebecca Alpert and Laura Levitt from Temple University in Philadelphia, provide their scholarly insights to courses at Kolot, just as songwriters like Raphael, Stein, Spitzer and other well-known local feminists—including Rabbi Sue Levi Elwell—do. The women mentioned here and other local scholars also share their songs, prayers, and rituals on Ritualwell.org, which is the most extensive website on contemporary Jewish rituals (Ritualwell 2015a). The website is owned, edited, and administered by the Reconstructionist Rabbinical College, at which Kolot is located.[8] Whereas Kolot offers a real site for feminist Jewish networking, the website is a virtual, but highly important, supportive space for exchanging contemporary feminist Jewish insights, experiences, and music. Levitt estimates that the connections between musicians and scholars are more of a social nature: "We like each other but live out very different feminist practices attempting to make connections at various moments" (e-mail interview April 2009). She pointed to the then-new issue of *Bridges* that dealt with feminist Jews and their fathers. In this issue Raphael (2009) published an essay in which she describes burying her placenta with her father. Her essay is next to essays on literary criticism by Lori Lefkovitz (2009) and other feminist articles on topics like local poets. Thus, Levitt, who sees herself "at an extreme on this [feminist Jewish] spectrum," presumes that this issue of *Bridges* reflects the situation of Jewish feminists, and their interrelatedness at its best with the Reconstructionist Rabbinical College, its students, and the larger Mt. Airy community of Jews (e-mail interview April 2009). Levitt continued:

> I am also thinking of Chava Weissler's work on Renewal and her connections to Philly as well. The point I would make is that these are loose connections and often the discourses and commitments are in conflict and given that, we don't directly confront some of the tensions which makes the relationships in many instances not as deep as one might hope. . . . I am perhaps the least connected to the music and ritual feminists. The point is we are all feminists, feminist Jews, and perform these commitments in radically different ways, and the kind of critical work I do and Deborah [Glanzberg-Krainin] and Lori [Lefkovitz] and Rebecca [Alpert] and others do is, in part, about appreciating these differences and tensions. (ibid.)

In sum, it becomes obvious how far and in what way feminist Jewish singer-songwriters are integrated into the local Jewish communities of Philadelphia—as rabbis or spiritual leaders, as musicians, or as feminist scholars and/or activists. I have discussed Philadelphia as an example. Now I use a translocal perspective to understand how feminist Jewish singer-songwriters are connected nationally and who is involved in those connections.

RELATIONAL NETWORKS

The songwriters discussed in this book are interconnected to and interact with other songwriters, producers, and audiences in distant places (see, for example, Peterson and Bennett 2004, 8–9). As demonstrated above, the aspect of locality, and thus the incorporation of feminist Jewish music into other local music scenes and networks, is indeed of great significance. However, although most of my informants are in the greater Philadelphia area,

I would argue that the feminist Jewish music scene in the United States is dominated by a core group of musicians who are scattered throughout the country. Besides Raphael, Stein, Spitzer, and Yofiyah, all located in Philadelphia, I have also discussed Linda Hirschhorn in San Francisco, California; Gold in Jemez Springs, New Mexico; Rabbi Hanna Tiferet Siegel, now living in Canada; and Friedman in New York City. There is often just one or only a few feminist singer-songwriters in one place, which in itself does not constitute a scene. That is why the feminist Jewish music scene in the United States is primarily constituted as a transregional, nationwide network of feminist Jewish singer-songwriters, as well as a national (and to some extent international) group of recipients. Thus, the feminist Jewish music scene spans the entire United States.

There are various possible ways of being connected to a particular music culture, or—as Mark Slobin puts it—there are "three overlapping spheres of cultural activity" (choice, affinity, and belonging) which lead to the formation of a subculture, Slobin's term for a scene (1993, 55–56). More precisely, Slobin's concepts of affinity group and affinity interculture are helpful when describing the translocal structure of the feminist Jewish music scene in the United States, which is by no means a tightly bounded entity but a constructed web of affiliation. Slobin's analytical category allows us to determine on what basis those singer-songwriters are interconnected (ibid., 55–56 and 98). The people who are related to feminist Jewish music in the United States are bound together not only as a community of like-minded music makers and recipients (an affinity group), but also by multiple, heterogeneous kinds of relationships within social and religious networks, which might be referred to as relational networks. Each network represents a particular kind of affiliation, and each kind of relationship may play a distinct role in a particular task and has different importance for various religiopolitical objectives.

Not only a certain kind of music, but also a common political aim—namely, the enhancement and integration of feminist consciousness through music[9]—is the reason for the affiliation. This mission, however, cannot be limited to one place or another but has to be conducted throughout the nationwide Jewish community. This is of course necessary to the formation of a recognizable affinity group, or a feminist Jewish music scene (Slobin 1993, 35 and 56). The aspect of belonging is a complex act, as it involves various patterns of commitment and thus different degrees of association, ranging from casual participation to professional engagement. What do these explanations mean with regard to the structure of the feminist Jewish music scene and its translocality in the United States?

National Networks

The general affiliation to Jewish feminism—more precisely, to feminist Jewish activism—is declared by some songwriters' membership in national feminist Jewish networks, such as B'not Esh and its offshoot Achiot Or, which are two of the major academically oriented associations of feminist Jews in the United States. The Reconstructionist Rabbinical College in Philadelphia might be described as the epicenter of feminist Jewish music making. B'not Esh has also had not only a deep religiopolitical impact on feminist Jewish singer-songwriters, but moreover has served as an important place for networking among feminist musicians. Compared to B'not Esh, Achiot Or is less academic and moreover welcomes women with children; these were issues that were of importance to Raphael at the beginning of her carrier, when her children were small (interview March 2008).

Another site of networking for feminist Jewish musicians is the National Havurah Committee (ibid.). Founded in the 1970s, the committee describes itself as "nondenominational, multigenerational, egalitarian, and volunteer-run" and as a "network of diverse individuals and communities" from across North America that are "dedicated to Jewish living and learning, and community building, and tikkun olam (repairing the world) (National Havurah Committee n.d.a). Hence, Gold offered a workshop on the practice of chanting at the committee's summer institute in 1995, and Hirschhorn (1993) and Tiferet Siegel (1994) have taken part in the committee's Poretsky Artist in Residence program (National Havurah Committee n.d.b).

An additional, even more important network, is that of ALEPH kallah, which is a biennial gathering of Jewish Renewal artists, activists, authors, and teachers offered by ALEPH, the Alliance for Jewish Renewal and drawn from all over the United States and abroad, sharing a week-long celebration of Jewish spirituality, prayer, music creativity and community and more (see KolAlpeh 2013). The Jewish Renewal–related pioneers of feminist Jewish music, such as Raphael, Gold, Tiferet Siegel, and Hirschhorn, have participated at past ALEPH kallah gatherings not only in their roles as rabbis or female cantors, but also as leaders in feminist Jewish ritual, prayer, and song.

How much feminism has been integrated into the Jewish Renewal movement and how much space the movement offers for the feminist Jewish music culture become obvious when we look at the eshet hazon ritual taking place at several gatherings of ALEPH kallah.[10] As Weissler describes (2006), the ritual was first created for Tiferet Siegel in May 1982 by a feminist circle called the Shechinah Sisters at a Shavuot retreat in Olympia, Washington. All of the roughly sixty men and women at the retreat attended the ceremony and gathered in a circle with a Torah (ibid., 67). The ritual is meant to honor the spiritual power of women who are not trained as rabbis, cantors, or rabbinic pastors[11] and who are "attuned to the work and joy of holding sacred energy in all its varied forms including the arts, teaching, organizational skills, healing, [and] music" (Tiferet Siegel n.d.). Thus, as seen in the *ketubah* (marriage contract)[12] that Tiferet Siegel received at the ceremony, the title eshet hazon expresses the idea of women's leadership and recognizes their artistic creativity, among other things, while the women are honored for teaching a "Torah of the hand and heart" (quoted in Weissler 2006, 67), rather than of the text and learning. Thus, Tiferet Siegel's document says: "Through dance and music, weavings and birthings, prayer and quiet revelations of learning and sharing, you radiate life's beauty to those around you and serve as a model, guide, and spiritual teacher to many. . . . May you be blessed with ever-growing strength and insight to express your vision of the Torah of the hand and heart" (quoted in ibid.). Raphael was one of the original visionaries who came up with the idea for the ritual long before ALEPH existed. At least thirty-six women have received the title of eshet hazon. Since 1982, Weissler writes, "the form of the ritual . . . has evolved, changing from a community-wide celebration to a small, private celebration among a group of women, and back again" (ibid. 63 and 66).

Ten younger women received the title of *bat kol* (daughter of the voice) at the 2005 ALEPH kallah. This title is given to young Jewish women who have inspired others with their work on the renewal of Judaism (Weissler 2006). Among those young women was Holy Taya Shere, who released an album titled *Wild Earth Shebrew* (2009). She wrote me:

> I was initiated, with 9 other young/next-generation women, as a Bat Kol (Daughter of [the] Voice) at the 2005 ALEPH Kallah. There was a ceremony—organized informally (in a non-official capacity) by many

> women spiritual leaders of the Renewal movement—in which they were naming women as Eishet Chazon (woman of vision). This is a ceremony they have been holding for a number of years, and four women were given this title during the 2005 ritual. They decided in addition to offering a ceremony for the women elders, they wanted to honor the women they saw as next-generation leaders: women picking up the mantle for the future. I felt tremendously honored and excited to be among this group of women, and to be initiated into this (informal) Bat Kol sisterhood. . . . Bat Kol . . . is also a phrase that invokes hearing divine inspiration (e-mail interview March 2007).

According to Tiferet Siegel, over the past twenty-five years, the ritual has also taken place in some local communities, as well as in spontaneous ceremonies at the various *kallot* (plural of kallah). At the 2007 ALEPH kallah, the eshet hazon ritual celebrated its twenty-fifth anniversary. In addition to Tiferet Siegel, Gold also attended the ritual and led the chanting throughout the ceremony (Tiferet Siegel n.d.). According to Weissler, Gold was not musically prepared for leading the ceremony. Thus, she explained to Weissler:

> I wasn't in on the planning for the ritual, but my friends know that I have a gift for making up chants to serve the truth of the moment. So they just asked me to jump in. The words were from B'reshit: ani b'derech nashim.[13] It's what Rachel says when she sits on the teraphim. It seems we were practicing "the Way of Women" and honoring that place in each other. . . . The music comes from just listening in to the moment and asking what's needed now to move the ritual to a higher, deeper level. When I create a chant like that, I surrender the melody to that sacred moment which will never be repeated (quoted in Weissler 2006, 85, note 40).[14]

However, the women who performed the eshet hazon ritual during Jewish Renewal kallot clearly state that it is very informal and that songwriters Tiferet Siegel, Raphael, and others are not acting on behalf of ALEPH. Lastly, it must be noted that several *n'shei hazon* (plural of eshet hazon) have been especially recognized for their spiritual leadership as singers and composers. In addition to Tiferet Siegel, Raphael, and Gold, who have been honored as n'shei hazon, Yofiyah and Shere, have received the title of bat kol (see Weissler 2006, 70 and 74).

The purpose so far has been to show how much feminist Jewish singer-songwriters are integrated into and engaged with national feminist and other Jewish networks, and to what extent their music is supported by recipients scattered around the country. To get a deeper insight into the scene and to understand who belongs to the circle of feminist Jewish singer-songwriters and who does not, it is worth looking at feminist Jewish musicians' self-constructed sense of belonging. This notion, however, seems to be built along the lines of their understanding of what feminist Jewish music is.

The Internal Network

Aside from the larger feminist and Jewish Renewal networks in which feminist Jewish singer-songwriters are engaged, I observed the ways in which women were linked to each other. Raphael, my main interviewee throughout my fieldwork, showed me the unpublished documents for a Jewish feminist songbook that she and other feminist composers had planned to publish in the mid-1990s. This material is of high value for this book, as it documents the feminist Jewish music scene between spring 1989 and summer 1994. It shows who was active as a feminist singer-songwriter and whose music was considered as feminist Jewish by the people working on the songbook, and thus what criteria were used to define this group. From today's perspective, the manuscripts also inform us who has remained active in the feminist Jewish music scene, and who has not. Finally, since Raphael, Rabbi Goldie Milgram, and I revived the project in October 2013 (Raphael, Ross, and Milgram forthcoming), it also shows who has joined the scene only recently.

According to the documents, the original team for the project consisted of five women, of whom four were knowledgeable about music, but all of whom were well informed about Jewish feminism, and the publication process. Shelley Mann, at that time an educator and song-leader at the Jewish Feminist Center in Los Angeles,[15] coordinated the project, and Raphael, Hirschhorn, the cantor Aviva Rosenbloom, and Elwell participated in the evaluation and selection of musicians and materials. Raphael was a prolific and spirited composer and singer of feminist Jewish music, while Hirschhorn was well known as a recording artist and major composer of contemporary music, including songs with a strong feminist Jewish perspective. In contrast, Rosenbloom was known first and foremost as a feminist cantor, although she contributed some of the songs she had composed to the project. Rosenbloom was also a frequent performer in a variety of settings and was very involved in feminist Jewish activities. Elwell was the only staff member with no musical expertise. Her contribution to the songbook was based on her experience as director of the Coalition for Women's Rights and a founding member and director of the Feminist Jewish Center in Los Angeles (Elwell et al. 1992).

The five women sought national distribution of their songbook, which served a specific purpose and vision. They wrote: "Music moves and educates people. In communities around the world, feminist Jewish songs carry and teach feminist Jewish visions and values. We propose to share these wonderful, inspiring songs with a broad audience through the production and distribution of the sourcebook of feminist Jewish songs. We believe that the music in this sourcebook will speed and enhance the integration of feminist consciousness into Judaism" (Elwell et al. 1992, n.p.). In a later paragraph they wrote: "Many contemporary feminist artists have been inspired to share their experiences and to express their visions in new songs. These songs have deeply touched the small groups of people who have been fortunate enough to share them. But most of these songs have not been shared beyond the community of the composer. This songbook will be an important vehicle for sharing this music with the larger Jewish community. . . . This is the new music of worship, celebration and communion. It needs to be shared and sung" (ibid.). Raphael confirmed that the core intention was to support and to collect the music of women who did not have enough songs written to record a whole album (e-mail interview May 2009). With this in mind, the members of the team identified up to a hundred songs written by contemporary composers, whose work had to meet the following basic criteria of feminist Jewish music to be included in the songbook: the song texts had to feature feminist Jewish content, and the songs had to be appropriate for community singing by adults or older children but still had to maintain a high level of musical quality. Last but not least, the music had to be in current use in feminist Jewish communities. Newly composed feminist Jewish music and traditional Jewish liturgical songs were chosen for inclusion, but in the latter case old sexist lyrics had to have been replaced by new feminist ones (ibid.). In a later draft of the songbook, another criterion was added: that the music "represents a geographical or cultural contribution." In the manuscript the word "geographical" was written in by hand, together with the word "Canada" (Elwell et al. 1993).

The following list shows which musicians in 1992 and 1993 the project staff members considered to be singer-songwriters with a strong feminist Jewish message in their repertoire. In preparing the updated version of the songbook, my colleagues and I have added women who are active as performers and singer-songwriters as of summer 2014 (Raphael, Ross, and Milgram, forthcoming). The last known (if any) geographical location and denominational affiliation of the songwriters listed below is presented in brackets.

LIST OF FEMINIST JEWISH SINGER-SONGWRITERS

Adelman, Penina (Newton, MA)
Avni, Fran (Berkeley, CA; Renewal/Reconstructionist)
Bachmann, Alan Scott (Salt Lake City, UT; Jewish Renewal)
Berkson, Laura (Des Moines, IA; Reform)
Berner, Leila Gal (Reconstructionist)
Brier, Sigal (Philadelphia, PA; Reconstructionist)
Capek, Batsheva (Toronto, ON)
Cohen, Tamara Ruth (New York, NY; Reconstructionist)
Damsky, Andrea Beth (El Cajon, CA)
Friedman, Debbie (New York, NY; Reform)
Gold, Shefa (Jemez Springs, NM; Jewish Renewal)
Goldstein, Elyse (Canada; Reform)
Goldstein, Sylvia F. (Hartford, CT)
Grodsky, Neshama (Jewish Renewal)
Hirschhorn, Linda (San Francisco, CA; Jewish Renewal)
Jedwab, Shoshana (New York, NY; Jewish Renewal)
Joanis, Susan Tamar (Canada)
Klein, Leslie Ginsparg (Baltimore, MD, area)
Levow-Krieger, Suri
Kummer, Judy (New York, NY, area; Reconstructionist)
Less, Naomi (New York, NY, area)
Lyons, Abbe (Ithaca, NY; Jewish Renewal)

Mann, Shelley (Jewish Renewal)
Martin, Jefferson (also known as Judah Prince; Philadelphia, PA; Jewish Renewal)
Moise, Elaine (Stanford, CA; Reconstructionist)
Newman, Benjamin (MA)
Perlman, Orit (Israel; Reform)
Rabinowitz, Myrna (Canada; Jewish Renewal)
Rabins, Alicia Jo (Portland, OR, and Brooklyn, NY)
Raphael, Geela Rayzel (Philadelphia, PA; Reconstructionist/Jewish Renewal)
Rogow, Faith (Reform)
Rosenbloom, Aviva (Los Angeles, CA; Reform)
Rubin, Petti Linsky (Northridge, CA; Reform)
Schwartz, Rebecca (Elkins Park, PA; Reform)
Shere, Holy Taya (Washington, DC; Reconstructionist)
Spiro, Hannah (Philadelphia, PA; Reconstructionist)
Spitzer, Juliet (Philadelphia, PA; Reconstructionist/Jewish Renewal)
Stein, Margot (Philadelphia, PA; Reconstructionist/Jewish Renewal)
Talo, Nancy Abraham (Scarsdale, NY; Reform)
Tiferet Siegel, Hanna (Canada; Jewish Renewal)
Turner, Ri J. (Boston, MA)
Tofa'ah Band[16] (Israel; Orthodox)
Yofiyah (also known as Susan Deikman; Philadelphia, PA; Jewish Renewal)
Zevit, Shawn Israel (Philadelphia, PA; Jewish Renewal)

The songbook material and the list above give an impression of how widely feminist Jewish songwriters are spread throughout the United States and beyond, and in what ways they are interconnected with each other. In January 1993, Mann sent a note to Hirschhorn, Raphael, Rosenbloom, and Elwell: "We have an incredible and varied collection of Jewish women's music from all over the world, including 60 songs which seem to fall into the realm of feminist Jewish music!" (the note is now in my possession). Twenty years later, in 2014, when the songbook was revised for publication, more than 300 songs were sent by the composers and songwriters to the new editorial board of the songbook (Geela Rayzel Raphael, Sarah Ross and

Goldie Milgram)—including songs of young singer-songwriters who are new to the scene of feminist Jewish music.

To conclude this discussion of the translocality of the feminist Jewish music scene in the United States, another aspect has to be mentioned, which is that of the distribution and reception of feminist Jewish music. Although the original songbook was never published, the music of feminist Jews nevertheless spread throughout the United States—mostly because of direct marketing, but also through the oral transmission. The networks of ALEPH kallah, the National Havurah Committee, B'not Esh, and others very effectively supported the distribution of feminist Jewish music, as has been shown above.

THE RECEPTION OF FEMINIST JEWISH MUSIC

At this point, we must refer back to Slobin and his concept of interculture, which he uses to describe music's potential to cross frontiers and the dynamic interaction of people within the boundaries of nation-states (Slobin 1993, 61). Slobin refers to three kinds of intercultures that work across frontiers and are tied to hegemonic powers—namely, the industrial, diasporic, and affinity intercultures (ibid.). The concept of an affinity interculture is the most interesting in the context of this study, as it refers to an interest group of performers and recipients that acts transnationally. According to Slobin, "musics seem to call out audiences across nation-state lines even when they are not part of a heritage or a commodified, disembodied network, and particularly when the transmission is of the old-fashioned variety—face to face, mouth to ear" (ibid., 68). Although I was not able to conduct a large-scale collection of data about the recipients of feminist Jewish music, I will nevertheless present a sketch of how feminist Jewish music is spread, received, and used in the larger American Jewish community. In doing so, I will draw on interviews I conducted with cantors and rabbis from a range of synagogue communities.

One important aspect of feminist Jewish music is its function as an educational tool. It was clear in the interviews I conducted, as well as in the documents I collected during my fieldwork, that feminist Jewish musicians see it as their mission to travel throughout the United States and abroad to teach Jewish communities their music. Raphael and Mann drew up a proposal for a workshop titled "A New Song: Jewish Feminist Music," to be held at the P'nai Or kallah, in which they wrote: "Music has great power to move, to inspire and to teach. . . . Our focus is on music that can be shared by communities, as part of Shabbat, New Moon rituals, lifecycle celebrations and every day celebrations."[17] This way of teaching Jewish communities new liturgical songs is known as song leading. Jewish song leading corresponds to the notion of face-to-face transmission mentioned by Slobin (2000, 68). Songwriters such as Hirschhorn, Raphael, and Gold can be hired as artists in residence and as lecturers on feminist Jewish subjects and Jewish spirituality, and at the same time perform their music.[18]

Even more interesting here is the aspect of mouth-to-ear transmission, as it reflects the success of feminist Jewish music in the larger Jewish community and in general synagogue worship, and its suitability for both. Music festivals (such as Shalshelet International Festivals[19] and the International Jewish Music Festival),[20] workshops, feminist Jewish conferences, and conventions (like ALEPH kallot) where some feminist Jewish songwriters perform at a regular basis can be regarded as a special type of translocal music scene (Peterson and Bennett 2004, 9). At such occasions, supporters of Jewish feminism, which is an essential part of Renewal Judaism, come together from all over the United States and have the opportunity to enjoy feminist Jewish music and the rituals and culture associated with it. These kinds of events "are most likely to take on the characteristics of a scene if festivals take place over a number of days in a risk-free environment, . . . so that participants have a chance to enact the ways of life idealized within the scene . . . away . . . from the agents of social [and religious] control" (ibid., 10). To some degree, these aspects can be claimed for events such as ALEPH kallahs and the feminist rituals taking place during the events. However, when I asked Raphael how else she distributes her music and is heard by other people, she replied that one of her strategies was to regularly send her songs to more popular Jewish singer-songwriters, such as Rick Recht and Craig Taubman (related to Reform Judaism), and ask them to perform her music at one of their concerts (interview June 2008).

Thus, in the words of Bruno Nettl, feminist Jewish music is "on the move"—it moves on the backs and in the heads of people who travel throughout America (2005, 334). This becomes even more apparent when we examine when and where the music of feminist Jews is integrated into Jewish liturgy. As most of my interviewees confirmed, their music is used cross-denominationally and worldwide—it often moves with other performers, cantors, rabbis, or worshipers from one synagogue to the other. Thus, Gold told me that people even call her music *mi Sinai* (revealed at Mount Sinai) and do not know that the songs they sing are contemporary compositions. Her music is thus considered traditional (interview March 2008). Other feminist Jewish songwriters told me about similar experiences, which were confirmed by the rabbis and cantors I interviewed about the musical arrangement of their services.

For example, I talked to Rabbi Ari Cartun[21] of the Congregation Etz Chayim, the first Reconstructionist temple in Palo Alto, California, which he founded. When I met him in February 2008, he was about to hold a special Shabbat service titled Shab-Beat-les Service,[22] in which he integrated original versions of different Beatles songs and other non-Jewish and Jewish pop songs by well-known performers (such as Taubman and, more important, Friedman) into the traditional Shabbat liturgy. Cartun thus invited his congregation to sing traditional liturgical songs, such as the "L'cha Dodi," to the tunes of the Beatles' songs (in this case, "With a Little Help from My Friends").

Cartun's Shab-Beat-les Service was only one of many folk-rock services held at Etz Chayim. As he told me, he regularly integrated the music of feminist Jewish songwriters like Friedman, Gold, or Raphael into his services. His handling of feminist Jewish music shows to what extent this music is accepted in regular synagogue communities. However, at Etz Chayim, song leading is mostly done by the female members of the community—often teachers working at the synagogue—who are more likely to draw on the music written by feminist songwriters, and to transcribe traditional liturgical songs into women's voices, than the male members of the community are. Cartun seemed to be a very open-minded and musically interested person, but he nevertheless confessed that sometimes he still struggles with the changing of traditional language in the prayer texts that most often form the lyrics of feminist Jewish songs. He said: "I do not use [for example] Marcia Falk's prayers, as they go a step further than the congregation does; . . . I think her view of God is too small" (interview February 2008).

The interviews I conducted with female cantors complete the picture of how well feminist Jewish music is integrated into synagogue worship. Angela Buchdahl, cantor at the Central Synagogue in New York City (a Reform congregation) told me that she chooses music first because it speaks to her personally, and then because it is prayerful, lyrical, democratic, and can be easily sung by the whole community. Feminist Jewish music meets these requirements. She said: "I seek a sense of history, but I also want to challenge my community by modern melodies. I want to push people by music" (interview February 2007). Thus, Buchdahl includes modern and eclectic arrangements of Jewish music in her services and sings pieces by Louis Lewandowski alongside Hasidic tunes and songs written by Friedman, Gold, and other female composers.

She further pointed to the connection between feminist Jewish music and the healing movement, which, according to her, marks an important and major shift in American Judaism. Here again she referred to the music of Friedman (interview February 2007). Buchdahl also mentioned that the music of Friedman is already considered traditional, a view confirmed by Katzew. Katzew said the music of Friedman in particular has become a traditional part of the Reform prayer- and songbook (interview February 2007). In my estimation, these statements are an important indication of the popularity, reception, and above all acceptance of feminist Jewish music, especially as helpful in healing.

But the integration of feminist Jewish music into synagogue services and the prayer books has not been as easy as it seems. Both Katzew and cantor Lori Corrsin from Congregation Emanu-El in New York City (a Reform congregation) talked about the initial resistance towards the use of women's music in synagogue worship in general, and feminist Jewish music in particular. For example, Corrsin told me that she cannot sing the songs of Friedman or other female singer-songwriters in general services, because of the community's resistance toward changes in tradition. Thus, one Friday night a month, she holds special services—called Shabbat Shalom services—for a small group of interested worshipers in an intimate setting. There, she sings Jewish women's music as well as other new Jewish and Israeli folk songs. Corrsin also referred to healing services. As there are no musical models available to show how to organize a healing service, rabbis and cantors had to create the programs for these services on their own. Corrsin told me that services such as her "Shirim: Poetry and Music That Heal Mind, Body, and Soul,"[23] which draws on the feminist Jewish music repertoire on healing and Friedman's song "Mi Shebeirach," are standard at every healing service (interview February 2007).

Raphael said that feminist Jewish music is most often integrated into the Friday night Kabbalat Shabbat service, as the liturgy's structure then is more flexible than on any other weekday or high holy day. Thus, it is no surprise that most of the singer-songwriters have a rich repertoire of new liturgical music for Kabbalat Shabbat (interview June 2008). Adin Steinsaltz writes that, according to the Kabbalah, which is considered to be an important textual basis of feminist Jewish songs, the Shabbat eve "is conceived of as Divine revelation in the aspect of *Shekhinah*, as the bride decked out in all her finery" (2000, 105). The reclamation of the Shekhinah is essential in feminist Jewish spirituality. However, as the liturgy of Shabbat morning (the *Shakharit*) and of high holy days, such as Rosh Hashanah and Yom Kippur, is too fixed in its order, the use of feminist Jewish music is thus mostly limited to such events as feminist rituals, healing services, or women's seders (interview with G. Raphael, June 2008).

PUBLISHING FEMINIST JEWISH MUSIC

Music scenes are most often regarded as informal gatherings, but once they flourish they become entrenched in the music industry (Peterson and Bennett 2004, 4). This raises questions about the success of feminist Jewish music in general and its integration into today's music business in particular. In this section I present a critical overview on the various options for and obstacles to producing and distributing feminist Jewish music, which are closely related to the radical change in the technology of recording devices and publication options.

Boundless Options and Insuperable Obstacles

At first sight, it would seem that feminist Jewish music could be released and distributed, using commercial marketing devices, as women's music, Jewish music, or world music. However, most of the feminist Jewish singer-songwriters discussed in this book face serious constraints created by the practical aspects of the music industry that eventually force them to fund, produce, and promote their music on their own (see Musleah 1995, 19).

In general, the music industry has various forms. On the one hand, there is the established corporate music industry, which is run and dominated by few media conglomerates (large music firms) that produce, market, and distribute music as a product to a dispersed mass of individual purchasers (Peterson and Bennett 2004, 4). On the other hand, there is a different form of music industry at whose core are music scenes. This "scene-supporting industry," also referred to as a do-it-yourself industry, is chiefly the home of "small collectives, fans turned entrepreneurs, and volunteer labor," and thus is in itself a valuable site for researching the dynamic forces of music scenes (ibid., 5). This so-called scene-supporting industry, which includes women's music record labels, for example, is of specific interest in an analysis of the possible options for publishing feminist Jewish music.

As already indicated in the discussion of the emergence of women's music as a new musical genre (see the introduction), a rare example of a commercial label that publishes feminist Jewish music is Ladyslipper, which continues to distribute the music of a few feminist Jewish songwriters such as Friedman, Julie Silver, and Hirschhorn. In the early 1990s, Ladyslipper also distributed the music of the Israeli band Tofa'ah and of MiRaJ (Ladyslipper Music n.d.; Elwell et al. 1992). Raphael told me that "MiRaJ was in the Ladyslipper catalogue for a while but they wouldn't take me as single recording artist—they only wanted groups that toured. When we didn't generate enough sales for them they took us out of the catalogue. I never tried to get them to produce the CDs" (e-mail interview May 2009). Although developments in Jewish feminism and its culture parallel many of those in mainstream feminism, Jewish feminists never founded their own Jewish women's music labels to produce and distribute their music.

The reasons for the exclusion of feminist Jewish music from the larger field of mainstream women's and feminist music publishing can only be guessed. The most reasonable assumption might be that the women's music record labels founded by various mainstream feminist and lesbian songwriters, because of their independent status in the general music market, could not afford to publish music other than their own. Futhermore, and as has already been mentioned, feminist Jewish music basically evolved due to the influence of mainstream feminist music—thus, most likely, it was not recognized in the larger women's music scene. The general ignorance of Jewish women's concerns by mainstream feminists might be another reason for the exclusion of feminist Jewish music from publishing. In addition, it is not clear how much feminist Jewish songwriters were interested in having their music published by mainstream women's music record labels or to what extent they tried to get a contract with one of those labels.

A typical example of the written replies by progressive presses and educational publishers Raphael contacted with regard to publishing feminist Jewish music is: "[We] have concluded that songbook will not fit into our present publication schedule. While we feel it is very interesting and well done, we just don't think there is a market out there for this kind of publication" (A. F. M.,[24] A.R.E. Publishing, letter to G. R. Raphael, November 20, 1989). A letter by N. K. at Houghton Mifflin, a leading American educational publisher, put it more precisely. N. K. expressed her thanks to Raphael for submitting her songs, which N. K. found "great!" Then she wrote: "I asked my friend to ask her friend at Beacon [Press] what was going on there; apparently Wendy, the Editor-in-Chief, is loath to take what she views as risks, and publishing a category, i.e. songs, that they haven't previously published, strikes her as risky" (N. K., letter to G. R. Raphael, June 13, 1991). N. K. continued: "I think there's a hidden element of anti-Semitism in the attitude of some of the progressive small presses; Jews are supposed to 'control' the media and the publishing world, so it's assumed that anything Jewish will get published and therefore there's no sense of political obligation" (ibid.). I do not use this quote to make a general statement about antisemitism as a major issue with regard to the publishing of feminist Jewish music. Rather, my purpose here is to outline different people's views on this subject, to give a sense of the various barriers raised by publishers. However, while the resistance of nonmusic publishers such as those mentioned above to the publication of Jewish women's music (considering it a "risk") is understandable to some degree, the same reasons for refusing to publish Raphael's music were given by independent and progressive music publishers, such as Sing Out!,[25] which is more surprising. Raphael's initial idea was to bring out a songbook on women and Judaism using popular music, such as folk-rock, as an educational tool. Thus, her project seemed to fit the mission of Sing Out!, which is "to preserve and support the cultural diversity and heritage of all traditional and contemporary folk musics, and to encourage making folk music a part of our everyday lives." Sing Out! describes itself as "a tax-exempt, not-for-profit, educational organization," (Sing Out! n.d.) and it is known for its long history of publishing songbooks. But even P. B., publications director of Sing Out!, expressed concerns about publishing Raphael's "Discussion Guide to Jewish Women's Music" (n.d.), another songbook project that Raphael tried to realize, and her Shekhinah songs. While P. B. suspected that her Shekhinah songs were "too specialized [as a] project to ever be appropriate for Sing Out's publishing mission" (letter to G. R. Raphael, October 3, 1991), he considered the discussion guide an appropriate project. But due to financial issues, he could not offer a contract to publish the songbook in 1991 (ibid.).

The music published by Sing Out! comes close to what has come to be known as world music, a significant marketing category that entered the realm of popular music and the mainstream music market in the 1980s and 1990s. World music made "musics from all over much more widely available than ever before, and much more influential and audible in more mainstream musics" (Taylor 2000, 163–64). The category generally refers to traditional folk and roots music, which is created and performed by indigenous musicians. It incorporates many musical forms "of various cultures that remain closely informed or guided by indigenous music of the regions of their origins," which makes it a part of "virtually every culture and society on the planet" (Nidel 2005, 2). Jewish music is generally considered as part of world music and is thus often published in this category. Moreover, world music includes by definition a plethora of hybrid and constantly changing styles and musical genres that emerged as a consequence of the impact of globalization on culture, together with new forms of collective identities such as ethnic or religious minorities (see Regev 2000, 259).[26] Feminist Jewish music, with its combination of original Jewish and other world music tunes, could be easily classified as world music. However, this new and successful marketing category did not make it more likely that feminist Jewish music would be published.[27]

Raphael is often in contact with various publishers in the United States and has written to several Jewish music and book publishers, as well as to other Jewish women's and educational organizations to ask for funding and about publication possibilities. But the same kind of rejections came from within the Jewish ranks, as it will be discussed in the next section.

Jewish Music Publishers in the United States

Raphael followed a certain strategy as she tried to find a suitable publisher for the Jewish feminist songbook and the "Discussion Guide to Jewish Women's Music" in the larger American Jewish community: she contacted publishers and organizations interested generally in Jewish women, Jewish education, and Jewish music. Jewish educational publishing companies such as Torah Aura Productions and Jewish organizations such as the National Foundation for Jewish Culture and the Mandell L. Berman Center at University of Michigan Hillel either questioned the discussion guide's "successful marketability" (J. L. G., Torah Aura Productions, letter to G. R. Raphael, November 28, 1989) or refused to sponsor it as there were no "funds available to support private initiatives" (T. S., National Foundation for Jewish Culture, letter to G. R. Raphael, November 22, 1989). In contrast, Jewish women's organizations recognized Raphael's manuscripts as "a much needed addition to our women's liturgy" (I. F., Women's Institute for Continuing Jewish Education, letter to G. R. Raphael, December 27, 1989), and considered the discussion guide to be a project that "really warrants more attention," as well as being a good component of a "curriculum for high school classes," where it would be "an ideal vehicle for this age group" (C. D., Hadassah, letter to G. R. Raphael, May 18, 1989). Although these organizations were not able to provide any funding either, they offered Raphael help and information, directing her to music publishers like Tara Publications and Sounds Write Productions. Biblio Press gave her the most specific information.

Biblio Press used to be a small feminist and academic-oriented press founded in 1979 that published nonfiction books for Jewish women, while focusing on the women's movement in Judaism (see Biblio Press n.d.). Biblio Press creator D. B. G. wrote Raphael that Biblio Press was not able to publish her music and the discussion guide either, "since it falls into a distinct 'text' category or is so specialized in its use that it would not be marketed well here" (D. B. G., Biblio Press, letter to G. R. Raphael, November 8, 1989). But D. B. G. suggested another way for Raphael to get her music out—an alternative that falls into the do-it-yourself part of the music publishing industry mentioned above. D. B. G. wrote:

> *Music* of any kind, esp[ecially] in Judaica, is truly a medium that needs a special publisher, preferably in the field of music. Alternatively, even experienced persons like *Ruth Rubin*, has decided to market her own new edition of *Yiddish folk songs*. We produced the work of 96 pgs. for her, and she is selling it to participants in groups she encounters. (There is a *Ladyslipper* women's music catalogue in which it is also listed, together with other Jewish women's music—the few items which exist.) You probably know that Jewish music in cassettes are sold in Judaica stores through one or two distributors, but there is still no demand there . . . for this kind of material. Reaching women directly seems the best way. Your material looks interesting, but seems that it

> might need many trial runs in places like CAJE [the Coalition for the Advancement of Jewish Education] and other conferences, to test further and to combine with existing curricula. (ibid.; emphasis in original).

In her letter, D. B. G. made specific suggestions, such as contacting Jewish music publishers, distributing the music through Judaica bookstores, and self-marketing. But all of these options also present problems with regard to Raphael's and other feminist Jewish music.

In 1989, Raphael was in contact with R. F., director of Sounds Write Productions, a well-known distributor of Jewish women's music, such as that of Reform singer-songwriters Friedman and Silver, and other contemporary Jewish music. Formerly an independent Jewish music publisher, Sounds Write Productions is now a division of the Union of Reform Judaism Books and Music (see URJ Books and Music n.d.). Although R. F. complimented Raphael's project proposal, she said that she "does not have the funds to do outside projects," as Sound Writes Productions' investment is "tied up with [their] own [. . .] and those of Debbie Friedman" (R. F., Sounds Write Productions, letter to G. R. Raphael, October 24, 1989).

As the members of MiRaJ told me in a group interview, the national Jewish music market, as well as the influential Jewish music publishers, is dominated by Reform Judaism. In addition, the rest of the music business—namely, Jewish music stores and Judaica bookstores—is dominated by Orthodox Jews (interview February 2007). The specific problem with the latter is Kol Isha, the Talmudic dictum that forbids Orthodox men to listen to women's voices (see the introduction). This creates enormous problems for Jewish female singer-songwriters in terms of distributing their music through these stores. Orthodox men refuse to carry and sell women's recordings (Musleah 1995, 19). Thus, the fact that Jewish music publishing houses and stores are affiliated with Reform and Orthodox Judaism is a great disadvantage for female songwriters related to the Reconstructionist and Jewish Renewal movements, which do not have their own music presses and distributors.

However, R. F. referred Raphael to Velvel Pasternak, the owner of Tara Publications, the largest distributor of Jewish music in North America. If Raphael could acquire funding, R. F wrote her, Pasternak—who had helped and encouraged a tremendous number of Jewish female musicians to make recordings and songbooks—would be the best person for Raphael to contact about selling her music (R. F., Sounds Write Productions, letter to G. R. Raphael, October 24, 1989). Three years later, Pasternak offered to publish the songbook, though nothing came of the offer (letter to G. R. Raphael, 1992). Thus, basically the only outcome of the correspondence between Raphael and several publishers was the idea of the songbook's creators' marketing it (as well as a supplemental recording) themselves, which would mean that they would have to produce it themselves and, at best, have it distributed by Sounds Write Productions, Jewish Family Production, or Tara Publications, as R. F. suggested (ibid.). The only reasonable and possible option for feminist Jewish singer-songwriters to publish their music thus seem to be through the do-it-yourself part of the industry. This became easier to do with the development of new technologies and the Internet (Peterson and Bennett 2004, 5).

DO-IT-YOURSELF: PRODUCING AND DISTRIBUTING FEMINIST JEWISH MUSIC

R. F. explained the process of self-publication to Raphael:

> Regarding publishing and producing—if you went into a recording studio and made a tape you would come out with a finished master recording which you would have 'produced.' You then take the master recording to some cassette duplicating company, along with any printed cassette J-card insert and have them package your product. Up to this point you would be responsible for all costs of the recording. JFP [Jewish Family Productions] could then get involved as your distributor to market the product if you had made previous arrangements with them to do so. If they heard the master recording and liked it, they would need to have their logo on the J-card and plastic tape, along with any other requirements. If they agreed to distribute your tape, they would become your publisher, which means they would take care of all royalty disbursements from sales of the product and they would handle future royalty contracts with anyone who wanted to use your work on another product. This is simply what the process is but there are complicated contracts to cover all these areas. (R. F., Sounds Write Productions, letter to G. R. Raphael, December 8, 1989)

In comparison with this very complicated way of producing a recording tape at the end of the 1980s, the digital revolution and its effect on recording processes facilitated the rapid development of the do-it-yourself music industry and further democratized the recording process by allowing musicians such as feminist Jewish songwriters to record their music without the financial patronage of record companies. High-quality recording technology is no longer only the property of extremely costly professional studios (see Peterson and Bennett 2004, 5–6).

Feminist Jewish singer-songwriters now make use of this new high-quality recording equipment. During my fieldwork in Philadelphia in March 2008, I had the chance to attend a session in the recording studio of Daoud Shaw, who owns the small recording studio Radio Active Productions that is located in the basement of his home. Shaw recorded some of the albums of Raphael and MiRaJ, offering them an inexpensive, uncomplicated, but professional way to publish their music. Unlike the style of publishing described above, in this case the copyright remains with the artists.

In addition, since the mid-1990s, the rapid development of the Internet has facilitated the democratization of distributing music. The Internet makes it possible for any innovative singer-songwriter or band to advertise and promote upcoming releases without having to sign with a major record company (Peterson and Bennett 2004, 6). The Internet-based way of selling recordings was especially beneficial for feminist Jewish singer-songwriters outside the Reform movement. Today, in addition to a songwriter's personal website that offers to sell albums directly by mail, independent online record stores such as CD Baby and OySongs sell the recordings of almost all of the feminist Jewish musicians discussed in this book.

Finally, it is relevant to refer to Philip Bohlman, who stated: "We have constructed the end of our century [the twentieth] in such a way that it would be difficult to imagine a past in which . . . the world was parsed between 'Europe and the people without history' " (2002b, 26). But, as he further argues, "in many cases, it has been those without history who have used Internet technology most quickly to claim and to construct history" (ibid.). This is very relevant to feminist Jewish singer-songwriters in the United States. As these musicians primarily promote themselves, their music is still, to a great extent, also distributed and sold at concerts, workshops, and conferences, which most often limits the distribution of their music to a local rather than a national or even international area. In addition most feminist songwriters necessarily "support themselves through other professions," as Rahel Musleah noted, adding that "non-parents like . . . Friedman . . . find it much easier to schedule performances than mothers with children" (1995, 19). The women of MiRaJ also identified the contradictions involved in being a full-time musician and a parent as a major problem (interview with MiRaJ, February 2007).

The major question that remains to be answered is why feminist Jewish music is not considered marketable. Does this music not contain the special and exotic "earmarks" of world music (Bohlman 2002b, 3)? Is the genre too heterogeneous in its style to be easily recognized by the ordinary customer, or does it blur every category on the music market? Or is the answer simply because nobody knows about the genre? These are the questions that the following chapters address.

PART TWO

The second part of this book discusses how text and music interact in Jewish worship and how feminist Jewish music is different from traditional synagogue music. As in any sung tradition, here text and music—two independent parameters of different origin—are temporarily bonded to create a specific type of songs or, in this case, prayers that are meant to constitute a personal Jewish religious experience for both men and women.

This experience, which is the relationship of the human being with his or her creator, is primarily expressed in Jewish ritual, prayer, and—in particular—the music of prayer. That music is conceived of as a sacred text, a ritual, and a performance, a conception that not only mobilizes a cultural field of meanings and emotions but also determines the worshiper's religious self-identity (Prell 1989, 166–67). Jewish prayer music enhances this process of spiritual self-positioning and defines how Judaism is experienced. But various factors (such as the problem of Kol Isha) have led to differences in the way in which men and women conceptualize and conduct their prayers (see, for example, Steinsaltz 2000, 26).

Thus, the second part of this book examines how feminist Jewish singer-songwriters invent new sacred songs that do not fail to recognize people who for the most part are ignored by Jewish tradition (such as women, gays, lesbians, and transgender people) to create an egalitarian community. By creating new gender-sensitive liturgical texts for various traditional and nontraditional (feminist) rituals, feminist Jewish songwriters place as much value on the shared cultural, historical, and religious memory called Jewish tradition as on the contemporary Jewish experience in America that includes questions such as how Jewish women can identify with a traditionally male-dominated Judaism, Jewish liturgy, and God; and which musical tunes can help them become engaged what they are singing about, since prayer and music are intrinsically tied together (see, for example, Marini 2003, 5).

The following chapters examine how Jewish feminism that explicitly addresses these questions is performed within Jewish liturgical music. I will argue that the core values and themes of Jewish feminism are the basis of the content of the lyrics as well as of the musical structure of the songs. Moreover, the following explanations are based on the hypothesis that the feminist reconceptualization of the normative structure of Jewish liturgy in general and Jewish prayer in particular is followed by a reconceptualization of Jewish prayer music, to create a feminist-informed, egalitarian Judaism and Jewish community.

3 Feminist Voices in the Lyricists' Choice

A Content Analysis

Rabbi Geela Rayzel Raphael once stated that "music is a nonthreatening tool, which when used correctly, can be used to soothe contentious issues while fostering discussions, [as it is] hard to argue when you are . . . entertained by song" (n.d., n.p.)—or, it might be added, when you are singing yourself. In other words, she argues that music has the power to slip a feminist message in that otherwise would meet resistance. Feminist Jewish songs differ widely in their sounds, but, as I will show below, they are held together by common ideas that are influenced by recent Jewish feminist discourses. Feminist Jewish songs can be outspoken or not about their political message, but the song texts represent a common understanding of the themes and values of contemporary Jewish feminism and thus also signify a feminist-informed "God–worshipper/God–world relationship" (Epstein 2004, 3). The latter relationship in particular becomes apparent in a religious context in which there is considerable interference in the interactions between the worshiper and God, such as restricting gender ideologies that have led to differences in the way in which men and women conceptualize and conduct their prayers (see, for example, Steinsaltz 2000, 26).

Accordingly, and although women and men in so-called liberal and egalitarian Jewish communities are to a large extent equal, most sacred texts, prayers, and sacred songs used in liberal worship still fail to recognize women and fail to create a truly egalitarian community. That is why the following central question arises: Assuming that worshipers seek to identify themselves with the shared cultural, historical, and religious memory called Jewish tradition as well as with the entity to which they are praying, how can Jewish women relate to a Judaism, Jewish liturgy, and particularly to a God who is conceptualized as the male Lord? It is worth examining how the political—in other words, the contemporary Jewish feminism that explicitly addresses this question—is performed in music. I will argue that the core values and themes of Jewish feminism are reflected in and shape the lyrics of feminist Jewish songs. For a better understanding of how the songwriters seek to affect not only the structure of Jewish liturgy and worship but also the social and cultural structure of the American Jewish community, the following analysis applies aspects of the theology of Judith Plaskow (1992 and 1994).

The content of the feminist Jewish songs can be classified into three major categories: (1) the reclamation of Jewish women's selfhood in Judaism, (2) the creation of an egalitarian Jewish community that honors diversity, and (3) an articulation of the feminist conception of the divine. This range of song topics can be equated with Plaskow's feminist Jewish theological conceptions of Torah, Israel, and God. In the following section, I will present a qualitative analysis of selected examples of these three ways of enhancing feminist Jewish theological consciousness and integrating it into Judaism through song.

RECLAIMING WOMEN'S SELFHOOD THROUGH SONG

Feminist Jewish theology holds that the Torah is the living memory of the Jewish people, from which women have been excluded. Accordingly, feminist Jews have raised awareness of the need to reclaim and highlight the uncovered histories and stories of Jewish women and their spirituality and religious experiences, a process that became known as the women's Torah. As Raphael (1998) states, the realization of the women's Torah requires the use of creative methods to communicate and teach Jewish women's issues from a contemporary perspective, as those subjects have been largely ignored by the Jewish tradition—that is, the common sacred texts. One of these creative methods is song. As the reclamation of the women's Torah (or the reclamation of Jewish women's selfhood in Judaism) was one of the first and most obvious goals of feminist Jews, it is no coincidence that a large majority of feminist Jewish songs honor the matriarchs and other women from the Tanach, tell the stories of historical Jewish female role models, and name and sanctify Jewish women's informal experiences and common events (biological, communal, and personal) that are generally ignored by Jewish tradition. In doing so, feminist singer-songwriters seek not only to honor women and teach them about their heritage and traditions, but also, as

Raphael put it, to "create cultural and theological change in the Jewish community" (e-mail interview June 2005).

The feminist Jewish music repertoire has further intersecting subcategories: next to midrashic songs about women from the Tanach and history, there are songs for feminist rituals (including healing songs) and other Jewish holidays, as well as songs categorized as miscellaneous.

Midrashic Songs about Women from the Tanach and Jewish History

More feminist Jewish songs are about women from the Tanach and Jewish history than about other feminist topics. The reason for this, and for why these songs are so important in the context of Jewish feminism and feminist ritual making, is that these women represent Jewish womanhood and the roots of Judaism. These songs present inspirational Jewish female role models and are considered art types for women's spiritual experiences. Moreover, these songs represent the range and diversity of the women's emotional and spiritual knowledge and can thus be used in different ritual contexts, such as Rosh Hodesh or the high holy days.

Consequently, the songs presented in this section might be considered less as an overtly feminist critique of patriarchal Judaism, since they do not primarily challenge male authority, than as a tool to reframe and reimagine Judaism in women's voices (see, for example, Prell 2007, 17). Feminist Jewish innovators in general, and feminist singer-songwriters in particular, have always evoked biblical and other historical Jewish women as powerful role models for Jewish women to transform the way women experience Jewish liturgy and to heighten their own sense of being Jewish (ibid.). In this context, the symbol of a woman's voice (Kol Isha) has a special connotation that has been repressed for many generations.

In relation to music and in the context of Jewish feminism, Kol Isha refers to women's spiritual expression through song, which is considered as a political statement since women have traditionally been excluded from performing prayer and sacred songs in public. This is yet another "motivating [factor] inspiring feminist Jews to sing out" (G. Raphael 1998, 2). Giving voice to Jewish female ancestors in song not only fills a lacuna in Jewish sacred texts but also is meant to give voice to today's Jewish women and to address the spiritual lacunae they feel (Ochs 2007b, 257). Almost all feminist Jewish singer-songwriters use the words of traditional sacred texts, such as the psalms, proverbs, and the Song of Songs, as well as Talmudic passages and other Jewish religious texts as the inspiration for and basis of their songs. Feminist Jewish songs thus also should be understood as a midrash, or an explanation of classical Jewish texts through song, which can moreover be interpreted as a discussion between Jewish women and Jewish tradition—or, in a broader sense, as women's conversations with God.

Referring back to the idea of the extension of the Torah through Jewish women's stories and insights, Raphael states: "We [feminist Jews] re-examine ancient texts not only to find ourselves mirrored in them, making them relevant to our lives, but the feminist agenda examines them to heal the stories themselves, adding new endings, interpretations or *midrashim*: this breathes new life into an old text" (1998, 3). Raphael also states that feminist Jewish songs about women from the Torah must be considered as a contemporary way of continuing the midrashic process—or, in Plaskow's words, as "the continuing revelation" of the Torah at Mount Sinai (1996, 105; see also introduction). Thus, it becomes obvious how important feminist Jewish songs are to the women's Torah and Jewish tradition in general.

The study of texts about biblical women provides an easy way for today's women to find themselves in the narratives of the Jewish people (G. Raphael 1998, 3). This message is reflected in several songs on women of the Hebrew bible, such as in Jack Schechtman Gabriel's song "A Web of Women" (1990), in which he sings about the courage and strength of biblical women—in particular, Shifra, Pooah, Yocheved, and Miriam—and of all Jewish women of today who are keeping the faith in general. Thus, his song goes:

A WEB OF WOMEN

© lyrics and music by Jack Gabriel, 1990

Based on Parshat Sh'mot, published on the album *Astonishing Is G!D: Holiday Songs*

EM AM EM
Long ago, on Egyptian soil,

G D
the Hebrew children multiplied,

C B7
the Hebrew children toiled.

EM AM EM
Nasty Pharaoh, he made a lot of noise—

B7
He told *Shifrah* and *Pooah*
to kill the baby boys!

Chorus

EM
It was a web of Women,

a web of Women,

B7
that kept the Hebrew children alive . . .

It was a web of Women,

a web of Women,

C7 AM
that helped the Hebrew children

B7 EM
to survive . . .

Shifrah and *Pooah*
ignored Pharaoh's scorn
they were loving midwives,
they helped life be born.
Pharaoh was a madman,
a monster through and through,
but women have the power
to do what they must do!

Chorus
The Hebrew women
in those dark years,
they kept having babies,
they pushed past their fears
Yocheved had a baby

Moshe was his name,
and he would lead his people
to freedom once again!

Chorus
Yocheved had a baby
she hid him on the Nile,
Miriam his sister
watched him all the while,
'til Pharaoh's kindly daughter
rescued him, so brave—
without these holy women
we might still be slaves!

Chorus
Shifrah and *Pooah,*
Yocheved, Miriam
Pharaoh's daughter—
the list goes on and on . . .
Long ago, as the Torah states:
Women made the difference,
Women kept the faith!

Chorus

With her recording *Bible Babes A-Beltin'* (1997), which contains thirteen songs about various biblical women, Raphael seeks not only to provide songs about female role models of the Hebrew bible but also to write—to some extent—a Jewish "herstory" that focuses on and emphasizes the role of women. This message is effectively communicated in her song "Who Were the Women?" As Raphael states in the liner notes of her album, she wrote this song for women in the Bible—namely Dina (Genesis 34:1), Hulda (Kings 22:14), Rahav (Joshua 2:3), Yael (Judges 5:24), and the daughters of Tzelophehad (Numbers 36:6)—who are mentioned only in passing, and whose complete stories are not told. The stories about these biblical figures are framed by the following verses that relate these narratives to the present day:

WHO WERE THE WOMEN?

Who were the women
  and where were their voices?
What were they doing
  and what were their choices?
Who were the women
  and what were they saying?
When were they singing
  and why are we praying?

Dina! Dina! Dina went out to the land, to the land,
Dina! Dina! She went out to meet the women
  of the land, of the land.
She was raped by the hand of Shechem, Shechem.
  She was never heard from again, again;
  She was never heard from again.

Hulda! Hulda! A prophetess of Josiah,
Hulda! Hulda! Proclaimed the law for Judah.
  To her we owe Deuteronomy;
The story of our people, our history.
  She was never heard from again, again
  Not a word from her again.

Rahav! Rahav! A harlot of old Jericho,
Rahav! Rahav! Hid Joshua's spies so the king wouldn't know.
  She gave them room and she gave them board,
Binding the sign of a scarlet cord.
  She was never heard from again, again
  Not a word from her again.

Daughters! Daughters! Daughters of Tzelophehad,
Daughters! Daughters! Wanted the land for their own blood;
  Married among the tribal brothers
Women of inheritance unlike the others.
  They were never heard from again, again
  Not a word from them again.

Yael! Yael! Put her hand to the tent spike,
Yael! Yael! Struck Sisera with all her might.
    She saved the Jews with bravery
Sporting the head of the enemy.
    She was never heard from again, again,
    Not a word from her again.

Women! Women! We've got the voices and we're out in the land,
Sisters! Sisters! We know our choices let's take a stand.
    Our biblical sisters were strong and bold.
Let's learn their stories, they must be told
    They want to be heard from again, again.
    We will be heard from again!

This example of Raphael's lyrics shows how the women of the Bible can be feminist role models, and how their stories are used in the feminist Jewish revolution to encourage today's women to speak out on their own behalf.

Songs About the Matriarchs

The *imahot* (the four mothers, or matriarchs: Sarah, Rebecca, Rachel, and Leah) play a particular role in American Jewish feminism, as their inclusion in the liturgy—in particular, the *amidah* (standing prayer; also referred to as the *sh'mone esre* [eighteen blessings], this is the central prayer of the Jewish liturgy) alongside the naming of the three patriarchs (Abraham, Isaac, and Jacob)—satisfies the most pressing demands of Jewish feminism. As I discussed above, once women were allowed to lead the community in prayer and song and to be ordained as rabbis and cantors (in non-Orthodox communities), the changing of traditional Jewish prayer to achieve gender equality not only in the performance of rituals but also in the words of sacred text was the next big step to be taken. The inclusion of the imahot into the amidah represents the emergence of a new, feminist-inspired liturgy that speaks to men and women alike by particularly recognizing "the contributions that both the Jewish Matriarchs and Patriarchs made to the Jewish future" (Smith 2012, 310). Consequently, the Reform, Reconstructionist, and Jewish Renewal communities and synagogues accepted the feminist demand to change traditional prayer texts—and thus the need to balance the community's commitment to Jewish tradition with today's social and cultural sensibilities—more easily than did the Conservative movement, let alone the Orthodox movement. The reason why those movements reacted differently to the feminist demand for a gender-equal liturgy is their differing stance toward Jewish law: Reform, Reconstructionist, and Renewal communities find it less binding than Conservative and Orthodox ones. Liturgical changes are traditionally implemented by the rabbinical leadership of each movement in a "top-down approach," the efforts of feminist Jews in general and feminist singer-songwriters in particular to change traditional sacred texts can be regarded as a "bottom-up action" (Smith 2012, 309–10).

Aside from the transformation of the amidah, the recognition of the imahot in Jewish tradition and liturgy has a deeper religiopolitical meaning, which is reflected in several feminist Jewish songs about the imahot and about Bilhah and Zilpah, as well as other women of the Tanach. This has to do with giving credit to these biblical women for their historical deeds, with their role in the Jewish nation's future, and with the fact that God is indeed present in the lives of Jewish women, even though God does not very often—as the biblical story reports—speak to the imahot directly (see Ramon 2005, 162–63). The singer-songwriters consider the imahot and other biblical women to be important in how Jewish women experience God and construct a Jewish women's identity.

Aviva Rosenbloom's song "Ode to the Matriarchs" (music by Aviva Rosenbloom, lyrics by Savina Teubal, 2004; see figure 3.1)[1] emphasizes the matriarchs' willingness to act at any cost and to demonstrate absolute faith in God in spite of all difficulties, which is relevant for today's society ("Let the matriarchs stand as a force in the land, let us sway with their grace and resolve / Let us sing of the past as a circle we cast, let the voice of their presence evolve"). The song also makes the statement that not just half of the society, but only the whole community, will be needed to transform Jewish communities in terms of gender equality and beyond ("The tent of our mothers is open to bless every daughter and son / Our people will be what our people can be, with the song that Shechina's begun").

Other feminist Jewish songs go more into detail about and interpret the biblical stories about certain matriarchs. The songs often explain the sometimes fateful and painful interconnections and relationships among the matriarchs as well as between them and the patriarchs. Thus, Hannah Spiro's song "Rachel and Leah" (2010, released on her album *Aliyah*; see

FIGURE 3.1: "Ode to the Matriarchs" (2004) by Aviva Rosenbloom

figures 3.2–3) as well as Margot Stein's song "Leah" (1999, released on MiRaJ's album *Counting Angels in the Wilderness*; see figure 3.4) can be considered a midrash on the biblical story of the matriarchs Rachel and Leah (see Genesis 29:16–49:31) and on their marriages to Jacob, which affected the two women and their relationship to each other. Jacob, who is the father of the twelve tribes of Israel, fell in love with Laban's daughter Rachel. They could not get married before Jacob had served Laban for seven years. Jacob did so and was finally looking forward to marrying Rachel. However, as it was the custom to have the older sister married before the younger, Laban betrayed Jacob in his wedding night and gave him Leah as his wife—although they did not love each other. Only after another seven years of work for Laban was Jacob allowed to marry Rachel as well. Leah was not only Jacob's first wife but also the first to bear him children, and Rachel was unfruitful for quite a while. As a result, she offered Bilhah, her maid, to Jacob in a "surrogate mother" arrangement. In turn, Leah gave him Zilpah, her maid, as a secondary wife.

Spiro's song (sung by herself and Chrissie Miller) shows the relationship between Rachel and Leah by pointing out what they were going through as a result of their father's betrayal. The song includes, Rachel desired Jacob; her giving him up to her sister; her worries about not being able to get pregnant[2] and her sharing of her beloved not only with her sister but also with her maid ("He [Jacob] told me: seven years and you are mine, just wait the time will fly because I'll see your face be faithful and patient and then one day I'll take you away . . . I lay with him, pray with him, love him like myself and yet I am barren and go up on the shelf. I'll give you my maid, just don't love her like me. Oh it kills me"). The song also tells the story of Leah, who was degraded as the second choice and Jacob's unloved wife. Her only cold comfort was giving birth to his children,[3] and even so she had to share him with her maid, Zilpah ("He [Laban] told me: Oh, my eldest, do not shed a tear, you'll wear his ring for only seven years, be faithful and patient and then one day, he'll take you away . . . I lay with him, pray with him, love him as best as I can, give him three children and he doesn't give a damn, so take my maid as well, do with her as you wish, I just can't take this, no, I just can't take this, it kills me"). Although Rachel and Leah were very different personalities and rivals, they showed compassion toward one another (chorus: "Oh they don't know how we live no, we're giving all we can give, sister, forgive me, I have what you lack and still I am empty, empty, helpless and trapped").

Stein's song "Leah" (1999, sung by MiRaJ; figure 3.4) is another song that takes up the story of the two matriarchs, while focusing on the anguish of Leah: her feelings of being ignored, alienated, and degraded ("He loves you for your beauty, He says my eyes are weak . . . I'm not a simple woman, pregnant through the years, I'm not the only mother smiling through her tears. I lock my pain inside me, no one has to know, father, husband, sister, son and nowhere safe to go, cuz I really want to say . . ."). Stein gives Leah a voice and lets her tell her own story. In doing so, and thus putting the focus on Leah's inner life, which is ignored by the Bible text, Stein gives a feminist interpretation of the matriarch Leah (chorus: "Take a look at Leah, tell me what you see, tonight you're gonna know me, what I'm like inside can you recall, if I'm gonna show myself at all, tonight you're gonna fall in love with me").

The same combination of music, midrash, and interpretive liturgy can also be found in Juliet Spitzer's song "Couldn't Do It without You" (1997),

FIGURE 3.2–3: "Rachel and Leah" (2010) © Hannah Spiro

FIGURE 3.2–3: (continued)

which completes the midrashic songs on Rachel and Leah by telling the story of Bilhah and Zilpah. It is said that Bilhah and Zilpah were half-sisters of Rachel and Leah. Spitzer's song ties together the lives of these four women, but her main point is that both Bilhah's and Zilpah's stories are hardly known and recognized, even when thinking about honoring and naming the imahot in the amidah ("Isn't it a shame, we don't know their names . . . We honor these women 'cause this story shows all of them are our foremothers"). Thus, her song points to the fact that even progressive communities who accommodated the feminist demand to include the imahot in their liturgy, still silence women.

COULDN'T DO IT WITHOUT YOU

© Juliet I. Spitzer, 1997

Bilhah was a child, she was only a babe
When Rachel's arms opened to receive her
Years of Rachel's pain and her suffering,
Bilhah agreed to conceive for her.

Chorus
Couldn't do it without you
Couldn't bear it alone
Couldn't do it without you, sister
You've been there all along

Zilpah was with Leah as her handmaid and friend
Held her close when her heart was breaking
Leah's womb was worn, it needed a rest
Zilpah stepped in for Jacob's taking.

Chorus

Class could have ruined them, for we are told
Two were wives, two were concubines
But for Rachel, Bilhah, Leah, and Zilpah
Their lives were intertwined.
Twelve sons of Israel and Dinah we claim
But here's a little story twister:
Isn't it a shame, we don't know their names
But each boy had a twin sister.

Chorus

We honor these women 'cause this story shows
All of them are our foremothers
And the blessing they have sent
From their birthing tent
Is that we all need one another.

Chorus

Another example of how the story of two biblical women can be transformed through midrash is the song "Sarah and Hagar" (1988; see figure 3.5),[4] written by Linda Hirschhorn and performed by Vocolot. Sarah and Hagar are considered the archetypal mothers of two enemy nations, the Jewish and Arab people. As Tirzah Firestone explains, Sarah and Hagar, who had once been intimate, were "divided by issues of competition for prestige and

FIGURE 3.4: "Leah" (1999) by Margot Stein

honor, and the Torah offers no story of reconciliation" (2009, 117). This is considered problematic, as their story has implications for today's beliefs about the Jewish-Arab relationship (ibid.). Hirschhorn thus changed the story—and with it the whole relationship of these biblical women:

FIGURE 3.5: "Sarah and Hagar" ([1988] 2002) © Linda Hirschhorn

We must tell each other's stories,
make each other strong,
and sing the dream of ancient lands
where both of us belong.

Oh, let us hear the prayers
where spirit first was sown,

that all of our children
may call this land their home.

As Firestone summarizes Hirschhorn's song, Sarah and Hagar realize that they have to listen to each other's voices and "understand that to survive they must finally speak each other's name, hear each other's prayers, share each other's dream of a homeland" (2009, 117). The idea is that Sarah and Hagar will be able to do so, since they can call on their similarities as women.

Another song by Hirschhorn that takes up the story of Hagar is "Kumi" (2005), which is based on Genesis 21:18, "in which Hagar is reassured that Ishmael will become a great nation" (Hirschhorn, booklet with *Becoming*, 2007, n.p.).

Songs about Jewish Prophetesses

In addition to the matriarchs, the prophetesses Deborah, Miriam, Hannah, Sarah, Abigail, Esther, and Hulda became important figures in the feminist Jewish revolution, as they played an important part in shaping the history of the Jewish people and served as inspiring role models for Jewish women of today. There are two songs in the Torah that inspired feminist Jewish songwriters to write a musical midrash on them: the "Song of Deborah" (Judges 5:1–31) and "Miriam's Song" (Exodus 15:20).

The story of Deborah, the prophetess, has been told in the in the "Song of Deborah"—which is basically a hymn of praise for liberation—and elsewhere in the Book of Judges (4:1–5:31). The song is said to be the oldest fragment of the Hebrew scripture (see Schroeder 2014, 2). These biblical reports about Deborah stand out, as there are no comparable chapters in the Torah that give such a detailed description of the deeds of any other one of the archetypal women. Furthermore, Deborah's reputation has nothing to do with such things as motherhood (in the traditional sense of the term), keeping the household, or nurturing the family; rather, she is famous for being an independent, forthright, and assertive judge and prophetess who plays a significant role in the military victory of the Israelites over the Canaanites (see Schroeder 2014, 1–2; see also bars 12–26 in Debbie Friedman's "Devorah's Song," below). It is only natural that Deborah's story is used for women and by women and men—and sometimes also against women—who aspire leadership roles and seek to justify their claims to political and religious authority. A brave leader and powerful woman, Deborah has also always been an inspiration to today's women (Schroeder 2014, 3–4). As the judge of Israel who kept the community through conflicts and adjudicated disputes with justice and fairness, the prophetess is considered to best represent the experiences and values of a new female soul.

Deborah's virtues are reflected in Friedman's "Devorah's Song" (music by Debbie Friedman, English text by Debbie Friedman and Tamara Cohen based on the Hebrew text in Judges 4:4–6; released on the album *Songs of the Spirit: The Debbie Friedman Anthology*, 2005; see figure 3.6–7). The third verse of Friedman's song (not shown in figure 3.6–7) highlights the most important characteristics of Deborah and thus the main plot of Judges 4–5:

> Devorah the prophet, a woman of fire, her torch in hand
> She led the Israelites to victory
> Barak said, "Devorah, I cannot fight
> Unless you are standing right by my side!"
> Devorah the prophet, Devorah the mother in Israel.

Here, Friedman first of all reacts to debates about how to translate the phrase *eshet lappidôt*. While some (mostly male) commentators translate the phrase as "woman of Lappidôt" (referring to Deborah's marital status), most feminist commentators interpret the same phrase as an attribute and translate it as "woman of flames," "woman of light," or "woman of spirit" who holds a torch in her hand. Translating the phrase as "woman of Lappidôt" masks Deborah's traits and deeds; the other translations are much more appropriate for her character as prophetess, treating her as an enlightened judge, inspiring poet, and woman of action. In the words of Leah Brunner, "Deborah was an 'inflamed and inflaming' woman in her own right, as a fervent and charismatic personality, and the term fits her without any need to connect her to a husband" (quoted in Schroeder 2014, 237).

After identifying Deborah as a prophet and woman of fire, as well as a powerful and charismatic woman who has the ability to lead the military forces of Israel, Friedman turns to another often debated phrase, "mother in Israel." In the biblical "Song of Deborah," Deborah calls herself this (Judges 5:7). Here again, interpretations of the phrase differ: while traditionalists read it as "Deborah's supposed maternal tenderness," feminists tend to interpret the phrase as her "protective military leadership," since it is more likely that this title was reserved for "women who lead Israelite males

FIGURE 3.6–7: Debbie Friedman and Tamara Ruth Cohen: “Devorah’s Song” (2005)

FIGURE 3.6–7: (continued)

to victory in battle" (Schroeder 2014, 2). The same verse in Judges 5:7 ("Villagers in Israel would not fight; they held back until I, Deborah, arose, until I arose, a mother in Israel") is also referred to in the chorus of Friedman's song ("Arise, arise, Devorah; Arise, arise and sing a song: Arise, arise, Devorah; Uri, uri dabri shir"). The chorus communicates the message that it was not Deborah's duty to fight in the battle against the Canaanites but to sing encouraging victory songs—a motive that is also relevant to the contemporary Jewish feminist movement, which is to some extent also a singing revolution.

The meaning of Deborah for today's Jewish women is reflected in Friedman's reports about how she wrote her song: "Devorah [the prophetess] came to be after not having written for a year and a half. She was an inspiration to me. She was a strong character who was peace-loving and whose values, integrity and leadership skills were particularly important examples to us, most especially in these turbulent times. It is my hope that when we sing this song we will find pieces of Devorah in ourselves and allow them to come to be in our own lives" (my transcription of Friedman n.d.a). The biblical character Deborah and Friedman's song also became part of a new baby-naming ritual called Devorah's Chair, which was influenced by Friedman's passing in 2011. This ritual for a baby girl replaces the male child's circumcision on the chair of Eliyahu the prophet (*kise shel Eliyahu*). The female child is placed on Devorah's Chair (*kise shel Devorah hanevi'ah*)—which is figuratively also understood as in the arms of the prophetess—while the community asks that the baby be endowed with Deborah's prophetic vision and hopes the child will be instructed "in the art of 'singing and dancing before the Lord'" (Ritualwell n.d.). It is important to know that the inventors of the ritual hope that Friedman is now sitting alongside Deborah and with the baby girl "to fill her soul with voice, spirit and joy" (ibid.) Throughout the ritual, Friedman's song is sung.

The lyricist Tamara Cohen reported that Friedman might have been drawn to write and sing about Deborah as part of her larger project to bring biblical women into contemporary Jewish life and also because, sharing the prophetess's name, she might have felt a particular connection to Deborah. After Friedman's sudden and untimely death in January 2011, Cohen told me in an e-mail message on November 8, 2013, that she thinks of the song as a way both to honor Friedman's prophetic voice and to teach about the life of the biblical prophetess and heroine.

Another prominent biblical woman is Miriam. She replaced Lilith, "the 'poster girl' of feminist Jews of the 1970s," as a role model for Jewish feminists (Ochs 2007b, 260).[5] Like Lilith—Adam's first wife, who energetically claimed equality with her partner and was thus banned from Eden—Miriam is a product of rabbinical legends. It is difficult to integrate Lilith into the newly constructed women's Torah, as she is simply not present in the five books of Moses (see ibid., 261). As Riv-Ellen Prell notes, "the feminist Miriam is the product of rewriting traditional narratives and imaginative engagement with the texts by scholars and writers who attempt to make Miriam and hence Jewish women central actors in Jewish life" (2007, 18). These rewritings, however, uncovered many important attributes of and background information about Miriam, which became relevant for the numerous songs that have been written about her since the 1980s by feminist Jewish songwriters such as Hirschhorn, Raphael, Penina Adelman and Suri Krieger, Elaine Moise, and Leila Gal Berner. These songs were mainly integrated into new feminist rituals such as Rosh Hodesh (see S. Ross 2004 and 2011).

What makes Miriam an appropriate feminist role model in liberal as well as Orthodox Judaism is first and foremost the notion that she is situated within the tradition: she facilitates and supports others while never challenging authority or traditional power (Prell 2007, 18). As Vanessa Ochs puts it, "Miriam works gracefully, yet critically, within the system. Powerful, but not egoistic, Miriam stands for a set of positive virtues that include healing, inspiration, foresight, courage, cooperation, nurturance, and the capacity to celebrate all victories along the journey. She mentors younger women and girls who have a dim memory of Judaism in which women count less, or not at all" (2007b, 262). For feminist Jewish singer-songwriters, it is not only Miriam's role in leading—together with Aaron and Moses, her brothers—the Jewish people out of Egyptian slavery into freedom that is significant, but also her role as the women's leader in singing and dancing. This image has its origin in what is called "Miriam's Song" in Exodus 15:20–21, where she sings about God's power of redemption while the whole nation walks across the Red Sea: "(20) And Miriam the prophetess, sister of Aaron, took timbrel in her hand; and all the women went after her with timbrels and with dances. (21) And Miriam sang unto them: Sing to the Lord, for He is highly exalted: the horse and his rider had He thrown into the sea." Norman Cohen (1984, 182) identifies in Miriam's song not only words that she sings to celebrate with her people the exodus from Egypt, but also—just as in Moses's song in Exodus 15:1—a pattern of future redemption. Both aspects of Miriam—as a leader in song and dance and as a symbol of the hope for future redemption—lead to the later idealization of Miriam as the mystical figure of feminist liberation and self-expression (see, for example, Magnus 1992, 337). These aspects became characteristic features of Miriam in feminist Jewish songs about her, such as Hirschhorn's "Miriam's Slow Snake Dance by the Riverside" (1989),[6] Raphael's "Miriam" (1984),[7] and Friedman's "Miriam's Song" (1988).[8] All these songs elaborate on Exodus 15:20–21, as shown below, to present Miriam as a feminist role model. Raphael stated that she dedicated her song "to people—both women and men—who are helping the dance of the feminist transformation of Judaism" (Raphael, booklet to *Bible Babes A-Beltin,'* 1997, n.p.). Thus, in each song we can find the image of Miriam dancing, singing, and celebrating with the Hebrew women at the Red Sea, when liberated from Egyptian slavery—a motif that is almost completely ignored by traditional midrashic texts (see, for example, S. Raphael 2010, 4–5). As Simcha Raphael explains, traditional commentators on Exodus 15:20–21 were interested only in the idea that these women were "confident God would manifest a miracle at the Red Sea," whereby the "Midrash makes this story about God and pays no attention to the experience of the women's voices and bodies in ecstatic celebration" (ibid., 8).

MIRIAM'S SLOW SNAKE DANCE BY THE RIVERSIDE

© Linda Hirschhorn, 1989

And Miriam the prophetess took the timbrel in hand
And led the women down to the sea,
And there they danced and they sang.

Shiru lashechinah [sing to Shechinah] a song of thanks for this day of liberation.

. . .

Oh, you were dancing the songs of freedom by the riverside.

MIRIAM

© Geela Rayzel Raphael, 1984

Chorus
And Miriam took her timbrel out and all the women danced.
. . .

They danced so hard, they danced so fast;
They danced with movement strong . . .
Some carrying child, some baking bread,
Weeping as they prayed.
But when they heard the music start
They put their pain away.

MIRIAM'S SONG

Chorus
And the women dancing with their timbrels,
Followed Miriam as she sang her song.
Sing a song to the One whom we've exalted,
Miriam and the women danced and danced the whole night long.
. . .

And Miriam the prophet took her timbrel in her hand,
And all the women followed her just as she had planned,
And Miriam raised her voice in song,
She sang with praise and might,
We've just lived through a miracle, we're going to dance tonight.

Miriam is considered not only to be a guide for music, dance, and drumming but also to be an archetypal prophet, as she predicts future redemption. Geela Rayzel Raphael states that "what makes Miriam a prophetess . . . is the word *kol*.[9] . . . For the new image of women is not one voice but the collective voice. All the women were drawn to follow her, for [Raphael imagines] she knew her descendants—both men and women—would be dancing in joy for centuries to come" (2001, 85–86). Today, Miriam is considered the female or feminist analogue of the prophet Eliyahu. Just like Eliyahu, Miriam is seen as a prophet of hope who promises the redemption of the world (ibid., 87). This becomes obvious in Berner's song "Miriam Haneviyah" (see figure 3.8). Berner sets her text to the melody of the traditional folk song "Eliyahu Hanavi."

As Ochs demonstrates, *tof Miriam* (Miriam's tambourine, or timbrel) is one of the most popular ritual objects used in feminist rituals, as it "is said to give witness to the voice of women that resists being silenced" (2007b, 268). Rabbis interpret Exodus 15:20–21 as being primarily concerned with the appearance and workmanship of the tambourine, and where Miriam got the instrument. Modern Jewish women follow their own interpretations of the same text and thus of the function of Miriam's tambourine. As Ochs notes, when the tambourine played in ritual contexts, mostly in feminist seders, it helps Jewish women "feel like Miriam or like the Israelite women who danced with her" (ibid.). Or as Elaine Moise and Rebecca

FIGURE 3.8: "Miriam Haneviyah" (1987) © Rabbi Leila Gal Berner

Schwartz say, "we take an entirely different road, using the framework of Passover and the liberation from Egypt as a metaphor through which to view the journeys and struggles of Jewish women. . . . 'Dancing with Miriam' means joyfully marking our milestones along the way, observing them in a Jewish context, and reveling in our womanhood" (2002, xvii).

In addition, Jewish women consider themselves to be successors of the women's community that followed Miriam in dance and song (see Adelman 1990, 69) and accept Miriam's heritage in the form of her song. Thus, rabbinical interpretations say that one reason for the fragmentary tradition of "Miriam's Song" conveyed through the Torah is that future generations have to complete her song (see ibid., 32 and 49). The function of feminist Jewish songs about Miriam, thus, is not only to honor her and to make her present in today's feminist rituals, but also to give women the chance to relive the Exodus and the event at the Red Sea (where Miriam celebrates the Israelites' liberation from slavery together with the women) through song. As can be seen in performances of the Rosh Hodesh ritual, the diverse aspects of the biblical woman Miriam are performed through a wide variety of traditional and feminist songs, as well as through instrumental music (see S. Ross 2004, 41). In comparison to Friedman's well-known "Miriam's

FIGURE 3.9: "The Water in the Well" (2001) by Debbie Friedman

Song" that celebrates the early part of the prophetess's life, Friedman and Tamara Cohen's "The Water in the Well" (released on the album *The Water in the Well*, 2001; see figure 3.9) brings to light and to voice—as Tamara Cohen explained it in an e-mail message to me on November 8, 2013—some of the midrashic interpretations about Miriam's well, and thus the association of water with the spiritual life of Jewish women.

Feminist Jewish songs on biblical women are hardly ever used in the general synagogue liturgy, and thus they do not replace traditional liturgical songs. In the liturgy the primary function is to signify the biblical figure's presence. As songs on women from the Tanach and Jewish history are not generally considered a fixed and traditional part of Jewish worship, they create new opportunities to honor Jewish women's leadership (social, liturgical, and creative) as a respected Jewish women's tradition with biblical roots (see, for example, Ochs 2007b 276).

Whereas most feminist Jewish songs are more or less easy to identify as midrashic, some feminist Jewish singer-songwriters, such as Yofiyah, tend to hide their interpretations of sacred texts. As Yofiyah told me, her feminism is much stronger than she would ever state in public; especially as Conservative and traditional communities very often book her. She does not want to "show the red flag," as she said, because people would get scared. Thus, she uses her music to slip her feminist interpretations of traditional texts into the community. This becomes obvious only through the specific combination of text and music, as I will show in the next chapter. However, her chants can thus be regarded as a midrash (interview March 2008).

Feminist Ritual Songs

Songs in this category are inseparable from innovative Jewish rituals, designed for ceremonies about pregnancy and childbearing, rites of passage, healing, growing older, death, and mourning (see, for example, Ritualwell 2015b). These rituals address individual spiritual needs as well as needs of the collective female Jewish body. The challenges related to creating feminist rituals are complex. Two topics of interest that are central to our discussion are the mind-body split in traditional Judaism and the lack of rituals honoring what is specific to the female body. Traditional Jewish thinking relates the world of the physical or the bodily (*gashmiut*) to the world of women. This is separated from the world of the spiritual (*ruhniut*), which is related to the world of men. The idea of the body opposing the spirit is a well-documented prejudice in Western culture, which infused traditional Jewish thinking as well. Nevertheless, the body provides access to the spirit, as Lori Lefkovitz and Rona Shapiro argue (2009, 69). This is proven by male rituals such brith milah, and other physical practices connected with prayer, such as the wearing of ritual clothing—a privilege that is traditionally reserved for men. Thus, in male-dominated Judaism, the body is celebrated as a medium for connecting one's spirit to the divine, but many of these practices traditionally exclude women. This reflects the age-old "prejudices that took for granted women's inferior potential for spirituality and the maleness of the Jewish spirit" (ibid.). Consequently, the achievements of feminist Jews can be seen in the creation of rituals opposing the traditional mind-body split by emphasizing that the female body can also be a vehicle of spiritual transformation, a fact that is reflected in many feminist songs.

However, the idea of the mind-body split has been challenged by feminist theory, which regards the body as a social construct and gender as a "matter of performance rather than essence" (Lefkovitz and Rona Shapiro 2009, 69). In the context of feminist ritual, and thus in feminist Jewish music, the question of whether to invent or imitate is of crucial importance, as it points to the overall question of women's participation in Jewish religious life. It refers to the fact that women must decide "whether to presume male Judaism as normative and adopt and adapt male practices, or to reinforce female distinctiveness by inventing distinct women's ritual expressions articulated in a Jewish idiom" (ibid., 70). Thus, alongside feminist rituals such as bat mitzvah, menopause rituals, Simkhat Chokhmah, or healing rituals—all of which include aspects that are ignored by Jewish tradition—the Rosh Hodesh ritual can be considered as one of the most popular and important. Indeed, Rosh Hodesh has generated many songs sanctifying women's biological, personal, and communal experiences.

Feminist Jewish songs for Rosh Hodesh generally emphasize the aspect of gathering in all-women groups to make a sacred time for communal praying, exploring spirituality, and singing women's songs, which must be understood as a metaphor for sharing personal stories. For example, Stein's song "Minyan of Women" (1994; see figure 3.10) says:[10] "Don't you know that we are a minyan of women; don't you know that we are ten women strong. Don't you know that in a minyan of women, each has time to sing her own song?" The song tells about individual women's character traits and events in their lives, but also contains moments of self-mockery.[11] In this way, participating in the minyan of women becomes a very personal experience (as noted above, women traditionally are not allowed to be part of a minyan; see the discussion on Kol Isha in the introduction to this book).

Other songs that emphasize Rosh Hodesh as a women's time include Tiferet Siegel's "Hachodesh Hazeh—Rosh Chodesh Song,"[12] Raphael's "Rosh Chodesh Moon" (1988),[13] and Gold's "In the Dark Rays of the Moon" (1989).

FIGURE 3.10: "Minyan of Women" (1994) by Margot Stein

Referring back to the discussion above about the potential of the female body as a vehicle for spiritual transformation, the focus on body issues in feminist Rosh Hodesh songs is significant. The equation of the moon's phases with women's menstrual cycles is one of the most important characteristics of the songs. It is not only related to a general renewal of body and soul, but it also celebrates women's fertility. Thus, Raphael's song "Red Moon Magic" (1992; see figure 3.11) is a good example of how feminist Jewish songwriters equate the phases of the moon with the female cycle (in this song referred to as the "red moon" or "red thread"), or more broadly with the phases of women's lives.

Another example of a feminist ritual emphasizing the body as a means of spiritual expression is the mikvah ritual. This ritual is often included in

FIGURE 3.11: "Red Moon Magic" (1992) by Rabbi Geela Rayzel Raphael

Rosh Hodesh ceremonies. The *tahara* (ritual purity) and *tumah* (ritual impurity), which are manifested in the niddah, traditionally determine the timing of sexual relations in a marriage. A woman abstains from sexual relations with her husband during her menstrual period and for a certain time (usually seven days) after it ends. After that she immerses herself in the mikvah and can resume sexual relations with her husband (see, for example, Zeigler 1996). Accordingly, the mikvah is inevitably marked by the concept of women's impurity and was for a long time one of the few Jewish practices that feminist Jews could not reclaim. During the past three decades, the ritual bath came increasingly under feminist scrutiny, and many women reversed their antimikvah position (Lefkovitz and Shapiro 2005, 106). Today, not only have the negative attitudes toward menstruation been reevaluated, but women have found ways to meaningfully integrate the practice of mikvah into their married lives or other relationships. In addition, some women have found creative uses for the ritual bath to mark other significant occasions in their lives, such as ordination as a rabbi, getting a divorce, and recovering from an illness.

Spitzer's "Mikvah Song" (see figure 3.12),[14] is based on the traditional prayer a woman recites on immersing herself in the mikvah. What makes this a feminist song is not only the subject but also the way Spitzer combines the traditional *b'racha* (blessing) "Baruch Ata Adonai, Elohaynu Ruach ha-Olam, asher kideshanu b'mitzvotav vetzivanu al ha-t'vilah" (Blessed are you Lord our God, spirit of the world, who has sanctified us with His commandments and commanded us on immersion) with a feminist version of the blessing that names Shekhinah alongside with the Lord: "Brucha At Shechina, Elohaynu Ruach ha-Olam, asher kideshanu b'mitzvoteha vetzivanu al ha-t'vilah" ("Blessed are you Shechina, Spirit of the world, who has sanctified us with Her commandments and commanded us on immersion") (not shown in figure 3.12). Both blessings contain the phrase "Ruach ha-Olam" instead of the conventional Hebrew terminology "Melech Ha'Olam," which can be translated as "sovereign [or king] of the universe." Because the Hebrew term *melech* is masculine, Jewish feminists prefer the more neutral term *ruach*, which means spirit. Also in the song the traditional prayer is complemented by an English verse that gives an interpretation of the meaning of the ritual: namely, that the waters of the mikvah symbolically purify not only the body but also the spirit, and are thus waters of rebirth.

FIGURE 3.12: Beginning of the "Mikvah Song" (1998) by Juliet Spitzer

Spitzer's song can also be regarded as a midrash. She sets the traditional mikvah prayer to music that is a blend of folk, spiritual, and New Age tunes, which makes the song a feminist invention in a Jewish musical idiom. In addition, Spitzer dedicates the song to her Rosh Hodesh sisters.

Healing Songs

The first feminist Jewish singer-songwriter who comes to mind when thinking about healing songs is Friedman. Both Friedman and her "Misheberach" song symbolize how closely the Jewish healing movement[15] and Jewish feminism are connected. The Jewish healing movement emerged around the early 1990s, when professional and lay leaders realized that, "as a consequence of modern life, many Jews no longer had easy or meaningful access to the spiritual and communal supports that had sustained previous generations of Jews through difficult times of illness and loss" (Prince 2009, 280–81). Although human well-being, in its broadest sense, has always been one of Judaism's most central concerns—as shown in the long tradition of scholarly and religious writing on the interconnectedness of physical and spiritual realms—the Jewish healing movement is meant to provide not only clinical but particularly spiritual and intellectual resources for those who are affected by stress, isolation, or loss or who simply experience hard times. The movement also provides services to those "who wish to foster wellness by enhancing the engagement of spirituality and framing the pursuit of well-being as a sacred journey. The Jewish healing movement, in its broadest sense, is thus a pathway to transcendence, mindfulness, and wholeness for individual Jews and for the Jewish people" (ibid., 281).

Thus, the Jewish healing movement shares several aims as well as ideas and values with the Jewish feminist movement and its particular interest in tikkun olam. As Michelle Prince explains (2009), Jewish feminism's impact on Judaism and the Jewish healing movement, which was largely created by women, has transformed the ways how Jews—particularly Jewish women—deal with illness, trauma, hard times, and communal tragedies. More than that, the healing movement conveys a feminist message, which, according to Rabbis Valerie Joseph and Alana Suskin, is that "healing women heal Judaism." Thus, by the time "when women became rabbis, the interest in spirituality increased. We came to see that not all rabbis are pulpit rabbis. . . . The unfolding of what is hurting a person through the art of active listening is an essential part of our tradition that took feminist healers to recover" (quoted in Prince 2009, 283).

Consequently, adherents of the Jewish feminist movement developed contemporary Jewish healing services that are focused on healing the soul rather than curing the body. These services consist of meditation and prayer as well as new chants, songs, and instrumental music. In the corpus of feminist Jewish healing songs, we find many that draw on traditional Jewish prayers for healing, such as Nancy Abraham Talo's song "Eyl Na R'fah Na

FIGURE 3.13: "Eyl Na R'fah Na La" by Nancy Abraham Talo

La" (see figure 3.13) and Raphael's "Ana El Na" (1995; see figure 3.14).[16] Songs drawing on new words, such as Andrea Beth Damsky's song "Heal Me, Oh My God" (1997), are also part of this corpus.

Both Talo and Raphael draw on the phrase "ana el na r'fa na la" ("God, please heal her"), which is part of what Moses said when praying for the healing of Miriam, his sister. Talo simply combines these words with the beginning of the traditional *Mi Shebeirach* prayer (see figure 3.13), one of the central prayers for physical and spiritual healing that asks for blessing, restoration, strength and compassion. In contrast, Raphael's song consists of three verses written for her father and dealing with the loss of a beloved person and mourning (see figure 3.14).

Damsky wrote new words asking God to heal one's pain and soul, help one get well, give one strength, and thus guide one's life:

HEAL ME, OH MY GOD

© Andrea Beth Damsky, 1997

Heal me, oh my God, please heal me
Heal me, oh my God, please heal me
Heal me, oh my God, please heal me
Heal me, oh my God, please heal me

Heal my pain, Holy One, please heal my pain
Make me well, Holy One, please make me well

Give me strength, Holy One, please strengthen me
Heal me, Holy One, please heal me

Heal my joy, Holy One, please heal my joy
Heal my love, my God, please heal my love
Guide my life, Holy One, please guide me
Heal my soul, my God, please heal me

Help me, oh my God, please help me
Hold me, oh my God, please hold me
Be with me, all my days, please be with me
Love me, oh my God, please love me

Mmm mmm mmm.

In comparison to the examples discussed above, the singer-songwriter Holy Taya Shere responds in her song "Dayenu" (2013; see figure 3.15) to the feminist request of tikkun olam.[17] Her song draws on the traditional upbeat

FIGURE 3.14: "Ana El Na" (1995) by Rabbi Geela Rayzel Raphael

FIGURE 3.15: "Dayenu" (2013) by Holy Taya Shere. © TayaShere 2014. Holy Taya Music

melody of the well-known Passover song "Dayenu" (a Hebrew word meaning "sufficient for us" or "we will be satisfied"), which appears in the Haggadah right after the telling of the story of the Exodus. While the lyrics of the traditional song are about the Jewish people's gratefulness to God for all he has done for and given to them (such as taking them out of slavery), Holy Taya Shere transforms the original phrase "if he [God] had brought us out of Egypt" into "if only we would protect earth mother." In doing so, she not only calls the attention to the people's own responsibility for tikkun olam but appeals for political action. She describes her song as follows: "Dreaming a deeper dayenu. A liberation lullaby. A loving-up liberation. A transformation of tribal trauma. An affirmation of abundance here & now. A vision raising vibration. A path of presence, possibility, play and peace" (n.d.).

Like songs for Rosh Hodesh and other feminist Jewish rituals, feminist healing songs (as well as the rituals in which they are sung) demarcate events that are linked to bodily experiences that have been previously ignored by formal Jewish tradition. In contrast to other feminist ritual songs, which most often deal with women's bodily experiences (such as pregnancy, giving birth, menopause, miscarriage, and infertility) or recognize the otherwise unmarked moments of a woman's life (such as becoming a mother, a widow, or a mourner), many healing songs address the physical and spiritual healing of women and men alike.

Songs for Shabbat and Jewish Holidays

The reclamation of Jewish women's selfhood through music and song does not exclude the realm of Shabbat and the Jewish holidays. There are a vast number of feminist Jewish songs dealing with the Shabbat liturgy and other customs and rituals performed on the day of rest, as well as issues of other Jewish holidays.

Feminist songs for Shabbat include different musical versions of, for example, the Hebrew hymn "Eshet Chayil" (Woman of valor), such as those by Fran Avni ("Eishet Chayil mi Yimtza"), Spitzer ("Gather In"), and Rabbi Rosalind Glazer ("Eyshet Chayil"), as well as feminist interpretations of traditional liturgical songs for Shabbat such as "Lecha Dodi" (Let's go, my beloved; see also the discussion of Hirschhorn, Fran Avni, and Marcia Falk's song "L'khu, Reyot V'rey'im" below) and psalms that are sung during Kabbalat Shabbat and the Shabbat morning service (for example, psalm 97 prompted both Raphael and Hirschhorn to write songs titled "Shama Vatismach Tsiyon"). One of the three mitzvahs that women have to fulfill is *nerot* (lights) or *hadlakat ha-ner* (lighting the lights), which is the lighting of the candles to mark the beginning of sacred time in general—the day of rest or any other Jewish holiday. We can also find musical alternatives to the blessing that is traditionally recited at the lighting of the candles, such as Marcia Falk and Hirschhorn's "Hadlakat Neyrot Shabbat" (1998, released under the title "Shabbat Candlelighting" on *Selections of Marcia Falk's Blessings in Song*, see figure 3.16). This song links the command to kindle the light of Shabbat with the refreshing of our spirit, which is—in addition to the mere rest from work—the quintessential reason of Shabbat.

During the Torah service on each Shabbat morning, a different portion of the Torah is read and studied until all five books of Moses have been read. As reading from the Torah is (at least within traditional and Orthodox communities) mostly reserved to men, women's writing and singing songs

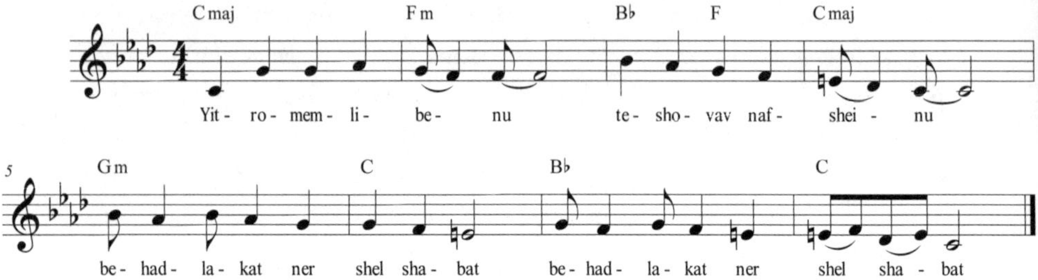

FIGURE 3.16: "Hadlakat Neyrot Shabbat" (1998). Words © Marcia Falk and music © Linda Hirschhorn

about the stories told in these Torah portions can be considered as an alternative Torah service. Moreover, we find feminist Jewish songs that draw on special collections of Torah readings that are read on festivals (for example, the Book of Esther, which is read on the festival of Purim) outside of this weekly order, and that give a feminist interpretation of a particular holiday or theme of a Jewish festival. Benjamin Newman's song "Masquerade"[18] takes up the story of queen Esther, and thus the story of Purim. This is a Cinderella-like story of love and of the deliverance of the Jewish people in the ancient Persian Empire, where a plot had been made to kill them. It is seldom presented as a story of not belonging, of masking and hiding one's Jewish heritage and identity.

MASQUERADE

© lyrics and music by Benjamin Newman, no date

I came to the palace with all the rest;
To win the king's favor, I've done my best.
The jewel of his harem, and soon to be queen;
And yet my true face I have kept unseen. . . .

My cousin reminds me it's not from shame,
But only from prudence that I play this game.
To my king I'm a goddess, with stars in her eyes,
And her name is my name, and it's my disguise.

The life of the palace is wine and dance,
But I don't belong—I just fell here by chance;
And yet, though I conceal all the fear that I feel,
Still, behind all these masks, is our love not real?

But I don't believe what I've just been told,
And behind all its splendor, the palace is cold:
No one steps out of place, no one shows their true face,
And the blood of my people's been bought and sold!

What can I do now? I'm so afraid!
G'd of my ancestors, lend me Your aid!
I could swallow my fear if I knew You were here,
But I can't find Your face in this masquerade!

So I'm making my way through the court, alone;
At the risk of my neck, I'm approaching the throne—
And I don't dare to ask: Strip my foe of his mask—
Only courage enough to take off my own.

Today there are other feminist Purim prayers, rituals, songs, and so-called Purim spiels that not only highlight the deeds and courage of Esther and Vashti but that also read between the lines of the biblical story.[19]

Miscellaneous Nonliturgical Songs

The next example given here points to a different way of Jewish feminist criticism that focuses on popular nonliturgical music, whose lyrics often present a rather misogynist image. It can be argued that the women's Torah is not restricted to the religious sphere only but can be extended to the broader Jewish culture. In contrast to the previous cases, the following example shows how Batsheva Capek, a Canadian singer, songwriter and concert artist, reclaims her selfhood as a Jewish woman in Jewish musical culture. By adding her insights and feminist criticism to traditional Yiddish folk songs, she transforms the songs into feminist Jewish songs and critique.

Capek is quite an unusual figure among feminist Jewish songwriters. She devotes much of her work and attention to the preservation of Ladino and Yiddish folk songs that have been honored throughout the United States, Canada, and Israel (Capek n.d.). But at the same time, as a feminist Jew, she takes a very critical view of the musical heritage she seeks to maintain. Capek's handling of musical tradition differs from that of other songwriters discussed above. Her feminist critique of Judaism is not presented in non-Jewish music genres but in the way she interprets Judaism's own musical legacy. She turns original Yiddish folk songs into sharp feminist satire. According to her, the best way to critique male Jewish culture is to present the music in a female perspective and expose the real (sometimes sexist) content of these songs, as she did, for example, in her song "Damn Little Yiddish Folksong" (telephone and e-mail interviews June 2008):

DAMN LITTLE YIDDISH FOLKSONG

© Batsheva Capek (lyrics), no date, Mordecai Gebirtig (music; melody of the Yiddish song "Margaritkelakh"), no date

In the woods by a river, picking some daisies
A maiden is humming along.
A handsome, young fellow is watching her walk
In this nice little Yiddish folksong.

Chorus
La, la . . .

"Where are you going? Can I be of service," he says.
"Is there anything wrong?"
"Oh, no," she says shyly, "I'm just picking flowers"
In this nice, little Yiddish folksong.

Chorus
By this time, they've told us his hair's
black and curly. Of course,
she's a virgin and blonde.
There's always a stud who's dressed up like a scholar
In those nice, little Yiddish folksongs.

Chorus
"No closer, my mother won't like it," she says
As he lowers her into the lawn.
"Your mother? What mother?
There's nobody here"
In this nice, little Yiddish folksong.

Chorus
"Do you love me?"
"Yes, I love you."

"Are you shy?"
"Yes, I'm shy."
"Then be shy, just lie down and be calm."
But the melody's charming and sucks you right into
Those nice, little Yiddish folksongs.

The next thing we see is our heroine clutching
Her daisies and bra on the lawn.
She's all "far-klemt" [choked up] 'cause the scholar's "far-shvunden"
[disappeared]
In this nice, little Yiddish folksong.

So, ladies, remember that offers of love
In this genre may just be a con.
They'll find you, deceive you
De-flower you and leave you
In those damned, little Yiddish folksongs.

Chorus

This song is a parody of a Yiddish favorite called "Margaritkelach" (Daisies), written by Zalman Shneour. This song is generally categorized as a song of love and courtship, but when we read the song in the original Yiddish, it is clear that neither love nor courtship is involved. It is a song about a rape. Over time, it has been popularized on recordings by artists like Theodore Bikel (*Theodore Bikel Sings Jewish Folk Songs*, 1958). It is sung lightly and with humor. When listening carefully to the version recorded by Chava Alberstein (*Yiddish Greatest Hits Volume 1*, 1969), one can hear that she interprets it correctly as a sad and painful interaction, which culminates in a rape. However, Capek took the song and did an almost verbatim translation into English to highlight the real meaning of the song. Finally, she added her ironic and satirical comments on it to stress not only the meaning of the song, but the poor treatment and fate of women in literature (telephone and e-mail interview with Capek, June 2008).

When Capek first performed the song, women were thrilled. But men were generally angry, demanding to know why she was destroying the holy canon of Yiddish songs. "Damn Little Yiddish Folksong" continues to cause controversy, conversations, and debates when she performs it in public

FIGURE 3.17: Leslie Ginsparg Klein. Courtesy L. Ginsparg Klein

(telephone and e-mail interview with Capek, June 2008). While the feminist songwriters presented above have to face the most resistance to the musical structure of their songs, Capek, who sings her song to the traditional tune, is chided for having the audacity to change the original masculine lyrics of the Yiddish song to the feminine perspective. In her view, the Yiddish language communicates male perspectives on the world, although the Yiddish language is generally described as the *mameloshen* (Yiddish for "mother's tongue") (ibid.).

Another song that should be mentioned in this context is "Aidel at Heart" by Leslie Ginsparg Klein (2006; released on *Girls' Night On: Live at the Makor*; see figures 3.18–20). Klein is the founder and director of Girls' Night On, an organization that promotes Jewish women in music and the other arts and organizes performances by women for female audiences (Girls' Night On 2006). She was inspired to pick up the guitar after going to a women's open mike night in Israel, and she started writing songs and singing in public a few years after that. Girl's Night On grew out of the Orthodox community, but it has a broader appeal: it pulls women in from across the American Jewish community (from Orthodox to secular, and everything in between) and of all ages, some of whom not only observe and appreciate the concept of Kol Isha but also like to share their voices and prefer the relaxed atmosphere of a performance by and for women only. The organization has released an album because, particularly for Orthodox women, recording is the only feasible way to distribute their music (Drusin 2005). Klein is also a professor of Jewish history and Jewish education.

FIGURE 3.18–20: "Aidel At Heart" (2006) © Leslie Ginsparg Klein

Klein is an Orthodox woman, but her very racy song "Aidel at Heart" knocks stereotypes of Orthodox womanhood and has thus a pretty irreverent tone, as she explained to me by e-mail on November 25, 2013. The main message of the song is that women should not be torn between their loyalty to Judaism, especially the Torah, and their desire to be true to

FIGURE 3.18–20: (continued)

FIGURE 3.18–20: (continued)

themselves—no matter what cultural and religious rules tell them who they should be: "Whoever said cool, funky and *frum* [pious] were mutually exclusive? So what if I know I'm sharp? Not afraid to show I'm smart. I love me the way that I am and I know I am *aidel* [precious, cultured] at heart. . . . I won't change myself for anyone, I refuse to play the part, I love me the way that I am, and I know that I'm *aidel* at heart."

As the examples have shown, feminist Jewish singer-songwriters felt the need to rewrite Jewish tradition and history to turn their feminist visions and critiques on Judaism and thus reclaim their selfhood as Jewish women. In doing so, these songwriters contributed to the transformation of the content of Jewish memory as well; or, as Plaskow (1996, 105) has put it, the content of the Torah. Hitherto invisible insights, teachings, and religious practices of women have been added to the canon, allowing the common, limited, and gender-exclusive understanding of Jewish tradition to be not only expanded but also challenged.

SINGING ABOUT DIVERSITY

This section is about how the feminist Jewish concept of community, and thus the material context for the creation and continuation of a revised Jewish memory (Torah), is represented in songs. As discussed in the introduction, feminist Jewish theologians argue that the Torah defines the actual structure of a community. Yet to create a women's Torah, a new community is needed that is able and willing to live and remember it, as the community is where God is experienced. That is why feminists demand a community in which women are no longer considered as "the other"; where the religious, cultural, and ethnic diversity of Jewish identities, beliefs, and practices is honored; and where different sexual orientations and gender identities are respected (see, for example, Plaskow 1992, 105). The commitment to tikkun olam in terms of ecological, peace, and social justice activism, and in terms of healing and repairing the community, is a crucial factor in feminist Jewish theology, and thus in the discourses of contemporary Jewish feminism. The idea of community involvement is of crucial importance. These ideas and values have been applied to feminist Jewish music.

At first, it seems difficult to separate songs written by feminist Jews that address the messages of social justice, peace, and diversity from the larger nonfeminist repertoire of new Jewish music that communicates the same values. Therefore, while some songs are very specific about their political message, the content of other pieces discussed here primarily results from the songwriter's individual understanding of Jewish feminism. In a large number of feminist Jewish songs, the wish for a broad Jewish community that honors diversity is apparent only when we look at the intention behind the songs or analyze their musical structures. Those structures will be discussed in the next chapter.

As far as the intention is concerned, Friedman clearly communicates the message of community building and bringing peace, freedom, and justice to all people and projects through song "a liberal and modern sensibility for Jewish life in America" (Kligman 2005, 370). This message and her commitment to the core Jewish value of tikkun olam are best reflected in her album and title song *One People* (2006). According to her, the album is about "the wish to acknowledge that what we share in common is far greater than what differentiates us" (quoted in Theiner 2008). Yet the chorus of the song "One People," as Debra Nussbaum Cohen notes, communicates the message of "a new anthem for people of all religious and political persuasions united in their prayers for peace" (2006). The chorus is:

> We'll be one people seeking freedom
> One people seeking justice
> One people seeking hope
> One people seeking peace.

The title song "One People" does not address a Jewish audience only, and makes no particular reference to Judaism and Jewish themes, whereas the song "Hear Our Voices" on the same album includes the phrase *sh'ma koleinu* (hear our voice), the plea to God to hear our prayer for redemption. This is the sixteenth blessing of the weekday amidah (see Steinsaltz 2000, 404). In her song, Friedman addresses the issue of connectedness and of working together in social action, and she emphasizes the strength of women by singing:

> Sh'ma Koleinu, hear our voices
> Sh'ma Koleinu, hear our song.
> When we rise up in the morning
> When we're walking, walking along.
>
> . . .
>
> It's within us, it's around us
> we will do and we will listen.
>
> . . .
>
> We are the women, we are the stories
> Each generation will pass them along.

Beyond the plea to God to hear our prayer for redemption, the phrase *sh'ma koleinu, hear our voices* sung in the chorus furthermore means the following: the Hebrew word *koleinu*, "our voice," is not plural as in many voices, but as in one collective voice. Thus, Friedman's song is not only about our voices being united to plead and be heard but also about raising our voices against the restrictive policies of, for example, the halakhic proscription Kol Isha (as discussed in the introduction) that creates congregations and communities without the voices of women. Friedman refers in her song to the power of music to both unite people in social action and create a third space (a new Jewish community) in which all our voices are heard, valued, and respected.

Friedman's songs are described as an "invitation—into a world that is repaired and whole" (Koenig 2007, 4). Similarly, the lyrics of the songwriter Chana Rothman speak not only to the essentials of Jewish tradition, but also to general subjects of feminism and social justice.

Rothman, who grew up in a Reconstructionist environment, considers herself a Jewish feminist, "insofar as that term is still bandied about" (e-mail interview September 1, 2008). She told me that "in my generation [people ages 20–30], people don't use it that much. But I identify with all the aspects of a feminist identity and outlook, and I think the feminist movement is extremely important, both historically and nowadays" (ibid.). Her musical style and approach to music is strongly influenced by female singer-songwriters, such as the Indigo Girls, Joan Armatrading, Suzanne Vega, and Ani Difranco. According to her, "my music is spiritual, honest, simple (at times), and groove-based. Sometimes it's bilingual/bicultural; sometimes it's focused directly on social justice. . . . Yet, I try not to opt for the simple answer. Usually, if I don't know the answer to something, I'll ask it as a question. That is why I'm not telling the listener or myself anything I don't actually believe" (ibid.). Rothman's album *We Can Rise* (2007) features protest songs about social and Jewish consciousness. In "More Than One Way" (2007), Rothman connects back to Jewish activism in the civil rights movement, singing "Marching through Selma in the blistering heat / A.J. Heschel prayed with his feet / You can't get no justice, so take it to the street / Because there's more than one way to be free." But she also emphasizes the importance of recognizing cultural and religious differences: "Buddhist and Catholic and a Muslim too / Atheist, Hindu, Rasta and a Jew / Whatever you believe, it must be true (to you) / Because there's more than one way to be free."

Rothman is always aware of tikkun olam and the fact that she, as a Jew, has no excuse for not looking for tools to repair the world—which, in her case, is music (e-mail interview September 1, 2008). She stated in an interview that because of her background in activism and spirituality, she feels the pain in the world, and that is why prayer and being openly religious in her music feels real to her (see MyJewSpot n.d.). The Jewish concept that the world is not perfect and needs to be repaired is communicated in her song "Ana" (2007).[20] Rothman stated: "Our planet is in trouble, it's no secret. We're killing each other. We have wars. It's not like we're saved" (MyJewSpot n.d.). Accordingly, the chorus of her song says "ana adonai hoshia na" (God, save us), which is taken from the Hallel (Psalm 118).[21] The song says:

> Deliver us
> We are broken
> Be our rock
> There's no solid ground
> And lift us up
> Let it be spoken
> Ana ana ana.
>
> Gather us
> We are scattered
> Return us
> We're so far from home
> And shine on us
> Show us what matters
> Ana ana ana.

As Rothman explained to me, this song has also been considered to be a particularly effective prayer for contemporary Jewish women, as it displays both the strength and fragility of faith (e-mail interview September 1, 2008). Rothman's music reflects to a great extent the themes and concerns of contemporary, postmodern Jewish feminism, and more precisely those of the younger generation of feminist Jews.

Another category of feminist Jewish songs must be mentioned here: ecofeminist songs. The most prominent example of this category is certainly Tiferet Siegel's song "Olamama," released on the album of the same name in 1995 (see figure 3.21). In the song, she praises the earth (also a metaphor for Shechinah) as the creating mother of all that exists. The first

FIGURE 3.21: "Olamama" (1995) by Hanna Tiferet Siegel. www.HannaTiferet.com

verse says: "Olamama, Olamama, I love you so. . . . You're the Mother of All, Spring, Winter, Summer and Fall, I love you so."

Shere also defines her music, including the recording *Wild Earth Shebrew* (2009),[22] as ecofeminist. She wrote to me:

> My music is definitely eco-feminist music, though I wouldn't have thought to call it that myself. The Kol Isha chants [on *Wild Earth Shebrew*] are earthy, tribal, Jewish chants celebrating the divine feminine. Most of the chants are either G!ddessified Jewish chants or Jewified G!ddess chants. Many of them take earth-based spiritual

> chants/melodies and set Hebrew words and/or Jewish theology to them. . . . When I say my music is earthy/tribal, [I mean that] it tends to have an ancient, raw kind of feel to it. Some songs are almost shamanic in quality or tone, with an eastern kind of vibe. Other songs are simply mellow and stripped down. You might imagine being in the forest or the desert, sitting around a fire at a full moon gathering, with your tribe, either now or thousands of years ago . . . everything is acoustic. All we need are our voices and some drums! (e-mail interview February 2007).

How much the agenda of Jewish feminism in general and thus the themes of feminist Jewish songs have been expanded since the 1990s is documented in an e-mail Raphael received from someone called Sara K.: "I admit to being somewhat puzzled by your description of the kinds of material you are interested in. You say it must 'contain reference to feminist Jewish material—i.e. lifecycle, new god language, liturgy, women of the Bible, etc.' This makes sense as far as it goes, but there are many other things I would think of as 'Jewish feminist material'—e.g., Jewish women in history, social justice issues (e.g., full civil rights for women, lesbians/gays, people with disabilities, people of color), peace struggles (in the Middle East and elsewhere), relationships with our families, etc." (Sara K., e-mail to Rabbi Raphael, June 27, 1994). The writer gives some examples of feminist Jewish songs that fit into these new categories of Jewish feminism. She mentions the songwriter Karen Beth,[23] who—according to her—wrote a song about feeling displaced in the world. Beth "draws connections between feeling dislocated as a woman in a male-defined world, as a white person on a continent that was stolen from others, and as a Jew living in *galut* [exile]" (ibid.). Sara K. states that while Raphael's descriptions seem to be focused on the religious aspects of being a Jewish feminist, she would expand the description to include more "secular" aspects of the lives of feminist Jews (ibid.). The songs discussed here, and the themes they communicate, support her argument.

"[Where] Jewish women were active in radical politics, there were often lesbians," as Faith Rogow writes, and these "Jewish lesbian feminists [also] find that creativity is a matter of survival" (1990, 68 and 76). This becomes apparent in feminist Jewish songs that discuss being a Jewish lesbian, how distinct lesbians' experiences of Jewish identity are, and how this influences the general vision of Jewish feminism (ibid., 76). In her song "Jewish

FIGURE 3.22: Cantor Abbe Lyons. Courtesy A. Lyons

Lesbian" (1990; see figures 3.23–24), the songwriter Abbe Lyons points to the fact that lesbians, gay men, and transgender Jews not only have often been ignored in the Jewish community but have also had to hide their true identity: "Hey, look at me! Do you know who I am? Look at all of me, I'm a Jewish lesbian. / And I'm longing for the day when I can openly and fearlessly stand as I am. / If you do not know of my life, you owe it to yourself to learn. . . . Jewish lesbian, two fires that within me burn, two strong blocks that build my foundation."

In this context, we must refer briefly to the contemporary band the Shondes (a Yiddish word meaning "disgrace"), whose members are Temim Fruchter, Louisa Solomon, Ian Brannigan, and Elijah Oberman. The Shondes combine classical and Jewish melodies with punk rock music, and the themes of their songs range from queer issues, feminism, and antiracism to Jewish tradition and Palestinian solidarity work. As Leah Koenig writes, "their songs serve the double purpose of the artistic and activist expression" (2007, 4). Thus the song "I Watched the Temple Fall"[24] (whose title refers to the Jewish holiday Tisha B'Av, commemorating the destructions of the First and Second Temples in Jerusalem, and which was released on the group's debut album *The Red Sea* [2007]) criticizes any form of apartheid.

The examples presented here outline the diversity of topics and subjects characterizing today's Jewish feminism. The main intention of these songs is to communicate the need for a just society in which the diversity of Jewish

FIGURE 3.23–24: "Jewish Lesbian" (1990) by Cantor Abbe Lyons

individuals in all respects is valued and honored. This society is a prerequisite for the creation of an egalitarian Jewish community, as envisioned in Plaskow's concept of Israel (1992, 105–26). I will end this section with Hirschhorn, who explains the more general intention of feminist Jewish songs through the biblical story of building a *mishkan* (a holy sanctuary).[25]

The word "mishkan" has many meanings in the Hebrew Bible. One is the tent build by Moses at God's command to house the presence of God amid the people in the desert. Later, the Temple in Jerusalem replaced this tent. Hirschhorn understands the mishkan not only as a physical place but also as the entire body of knowledge that constitutes Judaism. This is why she comes to the conclusion that all the things people put inside the mishkan, such as readings, writings, songs, and dances, are also part of it. For countless generations, these things (also referred to as Jewish tradition) have sustained the Jewish community. Thus, the mishkan is equated with the community—more precisely, with building and maintaining a Jewish community. That is why the community's sustainability, holiness, and richness depend on what people put inside, Hirschhorn concludes. This relates not only to songs, which she sees as her contribution to the mishkan, but also to the Jewish people. If half of the community (women) is kept outside, the mishkan does without half of its richness, strength, and meaning (Hirschhorn n.d.b). Consequently, for Hirschhorn writing songs—especially writing in harmony—means requiring people to sing with each other and to enter the mishkan.

THE FEMINIST CONCEPTION OF THE DIVINE IN SONG

According to feminist Jewish theology, the perception and description of God shared by a community represent its central values. Consequently, when addressing God only in the male form, a Jewish community may—unconsciously but implicitly—communicate the message that men are worth more than women. Accordingly, one central site of feminist theological criticism is the traditional concept of the Jewish God (expressed in established Jewish texts and liturgy) as male, which implies that the concept of God and prayer language must be transformed.

Feminist Jewish musicians contributed to the effort to reframe sacred singing in the Jewish tradition so that women's voices were heard. Thus, feminist Jewish songs are directly related to the dilemma of language. Seeking to transform customary God- and prayer-language, feminist Jewish singer-songwriters began to translate the language of their lyrics. They changed the masculine Hebrew in the verses they took from traditional sacred texts to so-called feminist Hebrew or another gender-neutral language, such as English. Especially in the context of feminist Jewish rituals, whose performances are closely related to women's traditional commandments, and also in the common Jewish liturgy, the use of exclusively male God- and prayer-language is felt to be "sexist" and "hierarchical" (Plaskow 1992, 142). That is why one crucial criterion for feminist Jewish songs used in Jewish worship is that the lyrics be written in a nonhierarchical language and make use of feminist images. The masculine may be included, but only if there is at least equal emphasis on the feminine (Elwell et al. 1993). One song that clearly shows how a traditional liturgical text is feminized and completed by a feminist English translation of the traditional Hebrew text is Hirschhorn and Avni's "L'khu, Reyot V'rey'im" (1998; see figure 3.25),[26] whose words are adapted from a poem by Marcia Falk. This song is the feminist version of the traditional L'cha Dodi (let's go, my beloved), the prayer to welcome the Shabbat bride. The chorus of conventional text is: "Lechah dodi likrat kallah / pnei Shabbat nekabelah" ("Let's go, my beloved, toward the bride, / and receive the presence of Shabbat.")

Hirschhorn and Avni's version of the song replaces the masculine term "dodi" with the feminine plural *re'ot*, which is mentioned alongside the masculine plural *re'im*, both of which mean "friends." All the verbs in the lyrics adapted accordingly. Hence, the chorus in Hirschhorn and Avni's song says: "Lechu,[27] re'ot likrat kallah . . . , Lechu, re'im likrat kallah . . ." (Let us go, friends, to greet the bride, Let us welcome the Shabbat).

Furthermore, the song omits every second verse of the original version. Elsewhere, verses beginning with phrases like "Kevod Adonai" (The glory of [the male] God) are transformed into more gender-neutral language like "Zohar haShekhinah" (the radiance of Shekhinah).

Raphael's *Friday Night Revived* (2005) is another of the many examples of how feminist Jewish songwriters have taken the traditional Kabbalat Shabbat liturgy for Friday night and transformed it into a feminized version. Raphael writes: "These songs reflect a diversity of G!d language staying somewhat true to the Hebrew, while rendering a gender neutral or feminist singable poetic language" (2005). This recording includes two of Raphael's most popular Shabbat songs, "Moving into Shabbos Time" (1984) and "Rock to the Rock" (1995).

FIGURE 3.25: "L'khu, Reyot V'rey'im" (1998). Words © Marcia Falk, music © Linda Hirschhorn and Fran Avni (SOCAN)

However, simply transforming traditional prayer language and using female pronouns to refer to God in the Jewish liturgy will not solve the whole problem. The most significant change in Jewish theology has been the reconceptualization of God. Feminists have pointed out that God is not only the God of our fathers and the patriarchs, but also of our mothers and the matriarchs. This message is communicated by Gold's well-known song "No More Big Daddy" (see figure 3.26), which she wrote in the 1980s when she felt discouraged by the traditional images of the divine that seemed to her extremely one-sided in a very hierarchic and male way. Her song thus must be understood as a response to this traditional view on God, seeking to come to terms with it by singing: "No more big daddy, the monarchy is dead. I take responsibility for the devils in my head. My love is like a circle that spins to set me free. My heart belongs to the Lord, who doesn't lord it over me" (figure 3.26).

FIGURE 3.26: "No More Big Daddy" by Shefa Gold. From *Abundance* © 1990. www.RabbiShefaGold.com

Feminists—in particular those related to the Jewish Renewal movement—became very active in revising traditional female images of the divine. They began to test new ways of visualizing and naming God in light of Jewish women's experiences and contemporary feminist insights. This led to the shift from referring to the divine as the Lord or the transcendent God, which denotes maleness and domination, to the concept of God as Shekhinah. The latter is understood as the immanent feminine aspect of the divine, as God's manifestation in the world. In addition to a variety of alternative metaphors addressing a more gender-neutral God, the use of Shekhinah in feminist songs has become very common.

"Shechinah, My Sister in the Wind" (1987; see figure 3.27) by Raphael is one example of a song that attempts to incorporate women's selfhood in Jewish spiritual life by also incorporating the feminine aspect of God and thus replacing the traditional male-focused idea of God. Phrases like "source of life" communicate the idea of God as an intrinsic presence in life. The song was recorded on a tape titled *Shechinah Songs* (Raphael c. 1987); a copy is in my possession. In addition to Raphael's solo singing, there is also a chorus of women (presumably the members of Raphael's former Toronto-based women's prayer group, B'not Levana). The song might be classified as country pop; it was arranged for keyboard, hand drum, claves, guitar, and bass. For most of the song, the women sing in unison, now and then shifting into a round and switching into harmony. The song closes with the name Shekhinah whispered in breathy voices.

Raphael considers feminine God-language and the reclamation of Shekhinah as essential to the development of feminist Jewish music. They not only provide an impetus for Jewish women to sing and create music, but they also meet the requirements for meaningful prayer in women's own words and for women's sacred music. The latter is required to express both the feminist concept of God and the emotional intensity that Jewish women feel in their relationships to the divine and to each other. In this context, music is inseparable from a feminist spiritual experience (G. Raphael 1998, 4). Here I must refer briefly to the legend that tells us that Shekhinah was exiled and has to be redeemed and reunited with the masculine aspect of the divine, to unite the cosmos as a whole. As Weissler concludes, "this myth formed part of the original motivation of . . . Renewal leaders from Hasidic background . . . to invite women into full participation. They saw the emergence of women's voices as the expression of the divine feminine, and they held that only women could call Shekhinah home from exile" (2007, 58). This is also one fundamental reason why we find more songs on Shekhinah written by feminist Jewish songwriters related to the Renewal movement, than by those related to Reform Judaism, for example.

Another popular feminist Jewish song that clearly shows the understanding of Shekhinah as an expression of women's power within the Renewal movement, and the affirmation of the holiness of qualities identified with the feminine, is Tiferet Siegel's "The Ways of a Woman," released on her

FIGURE 3.27: “Shechinah, My Sister in the Wind” (1987) by Rabbi Geela Rayzel Raphael

album *A Voice Calls* (1998). Here, Tiferet Siegel links "Shekhinah with a view of women that connects them with natural cycles and the earth" and communicates the message that a woman's ways are mysterious to men (Weissler 2007, 67):

> The ways of a woman a man cannot know,
> He does not understand
> The cycles, the seasons, the ebb and the flow.
> The prayers of the earth are the secrets women know.
> We sing the song of Shekhina, bringing us all home,
> Lifting us on wings of light to a place we've always known.
> We sing the song of Shekhina, waiting to be heard.
> The ways of a woman are the ways of life.
> There's power in our words.

As Weissler interprets the song, it "ends with a warning and an invitation," saying that "men should not suppress women's spirituality, but neither are they to be excluded from this women's world" (2007, 67). However, for feminist Jewish singer-songwriters of the Renewal movement, Shekhinah is far more than a metaphor, as is shown by the frequency with which they refer to the feminine aspect of God in their songs. By singing these words, they give voice to a missing expression of Jewish women's spirituality.

One image that is frequently used in feminist Jewish liturgy and songs is that of *tachat kanfei Shechinah* (under the wings of Shekhinah), which represents the immanent feminine presence of the divine while implying shelter and love that enfolds in a nurturing, feathered embrace. In Jewish feminism, Shekhinah is envisioned as a protective presence filled with motherly compassion, in comparison to the unseen male God. This image of Shekhinah is communicated by Adelman's song "Va'Anu Matzanu," which contains the line "menucha mitachat kanfei haShechina" (And we find rest and comfort under the gentle wings of Shekhinah) (see figure 3.28).

Another common name for God that is used in songs of Jewish feminists is *shaddai*, which is related to the Jewish Renewal movement. Gold's "The Majesty of Nurture" (2008), released on her album of the same name, is a good example of how feminist theology—more precisely, the feminist concept of God—influences feminist Jewish music. The chant consists of a translation of one phrase, "L'takayn Olam b'malchut Shaddai," from the tra-

FIGURE 3.28: "Va'Anu Matzanu" by Penina Adelman

ditional Aleynu prayer. Gold adds her insights to the traditional prayer text and expresses her relationship with God in her translation. A literal translation of the phrase is "to fix the world under the kingdom of God," but Gold translates it as "healing the world through the Majesty of Nurture." The ancient name for God, *shaddai,* normally translated as "the Almighty," is replaced here by the Hebrew word *shadayim* (breasts). From this perspective, Gold refers in her translation to a "God with breasts." In doing so, she feminizes the name and concept of God, linking it to the notion of nurturance.

To summarize: feminist Jews conceptualize God as the immanent one, who is affirmed as being around and within us, not above us. This idea is reflected in the linguistic texture of feminist prayer and song. These characteristics are regarded as being more intimate and relevant to Jewish women's immediate lives, since they have to do with women's stories, experiences, and common events. In addition, feminist prayer texts are commonly written in the plural and make no distinction between men and women. The act of praying is focused not only on the relationship between the individual and God, but also on the relationships among the congregants. The emphasis is on giving, rather than controlling, life (see, for example, Englander 2004, 27). Stein explained what feminist Jewish prayer means to her: "When I sing to the God within and around me I reflect more deeply, I take a more personal approach toward prayer. I see myself more clearly. . . . So that is . . . the 'felt experience' of praying to an imminent [*sic*] God. [While praying, I] want to be embodied, not disembodied. Connected, not disconnected. Brought forth, not overawed" (e-mail interview October 2008). Creating a spiritually fulfilling community for men and women is the central message of present-day Jewish feminism. Contemporary feminist prayer recognizes that music (as a social medium) is an elementary part of this message (ibid.), as the next chapter will show. So when singing to a God who is understood not only as the male Lord, what is required are both new prayer texts and new forms of prayer music that facilitate making the connections described above.

4 The Musical Conception of Feminist Jewish Songwriting

The feeling of invisibility that feminist Jewish singer-songwriters express with regard to male-defined sacred texts, as well as liturgies, rituals, and cultural ideas also applies to Jewish sacred music. One reason is that traditional music for Jewish worship is not written for women's voices. As shown in chapter 3, feminist songwriters used their lyrics to innovate customary sacred texts and Jewish prayer, while maintaining their individual connection with a tradition-based Judaism and Jewish community. In almost all of the songs written by feminist Jewish songwriters, the lyrics are based on traditional sacred texts, which have to some extent been modified and reinterpreted from a feminist perspective. However, the lyrics constitute only half of the religious experience. The other half, prayer music, is more than mere sound (see, for example, Epstein 2004, 1). Rather, it expresses the relationship of the human being with his or her creator, whereby it refers to a cultural foundation of meanings and emotions that shape, enhance, and reflect the process of spiritual self-definition and defines how Judaism is experienced (see Prell 1989, 166). Thus, to incorporate feminist politics into Jewish liturgy and its music, because prayer texts and music are intrinsically tied together, the feminist reconceptualization of the normative structure of Jewish sacred texts used as lyrics has to be followed by a reconceptualization of Jewish prayer music. In doing so, both Jewish women and men can become engaged not only with what they are singing about, but also with God (see, for example, Marini 2003, 5).

However, the power of Jewish tradition is clear not only in the lyrics but also in the music—though in a somewhat different way. Although feminist Jewish singer-songwriters do not dare to fully ignore or break with the written body of Jewish tradition, they have a thoroughly different attitude about musical customs. With regard to Jewish liturgy, feminist musicians do find some of the values espoused by established Judaism consonant with

Jewish feminism, but they consider traditional synagogue music as incompatible with their feminist politics, and thus with the realization of their feminist visions. This chapter discusses the musical concept of feminist Jewish music by presenting the variety of musical materials that have been borrowed and adapted from sources inside and outside Judaism and that have been incorporated into feminist Jewish songs. These materials are linked with various musical parameters and performance tools such as song leading, chanting, and singing in harmony. According to Ellen Koskoff, the process of musical acculturation in particular is not only usual but natural, as it is "part of all social, ethnic, and religious group interaction, especially within Jewish culture" (2001a, 77). From this perspective, the following questions arise: What is the intention behind this process of musical borrowing in the case of feminist Jewish music? Is the musical choice of those compositions only incidental or unconscious? Is it a mere product of acculturation or a politically motivated strategy? This chapter will show on which levels the redesign of Jewish liturgical music takes place. It will then discuss how this performative strategy legitimatizes the use of a cultural fusion of sounds to voice the political aims of Jewish feminism and to adjust Jewish liturgical music to the varied social, cultural, and feminized structure of the larger Jewish community and its modified spiritual needs.

PERFORMING FEMINIST RITUAL SONGS

Unlike song texts, which add a feminist sensibility to the words of prayers and liturgy, feminist Jewish music is primarily written in non-Jewish musical styles. Rather, its musical content is closely related to the songwriter's personal style of composition (see chapter 1), as well as to the cultural, religious, and political influences on her or him. Nevertheless, feminist Jewish music should be considered Jewish liturgical music and thus be added to the canon of synagogue music, even though it does not sound Jewish at all.[1] Contemporary popular and world music sounds have to be seen as part of the realm of Jewish liturgical music as well. This understanding of Jewish music is crucial for what follows in this chapter.

Aside from new Jewish music, there are no musical models available that give information about what songs written for feminist rituals or feminized egalitarian Jewish worship should sound like. This chapter will use the following musical examples to address what sounds Jewish women can relate to when singing feminist songs in religious contexts. It is worth returning to the so-called Miriam songs (see chapter 3). These songs are representative of feminist Jewish songs about biblical women not only with regard to the content and general structure of the lyrics, but also with regard to the idea of what today's women imagine that Miriam's song about the events at the Red Sea could sound like.

I begin with Debbie Friedman, who once explained that just as she cannot sing as a cantor in synagogue because she lacks professional training, she cannot expect an average worshiper to be able to sing the classical cantorial repertoire (see Friedman n.d.b). Of all the Miriam songs presented here, Friedman's "Miriam's Song" (see Elwell 2002, 150) is the catchiest and the easiest to sing. Composed in the popular style of new Jewish music, the song is written in a folk-song style (in B-flat major). After a short instrumental introduction, the song follows a classical A–B–A structure, alternating verses and a chorus. In comparison to the Miriam songs discussed below, in Friedman's song a band (including guitar, piano, trumpet, clarinet, violin, and cello, hand drums, and a range of other rhythmic instruments) accompanies the singer.

One unifying feature of all the Miriam songs discussed in this chapter is that the moment in the story of Miriam when all the women follow her is represented musically by a call-and-response formula of some kind, a feature that is often found in feminist Jewish songs. In the version of Friedman's song recorded in 1997 (which appears on the album *The Journey Continues*), the first iteration of the chorus and the first verse are sung by Friedman alone, whereas Friedman and a women's chorus sing all repetitions of the chorus in unison. Thus, the alternation of solo and chorus voices follows the call-and-response formula. In this way, the women's choruses sound like an echo of Friedman's solo voice.

While Friedman's song is written in the common style of the Reform repertoire (easy to sing folk-rock) that has the power to engage the listener and encourage group singing, the style of Geela Rayzel Raphael's song "Miriam" (1984) is, in comparison, less familiar. On *Bible Babes A-Beltin'* (1997), Raphael gives voice to the stories of biblical women in a unique folky, bluesy, and earthy voice, one that corresponds to her general music style—which is strongly influenced by diverse musical genres such as bluegrass, rock, and country. Moreover, it contains many changes of harmony and a few instances of hocket.[2] This openness to the use of diverse non-Jewish music styles, and especially Raphael's preference for country music that

FIGURE 4.1: Bars 7 to 12 of "Miriam" (1984) by Rabbi Geela Rayzel Raphael

infuses many of her songs, fits with her background in Jewish Renewal and indicates how much she has been influenced by the local music culture of Tennessee, where she grew up (see chapter 1).

Raphael's song is written in D-flat major (see figure 4.1). In comparison to Friedman's "Miriam's Song," Raphael's song is performed by only five people—Raphael, Rabbi Margot Stein, Juliet Spitzer, Aviva Bass, and Raphael's son, Yigdal—singing in harmony, accompanied by a hand drum and a xylophone played by Myriam Klotz and Daoud Shaw, respectively. The call-and-response formula is also used in Raphael's song, although not as obviously as in Friedman's. Phrases sung by Raphael, such as "red red sea," "light of the day," and "lit up the night," are immediately repeated by the soprano in an example of hocketing: that is the quick alternation of sung notes between the two voices. As indicated in chapter 1, characteristic of the whole repertoire of Raphael and MiRaJ.

Although the melody line of both chorus and verse is simple in structure, Raphael's song is not as catchy as Friedman's. Raphael's song, in 4/4 time, starts slow, then switches to double time, then triple, and then changes to a heavy $^{12}/_{8}$ time (not shown in figure 4.1). In addition, the whole song is characterized by a syncopated rhythm. Furthermore, it is full of interjections (for example, of the word "joy"), by hand clapping (on the word "clapped"), and improvisations (such as in the last chorus; not shown in figure 4.1.). Thus, it is not easy to determine the song's genre; it might be described as a mixture of swing and blues. However, it becomes obvious how the story of Miriam leading the women in song and dance is musically realized. Raphael's steady and low voice can be interpreted as the leading voice (Miriam's), followed by the higher voices of the other women, which—as the song progresses—become louder, freer in improvisation, and more joyful. With the swinging rhythm of the percussion instruments, one can imagine the scene at the Red Sea, where Miriam and the women dance with timbrels in their hands.

Another example of a song about Miriam is Linda Hirschhorn's "Miriam's Slow Snake Dance by the Riverside" (see figures 4.2–3). In contrast to Friedman, whose folk-rock music reflects her cultural, denominational, as well as political background, and to Raphael's country-infused music-mix, Hirschhorn's song is more closely related to traditional Jewish music styles, as indicated by the incorporation of a niggun. Moreover, her song is written in minor key (C-flat minor) and is divided into four sections: an introduction, sung by Hirschhorn's solo voice; part 1 ("Nigun"), sung by four women's voices in unison; part 2 ("The Call"), sung in a round by the women's choir (consisting of the four women); and part 3 ("The Celebration"), sung by all of the women in a round. Hirschhorn considers the most crucial aspect of the song to be the relation between the text or story and the music. While the introduction sets the scene of the whole song ("And Miriam the prophetess took the timbrel in her hand / And led the women down to the sea / And there they dance and they sang / *Shiru lashechinah* [sing to Shechinah] a song of thanks for this day of liberation"), the niggun is a song of thanks and liberation (beginning at bar 14, figure 4.2). As explained above, niggunim are wordless melodies originally sung by Hasidic Jews. They were performed at different occasions, such as *farbrengen* (gatherings of rabbis), weddings, Shabbat dinners, joyful holidays, and while someone spiritually prepares him- or herself "for prayer, study, and the contemplation of religious discourses" (Heskes 1994, 118; see also Koskoff 1987, 214). In conformity with the tradition, Hirschhorn's niggun

FIGURE 4.2–3: "Miriam's Slow Snake Dance by the Riverside" © Linda Hirschhorn

FIGURE 4.2–3: (continued)

is also sung on one to two syllables. A hand drum and a timbrel accompany it. The niggun is repeated over and over until the song ends. This is another characteristic of traditional (male) niggun performance, as described by Koskoff (2001a, 10 and 88).

"The Call" (beginning at bar 22, figure 4.2) uses the call-and-response formula seen in examples above. Hirschhorn's use of the formula is more obvious than Friedman's or Raphael's, as it directly relates to the text: "Miriam, bimherah, na' lamdinu, rikudayich" (Miriam, come quickly! Please teach us your dances!; bars 22–26, figure 4.2). One phrase is sung by Hirschhorn ("Miriam" in bar 22) and then repeated in the same manner by a second female singer ("Miriam" in bar 23) and so on, while the rest of the women's chorus simultaneously sings the niggun. The last section of the song, "The Celebration" (beginning at bar 30), repeats the call and the niggun again and adds a third melody that indicates the actual dance and song of freedom mentioned in the biblical story of Miriam. As the song progresses, the round and thus the harmony become richer.

In comparison to the previous examples, Hirschhorn keeps a musical connection to the Jewish tradition while taking a biblical passage as the basis for her lyrics. She also makes use of Jewish musical idioms, such as the niggun and the use of a minor key. The song is pervaded by harmonic minor thirds. Although this is not the same as the popular augmented second that is said to be characteristic of Jewish tunes (see Koskoff 2001, 85–88), the sound of the minor third is remiscent of the sound of the augmented second and helps make Hirschhorn's song sound Jewish. According to Mark Slobin (1982, 182–97), the musical parameters of Hirschhorn's song can be understood as musical codes. Like Koskoff (2001, 85–88), Slobin identifies the use of specific intervals (such as the augmented second), modes (Mark Kligman [2001a, 451] compares the function of the niggun with that of the Arabic maqām, and in this way with the cantorial nusach), scales, or certain performance preferences as "part of an in-group musical language" (Slobin 1982, 182). Those musical codes define a song as Jewish and contribute to a sound context that has musical, social, and religious meaning for Jewish and non-Jewish communities (Koskoff 2001, 88).

In this sense, Jeffrey Summit's concept of "melodic switching" (2000, 131) is instructive. We may also apply this concept to the melodic choices of feminist Jewish music. Summit adopted the idea of code switching from linguistics. It is defined as the use of more than one language in a single communication episode. In code switching, the speaker uses language as a code to connect with or keep a distance from other people. Summit writes: "Through linguistic switching, a speaker chooses the particular community with which he or she is identifying at a given moment" (ibid.). This is also true for music used in synagogue worship or feminist Jewish ritual (see S. Ross 2004, 57–59). The melodies chosen by feminist Jewish songwriters also bear a code, which means that they are inflected with symbolic meanings (as shown in the different Miriam songs) or certain associations. Contemporary folk-rock or other popular music styles are associated with the present (more precisely with the global shtetl of the American Jewish mainstream), while the use of traditional tunes, such as the niggun in Hirschhorn's song, is meant to create a connection to the past—in other words, to the historical experiences of the Jewish people. Thus, the songwriters' melodic choices must be understood as indicating their—and worshipers'—desire for spiritual, cultural, and historical authenticity (see, for example, Summit 2000, 154–55).

The songs about Miriam by Friedman, Raphael, and Hirschhorn do have some characteristics in common. They all portray the story of Miriam leading the women in dance and song, and use the call-and-response formula for prayer. However, giving biblical women a voice in the lyrics (by singing about them) is not enough; all three of these singer-songwriters integrate a women's chorus into their songs, singing in rich harmony—which can, against the background of Kol Isha, be understood as a political issue. In comparison to Friedman, however, Raphael and Hirschhorn renounce the use of full instrumental accompaniment, which is quite typical for music of the Jewish Renewal movement. In all three songs, the use of percussion instruments, such as the drums and tambourine, can be interpreted as a metaphor for Miriam's timbrel in the biblical story, as I have explained above in this chapter as well as in chapter 3. As I have shown, feminist Jewish singer-songwriters extend the content of the Jewish tradition and Jewish collective memory not only on the basis of their songs' texts but also on the basis of the songs' musical structure. Each of the songwriters discussed here takes a different approach to the question of how to give voice to the biblical women they are singing about, as well as to today's Jewish women and their concerns.

In the case of songs that have been written for the general liturgy—such as Hirschhorn and Avni's version of "Lecha Dodi," the song "Lechu, Re'ot," mentioned in chapter 3—it is crucial to note that feminist songwriters sometimes have fallen back on traditional tunes and motifs, but they have transposed those into women's vocal range, as the common repertoire of synagogue music is written solely for male voices. According to Hirschhorn, writing songs for women's voices is considered a feminist act (interview February 2008).

However, as it will become more obvious below, the crucial point is that feminist Jewish music speaks a multicultural language. The sounds of American folk-rock, country, blues, and jazz can be heard alongside Chana Rothman's world music mix or Holy Taya Shere's earthy, tribal, and shamanic tunes. Thus, feminist Jewish music represents an intersection of diverse Jewish subcultures.

FEMINIST PERSPECTIVES ON CONGREGATIONAL SINGING

The feminist concept of a Jewish community—in which the increased cultural fragmentation of the Jews that has occurred as a consequence of the accelerated changes in the U.S. cultural mainstream, is not only acknowledged but lived—is reflected in the way feminist Jewish songs are performed. As I have indicated above, the different voices in feminist Jewish music provide an important way for a Jewish woman to explore her own background as well as her relationship to other cultures, all within the framework of a Jewish context. The sound of feminist Jewish music used in general synagogue worship is not the most important point; rather, the musical practice of feminist songwriters is crucial in creating an egalitarian worshiping community. The community envisioned by feminist Jews today is one that reflects the ideal of not separate and equal on both secular and religious levels.

This section of the chapter is meant to provide a general understanding of the concepts of feminist Jewish prayer music—in other words, the musical practices that are characteristic of congregational singing. Shere stated that it is "very important for Jews . . . that they too can be agents of prayer" (e-mail interview February 2008). This is realized by focusing primarily on different forms of song leading, including divers chanting practices and choral singing.

Song Leading

The practice of song leading in American Judaism was born in Reform and Conservative Judaism's summer camps and uses songs that are written in a catchy folk style and are easy to sing and can be played on the guitar. Feminist Jewish songwriters such as Friedman were among the first to apply this musical practice to synagogue service (see, for example, Judah Cohen 2006b). The overall goal of song leading is to reengage people with—and integrate women into—Judaism, and thus to create a sense of community and feeling of connectedness among men and women, as well as between this integrated group and the divine. This is realized by the democratic nature and participatory character of popular music in general, and by engaging the worshiping community in collective singing in particular (see, for example, Kligman 2005, 367). Feminist Jewish singer-songwriters consciously make use of the transformative power of music, knowing that the worshiper remembers the song's message when he or she experiences the song through singing (see, for example, Love 2002, 74). When leading a community in prayer and song, feminist songwriters such as Shere also consciously exploit music's power to touch people's souls in their efforts to make prayer a soulful rather than an intellectual experience. Shere told me:

> For me, music is a hugely important element of prayer. It helps transport people to another space. It helps shut the mind off and open the senses, the body to Spirit. When music touches our spirit, our inner rhythms shift to match the rhythm of the music. Music can be such a powerful portal to G!d. . . . I see this happen in the Shabbat services I lead in the community that I serve. Many folks in this community have not engaged much with Judaism as adults. I see them open and come alive when we sing familiar melodies (usually the melodies that were most traditional in Reform and Conservative communities; which is what they grew up with). It touches something so deep in them. And they come alive in another, different sort of way, if we sing melodies that are more contemporary, or [funkier], or [jazzier,] etc. The melodies we choose to pray . . . affect our experience of the prayer, our ability to let go into it, and the kavannah that we hold for this prayer. (e-mail interview February 2007).

The form of song leading that is most associated with Jewish worship is that used in Reform Judaism, which is thus closely connected to a particular musical genre—namely, folk-rock. Friedman is the most popular of the feminist songwriters who use this form of song leading. Different concerts, rituals, and synagogue services that are used in *A Journey of Spirit* show Friedman standing on the stage or the bimah, with a guitar in her hands and occasionally a band behind her. She is not only performing her songs but also teaching her audience and asking the listeners or worshipers to join her singing. Friedman says: "You are doing something together as a community, you are not out there alone, and everybody in that room, everybody singing with you, has the opportunity to take part in this, and nobody has to stand by him- or herself" (my transcription of Coppel 2003).

Friedman actively involves people in her performances, making them feel special, and thus she turns every place in a secure and sacred space in which each person can just be whoever he or she is (Coppel 2003). Accordingly, the distance between performer and audience, or between clergy and worshiper, is erased. Peter Yarrow (a member of the group Peter, Paul, and Mary) stated: "Once you've looked in, it's like a conversation that moves from a tentative exploration to a deep mutual understanding. This is what her special gift is, additionally to write songs that allow it to occur" (ibid.).

As discussed in the introduction (see also Cohen 2006b; Kligman 2001b and 2005), the emergence of new Jewish music and song leading in Jewish summer camps and the advent of feminist Jewish songs are closely interconnected. Thus, Ellen Dreskin—a cantor who is coordinator of the new Cantorial Certification Program at the Debbie Friedman School of Sacred Music at Hebrew Union College–Jewish Institute of Religion in New York—remembers:

> I "grew up" (my high school years and beyond) at the URJ [Union of Reform Judaism] Kutz Camp in Warwick, NY. We sang every kind of song. In addition to whatever was taught at song sessions, or shared at services, the lobby area of camp was filled with guitars, and participants were up till all hours of the early morning, sharing popular tunes from home as well as from their shuls. Combine that with the deep Jewish value of diversity, inclusiveness, and unity, and you will have so many songs shared—social justice songs were, and continue to be[,] huge, whether they are feminist, civil rights oriented, feeding the hungry, sheltering the homeless, ending human trafficking, anti-bullying—camp is always a place where the youth begin to form independent opinions under the umbrella of their Jewish roots—it's a great thing. Debbie Friedman was certainly a huge influence in the Jewish summer camps. She was probably among the first to use more feminist language in her songs, such as "L'chi Lach," "Bruchot Ha-ba'ot," "Devorah's Song," or "Water in the Well." The first two are feminist in their language, the latter two highlight strong Biblical characters. (Not to mention "Miriam's Song.") There were many, many strong female role models as songleaders and teachers in all of the camps. Songleaders of the 70s [and] 80s included Merri Lovinger Arian, Benjie Schiller, Rosalie Boxt, me, Chana Rothman, and Debbie Friedman, to name a few (e-mail, March 4, 2014).

The essence of song leading, which includes taking in the atmosphere, raising the energy level of the community, and guiding the worshipers with the right choice of songs through synagogue service, resonates within contemporary feminist Jewish songs. Thus, one emblematic image of the Jewish feminist movement is the female singer-songwriter holding a guitar (see figures 4.4–7).

Today, there are young Jewish singers and songwriters, such as Hannah Spiro (a student at the Reconstructionist Rabbinical College), who follow Friedman's footsteps and write new interpretations of liturgical songs—songs that represent the mission and vision of song leading. Spiro's Jewish songs are characterized by a combination of "progressive midrash and interpretive liturgy with the music sentiment of a 90's kid raised on Fleetwood Mac and bubblegum pop" (Spiro 2015). Her music is thus a mixture of pop melodies and traditional Jewish tunes with a particular folk vibe added. Like other feminist songwriters, Spiro visits congregations for musical Shabbat services, teaching the worshipers her Jewish tunes and simultaneously "raising consciousness and energy levels among adults, teens, and kids alike" (ibid.).

Her interpretation of the Mi Chamocha prayer (released on her album *It Is upon Us*, 2012; for a notated version, see Eglash and Friedman 2014;

FIGURE 4.4: Alicia Rabins. Photo by Aaron Hartman

FIGURE 4.5: Cantor Aviva Rosenbloom. Courtesy A. Rosenbloom

FIGURE 4.6: Hannah Spiro. Courtesy H. Spiro

see also figure 4.8) contains the original prayer text plus verses to provide the obligatory translation and interpretation (for example: "You made us free, *b'nei chorin* [sons of freedom] / Hurled our captors into the sea ai yai yai / Who is like You, Adonai, Ai yai yai, / Who can do oo oo oo the things you do") that characterize songs in the tradition of new Jewish music and feminist Jewish music, respectively. People respond very differently to singing with a guitar than they do to singing with a piano, so most of Spiro's songs are provided with guitar chords to make it easy to use them for song leading.

Choral Singing or Singing in Harmony

The increasing process of individualization and cultural fragmentation poses a challenge to the creation of a communal Jewish identity. Gaps between men and women; differences between Jews of various religious,

FIGURE 4.7: Rebecca Schwartz. Courtesy R. Schwartz

ethnic, or cultural backgrounds; and limited Hebrew language skills, which make traditional texts and songs inaccessible to some people, are some problems that can divide a worshiping community or prevent the creation of a communal identity. Differences among the congregants, which is experienced as a stumbling block in removing all sorts of inequalities from a community, are also relevant for feminist Jewish singer-songwriters of the Jewish Renewal and Reconstructionist movements. Each singer-songwriter employs different musical practices to counteract this problem. For example, Hirschhorn works as an artist in residence, leading Jewish community choruses in singing her songs. For her, writing songs for several voices and singing in harmony is a model of how to respect differences among the congregants in a community, and thus of how to express the blending of diverse experiences, especially those of Jewish women. She remembers that "looking through the literature I found nothing that would give expression to the blending of diverse experiences particular to . . . women. . . . As I taught my new rounds and songs I saw how singing in harmony could have major impact on how we experience ourselves in relation to others and I saw how melody and harmony could [moreover] help deepen one's understanding of text" (Hirschhorn n.d.a).

FIGURE 4.8: Beginning of "Mi Chamocha" (2012) © Hannah Spiro

Through her music, Hirschhorn emphasizes "the strength of the individual voice to hold its own while recognizing that the whole sounds as good as the individual parts" (ibid.). This reflects her ideal of a Jewish community, in which each person acts in harmony with everyone else: "I write in harmony, you can't sing harmony by yourself so you are forced into community" (quoted in Musleah 1995, 21). This is exemplified in her three-part canon "Ilu Finu" (figure 4.9), whose words are taken from the Shabbat morning liturgy and can be translated as "Let us have songs to fill our mouth" (1989; released on the album *Gather Round*). For this song, Hirschhorn developed instructions for singing the round (not shown in figure 4.9), so that people will get the most out of the experience of singing in harmony. According to Hirschhorn, the whole community should start singing unison in English and Hebrew before they begin the round. The first group sings all the way through in Hebrew and then goes back to the beginning, singing in Hebrew again until bar 7 and switching to English at bar 8. This group then sings in English to the end and starts over, still in English. At the same time, the second group sings the whole song in Hebrew and then in English, and then sings bars 13–18 twice in English. The third group sings bars 1–14 in Hebrew, changes to English at bar 15 and continues to the end, then sings the whole song in English. This group then returns to bar 13 and sings in English until bar 18. The whole community ends the song by singing bars 15–18 in unison in Hebrew.

Singing "Ilu Finu" as instructed by Hirschhorn creates not only a blending of voices but also resembles the idea of tikkun olam and of the creation of an egalitarian and inclusive community through music. Both Friedman and Rothman are convinced that music can be an appropriate tool for repairing the world. Thus, Friedman states: "I really believe that each of us is an instrument of God, and each of us is been given certain gifts . . . that we are not here for a free ride. We've have been given gifts that we need to use to partake in tikkun olam and repairing the brokenness in the world" (my transcription of Coppel 2003). Rothman answered the question of whether she thought that music can heal the world this way: "I do. I don't know if it's music that will fix the world. But I believe that music tells the truth releases good energy. Even if it doesn't have words, just submitting a good energy. . . . I definitely believe music can create change" (MyJewSpot n.d.).

Chanting

Another way of dealing with the issue of difference is to seek equality and unity in the worshipers' particularity. Feminist songwriters, mostly those related to the Jewish Renewal and Reconstructionist movements, employ diverse forms of chanting practices. In synagogue services informed by the

FIGURE 4.9: "Ilu Finu" (1989) © Linda Hirschhorn

ideas of Jewish Renewal and feminism, the practice of chanting became an important version of song leading, which is often used in conjunction with other non-Western spiritual practices, such as yoga and Buddhist meditation (see, for example, Gold, 2006, 229–30). Chanting is the melodic and rhythmic repetition of a Hebrew phrase taken from a sacred text. It makes possible the exploration of the texts' deeper levels of meaning. For many, chanting has become a central method of spiritually opening up the mind, connecting with the community, and embodying the liturgy and scripture. Rabbi Shefa Gold considers chanting to be a feminist act (2006, 228; interview March 2008).

Gold and her former student Yofiyah helped develop the practice of chanting for feminist services and rituals. Gold differentiates between chanting and singing. According to her, chanting is primarily a meditative practice focusing on the inside (the spiritual state) of the performer, and it requires that the chant leader has a special "sensitivity to the energy of the group, and a willingness to serve the group" (1997). Consequently, Gold's music reflects these needs.

In general, her music is a hybrid of several musical genres, such as folk-rock, jazz, African American blues, reggae, New Age music, and Native

American music, which reflects the New Age orientation and ideology of Renewal Judaism. While drawing on common musical devices such as melody, harmony, and syncopation, Gold seeks to unlock the deeper meaning and power of prayer (1997; interview March 2008). In doing so, she is well aware of the fact that certain sounds and forms of rhythmic breathing have a powerful effect on the mind and body. Moreover, the integration of bodily movement into the performance enhances the effect of chanting.

Although her 1994 piece "Rani V'Simchi" (celebrate and rejoice), released on her album *Chants Encounter* (see figures 4.10–11), can be considered a song, its chorus has a structure similar to that of most of her chants. The lyrics are taken from Zechariah 2:14–4:7 (the haftarah for Hanukah): "Rani v'simchi, rani v'simchi, Bat Tzion ki/Hin'ni vah, ki /Hin'ni vah, v'shochanti b'tocheych, n'um Yah," which is translated by Gold as "rejoice, rejoice, daughter of Zion / for I am here, and I have come / to dwell within you. / These are the words of God." Written in D-sharp major, the chant-like chorus uses a typical call-and-response formula that is found in most of Gold's chants—as well as in those of Yofiyah, which I discuss below. Thus, the chorus opens with the call "rani v'simchi" in the high (leading) voice, sung on a particular melodic pattern in bar 1, which is followed by a harmonic response in the two lower voices in bar 2, after which the high voice repeats the call again in bar 3. All three voices come together in bar 4, but the leading voice starts a new call on "ki hin'ni va" (bars 4–5), which is again repeated by the other voices (bars 5–6).

This musical structure is typical of all of Gold's chants, which are accessible and consist of simple phrases that are easy to learn and that worshiper can join at any time. Gold's music is repetitive, meditative, and (in contrast to most of the traditional Jewish music repertoire) written in a major key, which she describes as an "uplifting key" (interview March 2008). Gold states that it is the responsibility of the chant leader "to understand the direction, function and potential of the chant in the context of a service or meditation and to know when to end the chant" (1997). This is important, as some leaders tend to stop the chant too soon, which ruins the chant's effect. As Gold explains, "the goal is to chant through the boredom, and through the momentary anxiety of losing control or losing fixed boundaries of self." After this moment of monotony has been passed, "there is a shift in consciousness, a sudden expansion, and a cohesion of the group" (ibid.).

FIGURE 4.10–11: "Rani V'Simchi" (1994) by Shefa Gold. From *Chants Encounter* © 1994. www.RabbiShefaGold.com

FIGURE 4.10–11: (continued)

Although most of Gold's chants consist of only one phrase taken from Jewish sacred texts, the strong relationship that generally exists between Jewish texts and prayer music is also relevant. She told me that in the Jewish tradition, everyone is meant to be in a conversation with the texts, God, and each other. Her chants have to be understood as a reflection of this conversation, in which the music is meant to emphasize her views on certain theological questions. Gold concluded that music in this context teaches people "to call up" to God (interview March 2008).

Chanting in prayer services has two functions. First, it has the effect of connecting the members of the worshiping community. As Gold writes, "it allows for the experiencing of praying in the voice of community as well as from an individual perspective" and allows a person to connect his or her individual spiritual practice to the traditional formalized Jewish prayer service (1997). Second, the practice of chanting permits a person to experience the presence of the divine in the world (see, for example, Caplan 2002, 149), and the music reflects the feminist conception of God as the immanent one. Gold adopted non-Western chanting practices.

For example, as described by Caplan (2002), Gold borrowed the concept of dhikr (see chapter 1), but not, I argue, its musical structure. In its original Islamic context, dhikr is the ritual invocation and remembrance of "the divine authority and power [of God] by Muslims through the repetition of God's names . . . , prayer, chant, and ritualized motions, including bodily movement and rhythmic breathing" (Shannon 2004, 381). During dhikr Muslims fulfill a Qur'anic obligation and moreover seek "to attain physical and emotional states that promote spiritual transformation" (ibid.). The ultimate goals of dhikr are to develop a deeper sense of the divine's pervasive presence (Caplan 2002, 149) and to allow the worshiper to forget his or her individuality, or inferior self, while simultaneously remembering God, the superior self, and seeking his or her unification with the divine reality (Shannon 2004, 384). Some of the central aspects and characteristics of dhikr can be found in Gold's chanting practice as well, such as the sequential chanting of God's names to a simple melody, the use of bodily movements and rhythmic breathing, and the search for spiritual transformation. But unlike dhikr, Gold's chants do not use the modal principles of Arabic music, which define the traditional musical style of dhikr.

However, to integrate the practice of dhikr into liberal Jewish worship, she takes, as shown above, biblical and Jewish liturgical phrases that can be used in a similar manner to the words in dhikr. According to Eric Caplan, the reason why Gold draws on the practice of dhikr is that it has the capacity to open up her heart and cultivate compassion, and it "helps her achieve a sense of her place in the universe" (2002, 149). It arouses such religious passion within her, as Caplan explains, that she "can never be content with bald religion, sentimental religion, or religion that engages the mind but excludes the body and the full range of emotions" (ibid.). Against the background of the mind-body split in Jewish liturgical traditions, and its effect on how women experience Jewish prayer and ritual, the unorthodox inclusion of the body in Gold's chants seems to be quite important.

Gold and Yofiyah share the same understanding of chanting as a feminist act, and their Jewish feminism can be described as a holistic feminism, which is highly influenced by Jewish mysticism (Kabbalah) and non-Western philosophies. Yofiyah is closely related to and thus influenced by the Jewish Renewal movement as well. This is why it is only natural that she draws on repetitive and ecstatic chanting practices. Yet she is the founder of kabbalistic kirtan, a combination of *kīrtan* (the participatory type of Hindu devotional singing, which involves the repetition of a mantra or a name of God) and the Kabbalah (interview March 2008). The result is an ecstatic kabbalistic practice based on the chanting of sacred Hebrew texts and the names of God found in Jewish tradition. Yofiyah is also the creator of vocal discovery, which is a method for personal transformation and community building that uses the power of sound and song (Kabbalah Kirtan 2015). Through her work with tone-deaf people, who are afraid of participating in any form of music making in a group setting, she recognized that the ancient practice of kīrtan gives deaf people a musical experience that is easy and accessible (interview March 2008).

Like original kīrtan, kabbalistic kirtan involves a calling out by the group leader and a response to this call by the rest of the group. The sound of kīrtan is not easy to identify as a particular music style as it is, according to Stephen Slawek, imitative in style and eclectic in nature (1988, 77 and 80). This is also true of Yofiyah's chants. It is interesting that anyone is allowed to take part in the performance of original kīrtan, "regardless of caste, sex, or voice quality" (ibid., 79). Yofiyah's performances often take place in Jewish Conservative and Orthodox contexts, where the separation of men and women persists (interview March 2008). Thus, she realized that people are excluded from participating in communal singing not only by deafness, but also by many other differences between worshipers, such as gender differences or different religious, ethnic, or cultural backgrounds. This is why Yofiyah decided to bring kīrtan into the synagogue (ibid.). Kirtan allows the simplicity and hypnotic energy of Yofiyah's music to help congregants forget their differences as well as their reluctance to participate in songs and prayer, which I will discuss in more detail below.

So far, I have shown that feminist Jewish songwriters draw on different forms of song leading to create unity among the congregants. How relevant these forms of congregational singing are for the musical implementation of the feminist concept of God will be discussed in the following section of this chapter.

ADDRESSING THE IMMANENT GOD THROUGH MUSIC

The last section of the chapter discusses how the relationship between God and the individual is manifested musically in feminist Jewish music. To get a better understanding of the relationship between music and the feminist concept of God, the section examines the feminist conceptualization of prayer music and some general thoughts on the relationship between word and sound in Jewish liturgy.

According to ancient Hebrew tradition, it is prohibited to represent God in images, as this is regarded as creating an idol.[3] That is why in Judaism the divine is conceptualized as an omnipresent but invisible God. Likewise, it is prohibited to say the name YHWH, but not to speak of God's existence as represented in the written word. Therefore, for Jews, God is a voice rather than a vision—or, as the philosopher Don Ihde puts it: "the very experience of the God of the biblical traditions is an experience of word in voice such as that the person of God is 'like' an intense auditory experience" (1976, 174). Thus, the use of various metaphors for the divine in Jewish texts and liturgy to try to capture the grandeur of God in human language comes as no surprise. It can be argued that the different names for God in Judaism—especially in Jewish feminism—refer to different concepts of the creator, particularly the understanding of God as transcendent on the one hand and as immanent on the other hand. These perceptions of God are manifested in and communicated through prayer, and especially through prayer music. Yet through the mere act of praying, the divine's presence in the world is already sensually experienced. Ihde takes this concept a step further, arguing that the omnipresent but invisible presence of God is a presence of sound in its most dramatic moments. Presumably referring to the performance of prayer in synagogue worship, he states that "the God of voice surrounds, penetrates, and fills the worshiper." Consequently, "in the drama of the liturgy the god is experienced *in* the presence of voice," he explains (1976, 174; emphasis in original). Ihde's remarks highlight the importance of the interconnectedness of word and sound in Jewish liturgy, even though he does not explicitly differentiate between the speaking and singing voice of the worshiper. Thus, I would like to use these points as a theoretical basis for my explanations that follow, when I consider the role of the singing voice in the feminist Jewish music of synagogue worship.

The text of standard prayers is designed to speak to the Lord—the male transcendent God—and so is the music that the prayers are set to. In traditional practice, standard prayers, hymns, and blessings are sung or chanted in the synagogue sometimes by the rabbi, but most often by a specially trained male cantor, employing cantillation. According to Stephen Marini, cantillation is "a simpler, freer structure than ordinary vocal music, closer to solemn declamation than to the structured, organized singing" that requires professional training (2003, 133). As a consequence, cantillation is not meant for the kind of congregational singing that feminist Jewish songwriters envisioned. Occasionally, this classical prayer music may be ornamented with rich vocalization. Its form is subordinated to the text and adapted to its syntax and punctuation. In this type of prayer music, the word has absolute priority over the music (ibid., 132–33).

Regarding the relationship between traditional prayer text and sacred music, the feminist singer-songwriter Stein explained that people who sing to a "Sky God," as she names the male-conceptualized Lord, are usually inclined to sing petitionary prayers and praise in "grand fashion with big musical flourishes" (e-mail interview October 2008). This lends grandeur and dignity to the religious ceremony. Stein added that "grand classical musical styles serve that more external God. It's not an accident that the congregation can't sing along. The (male) cantor is the conduit, and the rest of the group are the beneficiaries" (ibid.). Consequently, in normative synagogue service, the worshipers—especially women, because of Kol Isha—play only a passive role. Stein's statement shows how classical Jewish prayer music accentuates the heightened position of the Lord, as communicated by the prayer text, and how it concurrently creates a rather elitist and hierarchical form of worship. But this is opposed to the feminist understanding of Judaism and Jewish worship.

However, the description of the musical examples given above in this chapter might have raised the following questions: What makes popular music religious music? In other words, why does classical Jewish sacred music not serve the feminist concept of God and prayer? A rather basic answer to these questions is that music that does not move the congregants emotionally is not likely to be religiously effective either (see, for example, Marini 2003, 4). Thus, it can be stated that the concept of moving congregants emotionally is closely connected to the concept of active participation through antiphonal or group singing. Or, to put it differently, hearing one's voice in song means internalizing not only the lyrics but also Jewish prayer—and thus God—in general.

It is the folkiness and inclusiveness of popular music, especially folk-rock music, that feminist Jewish songwriters try to convey. They seek to be inclusive and appeal to those who used to listen to this type of music, particularly in its heyday in the 1960s and 1970s. Folky melodies that are easy to sing and that worshipers can easily join invite the formation of connections among the congregants that feminist Jewish singer-songwriters are looking for, according to Stein (e-mail interview October 2008). In comparison to worship using standard prayer, the worshipers take a more active role in synagogue worship. Thus, the religious beliefs expressed through female God-language can add an overtly sacred theoretical dimension to popular music (see, for example, Marini 2003, 4).

A more detailed answer from my interviewees to the questions above points to the aspect of kavannah, which denotes the intention, meaning, and attitude behind Jewish prayer. The feminist concept of God as immediate presence in the world puts the worshiping community more in touch with this aspect of Jewish prayer and emphasizes the worshiper's awareness of standing in the presence of Shekhinah.[4] Praying with kavannah invites the congregant's thoughts, ideas, and feelings to go beyond the prescribed text of the prayers. Thus, Stein says, kavannah has the function of leading the congregant to a higher state of mind and heart (e-mail interview October 2008). This aspect of Jewish prayer consequently requires forms of sacred music that offer worshipers the possibility of transporting themselves into a meditative state of consciousness. One of these forms, as mentioned above, is chanting, which became an important and alternative method of spirituality in feminist services. Gold writes:

> When we chant together with a community we create something so much more beautiful than any one of us could accomplish alone. . . . We can shape our differences to create fascinating harmonies. We can time our varying rhythms to create counterpoint. Each of us learns to bring the fullness of our presences to the group in ways that will enhance the overall feeling and tone of the chant. . . . As we enter the silence after the chant, each of us lays down our differences and experiences a collective silence that is framed by the highest intentions of everyone in the group. (2006, 230)

The practice of chanting, as described by Gold, contains elements that, according to Marini, are crucial in defining as sacred even something as mundane as popular music. Sacred song must possess a ritual intention and form, as this is its defining performance condition. Furthermore, Marini insists that "for song to be religious expression, it must be presented with sacred intentionality as part of effective ritual action." The latter embraces symbolic behavior, which moves the worshipers out of "everyday awareness into a state of shared mythic consciousness and creative community" (Marini 2003, 7). Let us return to Yofiyah and the practice of kabbalistic kirtan. The music of her chants does not necessarily allude to broader Jewish themes taken from the vast corpus of Jewish musical genres. However, the practice of kīrtan, which has no religious content, nevertheless allows her to consider kīrtan a Jewish practice. According to Yofiyah, it is not the musical form itself but the content that defines its Jewishness (see Yofiyah 2004). With regard to the feminist Jewish conception of God as an indwelling presence in the world, and thus to the overall intention behind the use of kīrtan chanting, the musical structure of kabbalistic kirtan is of crucial importance. Kīrtan invites people "to sing to, with, and ultimately as God," as Yofiyah explains, and so the music itself, but moreover the experience of singing, offers a direct encounter with the divine (ibid.). This is represented in her chant "Shechinah," which is on her album *OPEN* (2010) (see Yofiyah 2004; figure 4.12), which draws on the *Nishmat Kol Chai* (The breath of every living thing) prayer that is recited during the Shacharit (morning) liturgy on Shabbat and Yom Tov. The chant is written in the form of a Kali raga. The original prayer says "Shochen ad marom v'kadosh sh'mo" (God dwells forever, exalted and holy is God's name). Yofiyah's lyrics are a feminine version—"Shechina, shochenet ad marom v'kadosh" (Shechinah, indwelling [presence], exalted and holy [are you])—and might be interpreted as referring to the greatness of Shechinah that one can pray to, and thus as a congregational calling of the community to God. Thus, the role of Yofiyah or any other prayer leader is to pave the way for this call through chanting.

Yofiyah points to kabbalistic belief, saying that "hearing the sound of [the names of God and other sacred phrases], and the vibrational quality they establish when chanted, opens the small self, *mochin d'katnut*, to the spacious self, *mochin d'gadlut*, to allow you to experience the Divine" (2006). This bears some resemblance to the overall goal of dhirk, as described above. However, Yofiyah also writes that her chanting practice develops movements that connect these two perspectives: "Like the movement of breath, consciousness can shift fluidly, in and out, between the different levels of awareness" (ibid.). Yofiyah's chant "Hamakom Hazeh" (This place), released on *Kabbalah Kirtan* (2006), will be discussed as an example.

With regard to its musical type, this might be classified as a *nām* (name) *kīrtan* , which is, in special contexts, also referred to as an *akhand* (continuous) *kīrtan* (see Slawek 1988, 80). "Hamakom Hazeh" consists of a constant repetition of the various names of God that can be found in Jewish sacred texts. Typical Indian instruments, such as the harmonium, frame drum, tabla, oud, and *bansuri* flute accompany the antiphonal performance of the chant, led by Yofiyah. After a short instrumental introduction, Yofiyah's chant starts with a simple melodic phrase that is repeated over and over. In

FIGURE 4.12: "Shechinah" by Yofiyah. Words and music © 2009, Yofiyah Susan Deikman, all rights reserved BMI. www.kabbalahkirtan.com

the course of the chant, the tempo gets slightly faster, while the melody for a short time shifts to a second motif and reaches the climax of the chant, after which the whole process starts over again. Just as in an original *nām kīrtan,* the first melodic motif here is sung four times in a row, alternately by Yofiyah and the congregational chorus, before the chant proceeds to the next melodic motif (compare Slawek 1988, 80). As Slawek states, "the circular nature of rhythm . . . and of the melodies that are set to these rhythms is a central aspect of the psychological impact made by this [kīrtan] music" (ibid., 82). The circularity of the chants is also reflected in the typical circular seating arrangement of the performers (ibid.) that can also be found in Jewish kīrtan performances. Just as the power of kīrtan chanting is embedded in the actual sound (ibid., 84), the simplicity and hypnotic energy of the music of "Hamakom Hazeh," as well as the minimalism of words set into a call-and-response formula, quickly generate a feeling of spirituality and communal unity. In the traditional synagogue cantillation context, kabbalistic kirtan is just as original in conception and style as a minimalist piece of New Age music. Kabbalistic kirtan emphasizes the fundamental spiritual qualities of tone instead of the priority of the structure of sacred texts (see Marini 2003, 168–69), with their hierarchical chord functions. The meaning of the lyrics in Yofiyah's chants is also important.

In comparison to the lyrics of other feminist songwriters, Yofiyah's are "not overtly feminist, but at least not patriarchal," as she explained to me (interview March 2008). Referring to the reconceptualization of God in American Jewish feminism, Yofiyah's "Hamakom Hazeh" shows how God can be addressed without confining oneself to the patriarchal concept of the Lord. In the very short lyrics, several names of God—such as Adonai, Shekhinah, and Ya Rofe (the God who heals)—are mentioned:

> Hamakom, Hamakon, Hamakom Hazeh [the place, the place, this place].
> Adonai, Shechinah, Ya Rofe, Havayah [the Lord, Shechinah, the one who heals, Yaveh],
> El Elyon, Elohim [God most high, God].

Thus, Yofiyah offers the worshiper the choice to use whichever name of God he or she can most identify with. The rest of her lyrics consist of only two words that she has taken from Genesis 28:17: "And he was afraid, and said: How full of awe is this place [Hamakom hazeh]! This is none other than the house of God, and this is the gate of heaven." In a video of a performance of this chant (Yofiyah 2008), one can hear and see how Yofiyah set these two words to devotional chanting music. After giving some introductory explanations and personal interpretations of "hamakom hazeh," words that stand for the unnameable quality of God and how she experiences it, Yofiyah starts leading the chant. She begins by calling out the first words, to which the community responds immediately. Over a period of about seven minutes (the track on her recording takes twelve minutes and twenty-one seconds) the lyrics are repeated over and over.

When the camera turns around, the viewer can observe how the participants move their upper bodies back and forth or from side to side. Their eyes are closed. The energy of the participants is apparent in the flow of the chant and its rhythm, and thus the "consequent feeling of acting in synchrony with other people" (Clayton 2008, 142), also is an important element of feminist sacred music. As Martin Clayton notes, Ihde noted similar phenomena and wrote that to "listen is to be dramatically engaged in a bodily listening which 'participates' in the movement of the music" (quoted in Clayton 2008, 142).

However, while chanting, Yofiyah moves together with her worshiping community to another "place," one different from that with which the congregants are familiar, and this is what kavannah is about. In doing this, she offers the worshiping community a chance to add new ideas and interpretations to the meanings of the biblical words "Hamakom Hazeh." From Yofiyah's point of view, the words can be understood to mean the "Transcendent One," the "Immanent One," the "Healing One," the "One Who Is," the "High God," and finally God (Yofiyah 2006, 3). Like Ihde, who says that the divine is like an auditory experience (see above), Yofiyah states that the power of *Kabbalistic Kirtan* is to invoke the attributes of God, and thus to put the singer in direct relation with them (2004).

Yofiyah's chant is one of many examples that clearly communicate the feminist concept of the divine as the infinite and immediate presence in the world. She says: "'Hamakom Hazeh' (This very place) is an affirmation of God's presence in the world, as the world. There is nowhere to go to find God. God is here, now, and always. There is only this place, this moment, this breath. There is nowhere else to be. There is no one else to be" (ibid.). Thus, she aligns herself with the tradition of Jewish feminism in offering alternative views of the divine. During my fieldwork in Philadelphia in March 2008, I could experience the effect that kīrtan had on Jewish communities. When I attended another kabbalistic kirtan Shabbat service, I observed how just a few words of a traditional prayer text combined with kīrtan chanting engaged the most resistant congregants and evoked feelings of unity and spirituality that went far beyond the traditional recitation of one particular prayer.

One day during my fieldwork in Philadelphia in 2008, Raphael explained to me how to find the difference between a God who is the Lord and one who is Shekhinah, or the eternal. She told me that one should step in front of a mirror and, one at a time, write the different names of God on the mirror with lipstick. When I got back home, I conducted the experiment. By looking at myself and reading God's names, I found the name I could most identify with. The lesson I learned was that in comparison to normative Jewish prayer and sacred music, sacred singing in American Jewish feminism offers choices and opportunities. Furthermore, feminist Jewish songs are a form of prayer that fully recognizes women and their religious needs. Thus, they allow a reinterpretation of the traditional concept of Kol Isha as a symbol of women's voices freed from its original repression. By communicating different views of the divine, the songs give every worshiper a chance to find out what name or concept of God fits his or her own Jewish identity. At the same time, by drawing on popular music styles, feminist singer-songwriters make God real in relation to the worshipers' circumstances. The songs draw the worshiper into prayer and offer congregants a chance to engage their emotions. In doing so, the songs create a fulfilling and egalitarian religious experience that recognizes the worshipers' personal connections to prayer and to an image of God that is immanent.

DEFINING FEMINIST JEWISH MUSIC AS GENRE

The explanations and discussions above examined the historical, cultural, and political backgrounds of the emergence of feminist Jewish songwriting in the United States and showed how this feminist Jewish music is structured by content and sound and, thus, how the genre of feminist Jewish music developed since its emergence in the 1970s. This music cannot be defined as fitting in one genre or another; instead, as I showed above, it consists of a multicultural fusion of sounds. Thus, it has the same problems as so-called women's music, or what is more generally labeled as "music for women." Music for women is a highly controversial category, as the name does not describe a closed and homogeneous concept of a work of art. This is also true in the case of feminist Jewish music. Therefore, a classification according to merely aesthetic, formal, or technical aspects of feminist Jewish music is not possible. American feminist Jewish music as a genre has to be understood as a social practice, which can be defined only by factors such as authorship, performance context, content, intention, and the identity-establishing effect of the music, as well as by its overall function in Jewish religious contexts (see S. Ross 2009a).

However, this following section seeks to provide insights into individual understandings of this musical genre, summarizing the most crucial characteristics of feminist Jewish music. When I asked Shere how to define feminist Jewish music, she said:

> I don't know that I have a definition of Jewish feminist music. For me, it's more about listening to and supporting women making sacred Jewish music. While some of these women, like Geela Rayzel Raphael for example, whose music as midrash I think is brilliant, are explicitly feminist in the content of their music, other women are being radical simply because they are women making Jewish music. This act itself I think is a feminist act. Being a woman willing to create, share and record her music is a radical act, [particularly] in a Jewish context where liturgy has been so often (except for Tekhines [Yiddish prayers written for and by women], etc.) been dominated by men. . . . Among the women in the Kohenet program, which I co-lead, I see how powerfully women are affected by creating their own music, chants and liturgy. Particularly among the Kohenet women, there's a focus on feminine G!d language and grammar structure, not simply in English but in Hebrew as well. So when we pray together, we are often praying in Hebrew that is entirely in the feminine gender (e-mail interview February 2007).

While Shere's answer touches on most of the aspects mentioned above, such as authorship and performance context, as well as the intention behind the music and its effect on Jewish women, Raphael's answer to the same question ("what is feminist Jewish music?") points to the content of the music: "There is a theory by Linda Hirschhorn saying that music should not only address God; music itself is a spiritual round and a circle that carries feminist concepts and theology" (interview February 2007). The following general characteristics can be identified as defining feminist Jewish music.

Most of the characteristics are related to the music's content. A song is considered as feminist if it (1) uses feminist language (feminist Hebrew or any gender-neutral language), (2) uses feminist images (for example, gender-neutral terms for the divine, such as "the beloved"), and (3) addresses the feminist aspects of God (such as Shekhinah, the immanent God, or God's presence in the world and the community). Feminist Jewish songs also (4) portray the role of Jewish women in history and Jewish tradition, and (5) are related to specific Jewish women's rituals and experiences. The primary intention behind these songs is to give a voice to Jewish women, in the past as well as in the present.

In addition, new perspectives on Jewish liturgy and on a vision of what Judaism and the Jewish community might look like in the future are incorporated in the songs. As Raphael put it, "Jewish feminist music is meant to heal the past and to create the future" (interview February 2007). Those are criteria that are given in both versions of the *Jewish Feminist Songbook* (Elwell et al. 1992 and 1993). However, the examination of feminist Jewish music in this book has shown that songs addressing issues such as healing, social justice, tikkun olam, peace, ecofeminism, and multiculturalism in its broadest sense are also defined as feminist Jewish songs. The different forms of feminism of the singer-songwriters discussed in this book determine what themes are most commonly represented in their various repertoires.

My informants also told me that the music should be written in a way that can easily be sung by groups of untrained people; it should be limited in range and easy to master; its sound should be neither boring nor repetitive; and the music should match the lyrics (see, for example, Elwell et al. 1993). In addition, the mere act of writing and performing music is considered to be a feminist act, as most of the repertoire of synagogue music has been written by men. The style of feminist Jewish music, however, is determined by the musical conventions of the denomination of the singer-songwriter and by the influence of local musical cultures, or by the individual's interest in other musical cultures.

Finally, a general question arises: what role does this music play in contemporary Jewish feminism? The plurality of the Jewish feminist movement is apparent in the issues it addresses, such as gender equity, social justice, multiculturalism, and identity politics—all of which have been part of the content of feminist Jewish music since the beginning of the Jewish feminist movement. The major difference between the music of the early years of Jewish feminism (the 1960s and 1970s) and the music of today is that feminist Jewish music—and the political statements that it contains—is now more integrated into general Jewish worship and the cultural terrain of American Judaism.

Furthermore, popular culture and new media are increasingly used as ways to bring about social and religious change in today's Jewish feminism. In response to Judith Plaskow's (2009, 11) critique of the missing link between feminist theory or theology and feminist Jewish activism, I would say that feminist Jewish music is indeed a central site of feminist activism because music, and particularly chanting, has the power to forge a community while allowing its members to assert their individuality. Furthermore, it enables people to imagine a new Judaism in general, as well as alternative ways of Jewish worship (egalitarian or informed by feminism) in particular. In doing so, feminist Jewish music functions as an educational tool.

Finally, and most importantly, the variety of Jewish identities is to a large degree reflected in the sound—and, more precisely, in the diverse styles—of feminist Jewish music. This bears witness to the cross-cultural nature of American Judaism in general and contemporary Jewish feminism in particular. Feminist Jewish music not only keeps Judaism real in the age of globalization, but it also becomes a central site for exploring the key concepts of contemporary Jewish feminism. It should thus receive more attention in scholarly discourses.

Conclusion: Feminist Jewish Music

Balancing between Jewish Tradition and Feminist Innovation

> *It was the Jewish feminist movement in particular that inspired me to speak out on behalf of all girls and women who had been consigned to the balcony of synagogues for so many years. Jewish feminism with its insistence on, and permission to be an honest expression of one's deepest self without shame or inhibition helped me integrate my political and Jewish roots, made me determined to sing in Hebrew to all my audiences, Jewish and non-Jewish alike[,] and convinced me that it was time to bring social concerns back into my Jewish world—the concerns that had been so deeply ingrained in me by my years in the Labor Zionist movement. Using traditional Hebrew and original English texts, my music became my contribution to Midrash at a time when more and more women were reclaiming, rediscovering, recreating and inventing Midrash, liturgy, dances, poems and songs to add onto the vast wealth of Jewish texts.*
> E-mail interview with Linda Hirschhorn, July 2005.

As this study has shown, and as is apparent in Linda Hirschhorn's statement above, Jewish feminists singer-songwriter made significant improvements by strengthening the position of women in Judaism, yet they were aware that it would be impossible to ultimately make women equal to men on all levels and in all denominations of Judaism. They nevertheless chose to remain Jewish, to remain part of an inherently patriarchal religion. Consequently, there have been limits in the feminist transformation of Jewish liturgy, and the resistance to the feminization of the Jewish belief system and synagogue worship and its music did not come only from men. Furthermore, feminist Jewish women had to acknowledge to themselves that even the male-dominated and patriarchal sacred texts, liturgies, rituals, and cultural ideas that they sought to transform were still personally powerful and meaningful to them, and were moreover virtually inseparable from Jewish history (see, for example, Prell 2007, 10). Almost all of them were strongly attached to their religion, and Judaism and its religious traditions had long been an important part of their identity (see, for example, Ackelsberg 1986, 109–11). For the most part, the contradictions between their Judaism and their feminism became obvious with regard to the question of how to preserve Jewish tradition while simultaneously promoting religious, cultural, and political changes—which is also a key question in this study of feminist Jewish music.

The relationship of new Jewish music, including feminist Jewish music, to Jewish tradition is created through the use of traditional liturgical texts, as those establish continuity with the past. However, the employment of non-Jewish, and thus nonstandard, melodies creates a connection to the present and thus to the surrounding "superculture," as Jeffrey Summit calls it (1993, 52). The feminist Jewish songwriter Holy Taya Shere explained to me how she not only establishes a relationship to the present by the choice of her music, but also adds English and feminist-inspired translations of the original Hebrew text to her lyrics:

> I needed an accurate expression of my experience of G!d, and I needed language (and melody) to pray in that matched and was an appropriate vessel for my spiritual experience. I needed the earthy, divine feminine songs, to be wholly connected to these prayers. For this reason too, most of my chants . . . have both Hebrew and English sections. This is a reflection of my experience [of] the most powerful ways for me to pray. It is important to engage the prayers that my ancestors have been praying for so many years—the traditional Hebrew—as well as to [engage] prayer in English that reflects my heart-conversations [*sic*] with G!d. Most of my chants are a line or two of (traditional) Hebrew with a corresponding earthly, woman-honoring translation. (e-mail interview February 2007)

To further understand the relation between tradition and innovation, and thus how the political is actually performed in feminist Jewish music, the concept of discursive traditions[1] as introduced by the anthropologist Talal Asad seems to provide a fitting model. In "The Idea of an Anthropology of Islam" (2009), Asad more specifically defines the general concept of tradition by emphasizing the interrelatedness of and interactions among different coexisting traditions. Therefore, his concepts allow us to examine the interconnectedness of feminist Jewish theological discourses, Jewish liturgical music, and the function of other religious and cultural traditions, such as kīrtan. According to Asad, tradition is not a static concept, but a lively model that refers to an ongoing process of change. Thus, the path from scared feminist Jewish knowledge to a performed ritual and its music leads through multiple and continuing reconstructions of religious traditions on the basis of discursive debates, which "relate conceptually to *a past* (when the practice was instituted, and from which the knowledge of its point and proper performance has been transmitted) and *a future* (how the point of that practice can best be secured in the short or long term, or why it should be modified or abandoned), through *a present* (how it is linked to other practices, institutions, and social conditions)" (ibid., 14).

When we apply Asad's concept to the study of feminist Jewish music, the following factors become important: Previous studies of American Jewish music confine their explanations and analysis to the question of how American Jews, through the integration of American tunes with Jewish sacred texts, integrate the superculture and subculture. Thus, the discussion concerns to what extent someone uses the music as a tool to blend his or her American and Jewish identities and to create an "inclusive interlanguage . . . that facilitates broad participation" in Jewish worship and ritual (Summit 1993, 55).

In Summit's study (1993), two aspects of Asad's concept are emphasized—namely, the past (Hebrew text) and the present (American tunes), which become related through music. The main focus of feminist Jewish music, I argue, is on the future, and thus on how to incorporate feminist values into future structures of Judaism. Summit explains that American tunes are used only occasionally in a Simkhat Torah (Rejoicing in the law) ritual, and that use is not meant to become a tradition in the general service of the synagogue community he studied. Mixing liturgical and melodic codes as discussed by Summit and others nevertheless makes a political statement: Jews are culturally loyal to the American mainstream. In comparison to feminist Jewish music the use of American popular tunes alone is not necessarily meant to bring about a radical and lasting change (see, for example, Summit 1993, 52–57).

The establishment of a relationship of Jewish women to Jewish tradition, and thus to Jewish cultural and religious heritage, is of particular importance for Jewish women, as they have been for the most part excluded from participation in Jewish rituals. But this does not mean that they categorically had less of a connection to these rituals than men. As I discussed at length in chapter 3, feminist Jewish singer-songwriters draw their lyrics from traditional Jewish texts to establish a relationship between their songs and their religious, cultural, and historical heritage, and they set those texts to diverse modern and non-Jewish forms of music (as discussed in chapter 4). Thus, feminist Jewish music (understood as independent discursive tradition) follows the pattern of new Jewish music, as described in the introduction and chapter 4. I argue that the moment of performing the political in feminist Jewish music, and thus the moment of negotiating the relationship between Jewish tradition and feminist innovation and finding a balance between the two, is particularly realized in the expression of the future—and thus in the claim that an egalitarian Judaism inspired by feminism can eventually be created through music. To elaborate on this argument, I confine the following explanations to the question of to what extent feminist Jewish visions are reflected in the songwriters' choice of music itself, and I will give my impression of where the limits of feminist Jewish music used as a political tool are.

The songwriter Chana Rothman told me that "there are spiritual challenges in trying to create music which addresses relevant questions and feelings, using both the strength of tradition and also recognizing the need to 'update' and add voices which have been excluded" (e-mail interview September 2, 2008). The problem described by Rothman applies to all feminist Jewish music in the United States and raises the overall question of whether songwriters should imitate Jewish traditions or innovate. In their desire to produce a change in the Jewish religion, and thus to establish feminist Jewish principles in the Jewish liturgy, feminist Jews were trapped in the structure of traditional prayer and ritual just as feminist Jewish songwriters were caught in the traditions of standard cantorial music. Neither traditional liturgy nor synagogue music left room for feminist input. Accordingly, the mere imitation of established (male-defined) traditions by Jewish women failed to permanently transform synagogue worship. This caused Jewish feminists to search for innovative, rather than modified, musical traditions that could represent the themes and values of contemporary Jewish feminism.

Such a search, which Timothy Taylor (1993, 388) identified in the music of the feminist songwriter Pauline Oliveros, was closely tied to the question of identity. The choices of music by the feminist Jewish songwriters featured in this book were related not only to their identity as Americans and as Jews, but also to their identities as, for example, members of Reform Judaism, the Reconstructionist movement, or the Jewish Renewal movement. Thus, and acting on the premise that Jewish prayer does not belong to the cantor or the rabbi, but to the people (my paraphrase of Cantor Annie Bornstein's statement in Coppel 2003), Debbie Friedman stated: "I'm not interested at all in throwing away tradition, but I'm also not interested in throwing away all the numbers of people who can't relate and can't connect with the tradition" (my transcription of Coppel 2003).

It has been the main argument of this book that the transformation of the Jewish narratives and sacred text in lyrics alone has not been entirely effective, and that it must be followed by a transformation of Jewish prayer music to achieve long-lasting changes in the American Jewish liturgy. Thus, the rather unorthodox musical choices made by feminist Jewish songwriters (to use folk-rock, country, blues, and New Age sounds and practices such as Hindu devotional chanting) were not only meant to make their music sound contemporary, in comparison to the work of other American Jewish songwriters, but also to emphasize feminist values and visions that had been ignored, left out, hidden, or denied by Jewish tradition. As a consequence, the integration of a cultural fusion of sounds into the repertoire of feminist Jewish music worked only against the norms of classical synagogue music and worship, as it purposely challenged the traditional Jewish "aesthetic and commodification of music" (Taylor 1993, 391). And feminist Jewish music itself became very closely tied to the goal of creating community and meaningful religious experiences that included feminine religious insights and empowered people to engage in ritual and prayer.

Feminist Jewish music thus must be understood as the performance of feminist politics, as feminist values are not present in the classical cantorial repertoire. In contrast to feminist Jewish songs, cantorial music pays more attention to formal issues, such as nusach, than to the relationship of the composition to its larger social and religious context (see, for example,

Taylor 1993, 388). Rabbi Geela Rayzel Raphael stated: "I'm one [for] making sure the music is relevant and people can sing along and feel part of it, but I know that some folks just like the old tunes, [as] it makes them comfortable" (e-mail interview January 5, 2007). She remembers what one of her congregants once wrote to her: "I very much like some of the new music you've added, but I don't want to sing and clap and beat drums throughout service. What I want to do is pray. I want the solace and comfort of the Friday night prayer service. I enjoy the responsive readings. I enjoy the familiar melodies, and welcome the infusion of some of your lovely songs" (quoted in ibid.). Responding to her congregant's statement, Raphael told me: "They don't associate upbeat music with prayer—they like the soulful sound of traditional nusach. [But] the issue will be what will the next generation want or like? I'm only doing my part, which is to take advantage of my goddess given gifts to write music. How much of it will last now I don't know. I do try to balance things in my congregation to keep everyone happy, but left to my own devices I'd transform everything and really raise the roof!" (ibid.) As these comments show, the sound of feminist Jewish music is not always satisfying for all worshipers. But as a religiopolitical medium, and at least in some liberal Jewish and feminist contexts—that is, as a "site of audience participation and meaning" (Taylor 1993, 392)—feminist Jewish music makes a powerful statement. With regard to the criticism that feminist Jewish music lacks nusach, and also to the charge that feminist songwriters lack knowledge of *chazzanut* (cantorial performance), Friedman countered: "The word chazzan [cantor] means visionary, chazion is a vision. It's to be a visionary, it's to lead people . . . [to gain an] insight [into] themselves . . . , to help people find their way [to] insight" (my transcription of Coppel 2003) and thus to help them finding meaning in contemporary Judaism. Despite all the criticism, it can hardly be denied that feminist Jewish songwriters make traditional prayer and liturgy meaningful to all worshipers—men, women, lesbians, gays, and transgender people alike. And in doing so, they transform Jewish tradition into feminist visions of a future Judaism, which is communicated through their music.

In my work, I sought to develop the genre of American feminist Jewish music for the first time, making it accessible for further research. My primary focus has been on the creators of this music—on the feminist Jewish songwriters themselves—instead of on its recipients. Thus, I have primarily presented here the insider's, not the outsider's, perspective. In this regard, one crucial aspect of my fieldwork was the meaning of singing as an emotional and spiritual act in Jewish worship, which sheds new light on the issue of whether to revise tradition or innovate, as it refers to nonrational reasons (such as a worshiper's personal musical taste or associations with the tunes sung throughout synagogue services) for why new liturgical sounds are met with resistance or not.

Some of my interviewees, such as Rabbi Ari Cartun, expressed their sincere reservations about the transformation of the liturgical text and accepted with interest the new sounds introduced by feminist songwriters (interview February 2008). While some people ignored the feminist messages communicated by the songs that Raphael and Rothman sang (interviews with Raphael and Rothman, June 2008), a considerable number of congregants expressed their concerns not only about the musical style of feminist Jewish songs, but also about the presence of women leading prayer and song services. Cantor Naomi Hirsch told me that even when she sang traditional cantorial music, she met with resistance on part of the community. As classical cantorial music is only written for men, Hirsch reinterpreted the music so it could be sung in a woman's voice. Thus, as she told me, her approach to the music is "soft," meaning that the repertoire sounds softer when it is sung by a woman. She said some congregants complained that they could not sing along with her because her voice is "too high" (interview June 2008). Other feminist Jewish songwriters I interviewed reported similar experiences.

Although Jewish feminism has entered synagogue worship, the most resistance to feminist transformation seems to be about aspects of worship that engage spiritual or religious feelings, such as liturgical music. It seems that recipients of feminist Jewish music have different levels of tolerance for changes in music, compared to changes in women's role in leading worship. This topic is ripe for further research.

This analysis of feminist Jewish music has shown how Jewish women negotiate long-standing traditions and religious practices of the past, and those they want to see in the future, through the present—through sociopolitical discourses such as those of today's Jewish feminism. In particular, Plaskow's (1992) explanations of the realization of the feminist Jewish theological concepts of Torah, Israel, and God in the textual and musical structure of feminist Jewish songs revealed the arguments that feminist singer-songwriters have developed to legitimize their transformation of long-standing religious practice and to redefine what can and what cannot be considered Jewish liturgical music. Especially through the diversity of their music, feminist Jewish songwriters have redefined traditional synagogue music and have called attention to the fact that the value of liturgical music, no matter what it sounds like, is related to its time and context. However, what is important now is that feminist Jewish singer-songwriters have created new listening habits in the American Jewish synagogue, whose effects on the worshipers still need to be studied.

This emphasis on human decision making is exactly what Asad's concept of discursive traditions is about. Asad combines essentialist and relativistic perspectives on tradition, a combination that points beyond the controversial and disputed term "discourse." Unlike Michel Foucault's understanding of discourse (1981), Asad's concept allows us to consider nonverbal phenomena like emotions and religious experiences as discourse. Thus, his argument not only allows us to simultaneously examine the unity and diversity of feminist Jewish music, and to single out the various traditions merging within it—or, more precisely, how feminist Jewish theological discourses are processed within the music (for example, when asking about the relationship between text and music). It also allows us to regard music from a discourse-theoretical perspective not only as text, and to ask how music is experienced.

This study of feminist Jewish music has shown how feminist Jewish singer-songwriters in the United States perform feminist politics in Jewish liturgical music, and how new and future visions of Judaism and Jewish community are negotiated in music.

APPENDIX A: *A Note on Fieldwork*

From my perspective as a European ethnomusicologist, and thus as an outsider, I have tried to understand and present here the ideas and values of contemporary American Jewish feminism as represented in the music discussed in this book. Consequently, and because of the study's exploratory nature, an investigation of qualitative character in the form of a data triangulation was considered the appropriate research method (see Flick 2008). This consists of expert interviews, fieldwork (participation observation and narrative interviews), and document analysis (see Schütze 1977).

I was first exposed to the field of American feminist Jewish music in Europe. In 2003 and 2004, I was studying the music of Jewish women that is used in the context of the feminist Rosh Hodesh ritual for my master's degree, and I conducted fieldwork in a Rosh Hodesh group in Utrecht, the Netherlands. Through the songs that had been incorporated into the rituals of the Utrecht group, I got to know at least a few Rosh Hodesh songs written by American Jewish women such as Geela Rayzel Raphael, Linda Hirschhorn, Hanna Tiferet Siegel, and Shefa Gold.[1] Most of the other music used by the women in the Utrecht group was traditional Jewish music. In comparison, the songs written by American Jewish feminists spoke an overtly feminist language (see S. Ross 2004). Thus, my preliminary study of Jewish women's music used in the feminist Rosh Hodesh ritual provided not only a theoretical basis for this book, but it also provided me with my first contacts with feminist Jewish songwriters in the United States.

Once I had the names of some feminist Jewish songwriters in the United States, I was able to get the necessary contact information online. After my first e-mail interviews on Rosh Hodesh songs in 2003 and 2004, I stayed in contact with my informants until I began my doctoral research and fieldwork in October 2006. My choices of interviewees in the United States were determined by several criteria: first, the songwriters I interviewed had to consider themselves and their music as feminist Jewish; and second, their work had to be related to the focus of my research. I met some of my interviewees through others I had already interviewed, and met some only by chance. In addition to the data I collected in interviews, I also relied on written materials found in private archives, newspapers, and material on the Internet, as well as a range of audio and video recordings.

As I learned in several conversations, a large number of feminist Jewish songwriters are related to the Jewish Renewal movement. This motivated me to try to find other interviewees through ALEPH, the Alliance for Jewish Renewal. In January 2007 I put a call for interviewees in the organization's e-mail newsletter, and I got some positive responses and further contacts. Quite soon it became obvious that my informants were spread out geographically as well as denominationally. During my fieldwork between January and April 2007 and in February, April, and June 2008 in Philadelphia, New York City, Boston, San Francisco, and New Mexico, I conducted twenty-nine interviews, either in person or by e-mail or telephone. In addition, I conducted participant observation and attended several synagogue services, performances, and rituals.

One crucial issue in scholarly discourses about ethnographic fieldwork is the question of self-reflexivity and representation—that is, the analysis and interpretation of the data collected in the field, and how much this is influenced by the subjectivity of the researcher. This problem has been described as the "crisis of representation" (see, for example, Cooley and Barz 2008). I am well aware that fieldwork is the integration of "scholar, scholarship and life," and that I am, as an ethnomusicologist, also positioned as a "social actor" in the musical culture I studied (Cooley and Barz 2008, 4 and 5).

Given the interdependency of "scholar, scholarship and life," it was not always possible in my fieldwork for me to separate my roles as researcher and friend or to distance myself from the field. The loyalty I showed to feminist Jewish songwriters and their work, and vice versa—as well as the whole world of American Judaism that I was experiencing for the first time—occasionally made me forget that I was at work. In comparison to most ethnographers, I did not experience culture shock in the strict sense; rather, I embraced the new cultural terrain (the field) with curiosity and interest (see, for example, Koskoff 2001a, xiii; Nettl 2005, 184). Although I did not experience life in the United States as significantly different from the life I had been used to, the cultural sphere of American Judaism was new to me. However, the openness of the people I met made it fairly easy for me to enter and participate in their culture. Furthermore, my being female helped me establish contacts with American feminist Jewish songwriters. Nevertheless, I constantly had to identify myself as an ethnomusicologist. Whenever I visited a new Jewish community and attended its services, the rabbi (or whoever led service at that time), called me up to the bimah and asked me to introduce myself and to talk about my research project. The congregants got the chance to ask me questions and to observe me throughout services. This helped build their confidence in me and my research project, and their willingness to participate in it. Although I did this many times, I never got used to it. These moments always reminded me of the job I had to do, and pulled me back into objectivity. Going back and forth between Germany and America also helped me regain the necessary distance from the field, both literally and figuratively.

APPENDIX B: *The Source Materials*

In addition to the interviews I conducted throughout my research, the book draws on a small but valuable corpus of source materials ranging from manuscripts, both published and unpublished, to audio and video recordings. The most important part of this material came from the private archives of my informants, who had collections on Jewish feminism in general and feminist Jewish music in particular from the early 1980s to the present. Further important contacts during my research were with the Jewish Women's Archive in Brookline, Massachusetts, which is a nonprofit organization founded in 1995 whose mission is to discover, chronicle, and spread to a broad public the history of American Jewish women. The Jewish Women's Archive is not a physical repository but a virtual archive. Its rich resources, including primary sources, are thus accessible online and can be downloaded, at least in part. In addition to the archive, the library and the Department of Music of Harvard University proved useful, as both have very large collections on Jewish music, especially contemporary popular Jewish music such as the recordings of Debbie Friedman (see Dreyfus 2001). The libraries of the School of Sacred Music of the Hebrew Union College–Jewish Institute of Religion (HUC)[1] and of the Jewish Theological Seminary, both located in New York City, also have rich collections on Jewish music in general and cantorial music in particular. The ethnomusicologist Mark Kligman, back then at the HUC School of Sacred Music, provided me with an abundance of material on Debbie Friedman. Another important contact person was Judith Pinnolis, a librarian and musicologist at Brandeis University, in Waltham, Massachusetts. Pinnolis hosts the Jewish Music Web Center, which includes a section on the contributions of Jewish women to music and of women to Jewish music. She directed me to some rare source materials on Jewish women's music in the United States. A final and important contact point at Brandeis University was the Hadassah Brandeis Institute, which is a well-known research center for Jewish women's and Judaic studies.

At the time of my fieldwork no in-depth research on feminist Jewish music in the United States had been conducted, and thus there was no reliable corpus of resources to rely on. As a result, I will give a short description of the material I used for this study.

The written material on feminist Jewish music is rare and not always recognizable at first sight. Besides a rather disorganized pile of sheet music of thirty-four female composers and songwriters, most of the source material used in this study consisted of prayer books, Passover haggadot, and so-called ritual sheets. The latter are drafts and outlines of feminist Jewish rituals and services that show how the music is incorporated into the liturgy.

At first sight, the official prayer books of each denomination show how much the music of feminist Jews is already used and thus accepted in general synagogue service. The Reform movement, for example, did not publish a gender-neutral liturgy until 1993, which was meant only to supplement the movement's 1975 prayer book, *Gates of Justice*. In the 2007 siddur of the Reform movement, *Mishkan T'filah*, changes in the Hebrew prayer texts were limited to the addition of the names of the matriarchs to liturgical references to the patriarchs (Goldman 2007, 124). As Karla Goldman explains, some people have been uncomfortable about even those revisions, regarding them as too awkward and radical. In contrast, Friedman's tunes have naturally been included in the prayer book. As the cantor Alane Katzew told me, Friedman's songs are already considered a traditional part of the Reform prayer book and songbook (interview February 2007).

However, the official prayer books of American Judaism's four denominations are rather unimportant in any attempt to understand the nature and use of feminist Jewish music. Far more profitable source texts that reflect the use of feminist Jewish music are feminist Passover haggadot written and compiled for women's seders (see, for example, Elwell and Weisberg 2002; Moise and Schwartz 2002). Most of these feminist haggadot are for informal women's seders and reflect the roles of women like the prophetess Miriam in the Passover story (in contrast to traditional Passover haggadot). In addition to the Passover story, which is mostly rewritten from a feminist perspective, the feminist haggadot contain drafts of an alternative Passover ritual that consists mostly of singing and dancing. The songs used at women's seders, such as the many different songs about Miriam written by various feminist Jewish songwriters, are discussed in chapters 3 and 4.

In the same category of source materials are the ritual sheets. In addition to using the official prayer book of their denomination, rabbis and cantors, as well as lay leaders, often compile their own drafts for synagogue services, as supplements to the siddur or as independent ritual sheets. Ritual sheets are often compiled for special services, such as healing services and folk-rock Shabbat services. Traditional sacred texts and resources do not offer any models for those kinds of services. The latter point is especially significant in regard to feminist Jewish rituals and women's services. I found a considerable amount of material compiled for the Rosh Hodesh ritual, which is by far the most popular feminist ceremony, as well as sheets on other rituals, such as the 1999 "Shabbat Shira: Biblical Women—Our Spirit Guides" edited by Rabbi Raphael. This special Shabbat ritual was devoted to the worship, study, and celebration of Jewish womanhood. In the sheet Raphael included some of her original songs as part of a redefined Shabbat service. The website Ritualwell.org (Ritualwell 2015a) offers extensive sources for innovative, contemporary Jewish rituals. It also offers a unique and very important platform feminist Jewish songwriters can use to share their songs. The website has sections devoted to rituals for life cycles, holidays, Shabbat, and daily life, as well as to music and liturgical melodies.

The most important discovery I made, however, is the *Jewish Feminist Songbook* (Elwell et al. 1992 and 1993), a project initiated by Rabbi Geela Rayzel Raphael, Linda Hirschhorn, Shelley Mann, Rabbi Sue Levi Elwell, and the cantor Aviva Rosenbloom, who wanted to publish a collection of feminist Jewish music. Besides sheet music, drafts of the songbook concept, and notes from possible publishers, the material also includes personal communications between the musicians, such as letters, postcards, and printed e-mails. The particular value of this corpus of material is that it gives insight into a unique project conducted between 1989 and 1994, in which the most relevant actors on the feminist Jewish music scene were involved. Given the state of technology at that time, it is amazing that this project got as far as it did. The material contains the songbook's mission statement, information about the background of the project and the selection criteria for what was considered to be feminist Jewish music, notes on the possible target audience, biographical information about the composers and contributors, and information about the expenses and funding of the project. All this is important information for future analysis of feminist Jewish music.

Last but not least, the corpus of my research materials included audio and video recordings. The larger part of this category of source material consists of CD albums of feminist Jewish songwriters—both their own productions, as well as professional productions distributed by Jewish music publishers—most of which were released between the early 1980s and the present. I also found in private archives tape recordings made by my informants that reflect the great variety of feminist Jewish music, in terms both of content and of musical style.[2] Finally, for further analyses of the music, I used Ann Coppel's (2003) documentary about Friedman, *A Journey of Spirit*, and several private video recordings of performances of some of my informants available on the website YouTube.com.

APPENDIX C: *A List of Selected Feminist Jewish Songs*

The following list contains a selection of feminist Jewish songs classified into different categories. Each category represents one of the major themes of Jewish feminism as well as the ritual and liturgical contexts to which feminist Jewish singer-songwriters have contributed their songs.

WOMEN AND JEWISH HISTORY

(Songs reflecting women's activism and/or presence in the history of Jewish life and learning)

"Behind the Mechitzah" (Shefa Gold)
"Donia Gracia" (Geela Rayzel Raphael)
"Each of Us" (Marsha Attie)
"Each of Us Has a Name" (Marcia Attie)
"No More Big Daddy" (Shefa Gold)
"Our Cantor" (Sylvia F. Goldstein)
"Women of the Wall" (Sylvia F. Goldstein)

SONGS ABOUT WOMEN OF THE TANACH

(Midrashic songs reflecting the lives, feelings, actions and concerns of women of the Torah and other Jewish sacred literature and lore)

The Matriachs

"Balancing Act" (Terry Horowitz)
"Café Forever" (Linda Baer)
"Eshet Chayil" (Judith Tellerman)
"Judith" (Judith Tellerman)
"Leah" (Margot Stein)
"Lullabies for Moshe / Yocheved Song" (Linda Baer)
"Ode to the Matriarchs" (Aviva Rosenbloom and Savina Teubal)
"Rachel and Leah" (Hannah Spiro)
"Sarah and Hagar" (Linda Hirschhorn)
"Song of Ruth" (Linda Baer)

Miriam the Prophetess
"The Ballade of Miriam's Well" (Penina Adelman and Suri Levow Krieger)
"How Did We Know? (Matia Rania Angelou)
"Miriam" (Laura Berkson)
"Miriam" (Elaine Moise)
"Miriam" (Geela Rayzel Raphael)
"Miriam Haneviyah" (Leila Gal Berner)
"Miriam's Song" (Debbie Friedman)
"Miriam's Slow Snake Dance by the Riverside" (Linda Hirschhorn)
"Song of Miriam" (Jeff Marder)
"Va'tikakh Miryam Ha'Niveah" (Marsha Dubrow)

Other Women of the Tanach
"A Web of Women" (Jack Gabriel)
"Al Tif Givi" (Terry Horowitz)
"Bat Yiftach" (Geela Rayzel Raphael)
"Batya" (Geela Rayzel Raphael)
"Couldn't Do It without You" (Juliet Spitzer)
"Daughters Dancing" (Geela Rayzel Raphael)
"Devorah" (Geela Rayzel Raphael)
"Devorah's Song" (Debbie Friedman and Tamara Ruth Cohen)
"Don't You Sit There Weepin' No More" (Judy Kummer)
"Judith" (Geela Rayzel Raphael)
"Kumi" (Linda Hirschhorn)
"Lech Na" (Geela Rayzel Raphael)
"Lilith" (Elizabeth Swados)
"Masquerade" (Benjamin Newman)
"Naomi" (Beth Sass)
"Ritzpah" (Geela Rayzel Raphael)
"She Said No" (MiRaJ)
"Shifrah and Puah" (Geela Rayzel Raphael)
"Tamar" (Geela Rayzel Raphael)
"Tzlophanit" (Geela Rayzel Raphael)
"Who Were the Women?" (Geela Rayzel Raphael)
"Yiftach's Daughter" (Batsheva Capek)

SONGS ABOUT FEMINIST RITUALS AND RITES OF PASSAGE

(Songs about and/or for women's physical changes, feelings, issues, rites of passage, and so forth)

Rites of Passage

"Daughter of Mine" (Beth Hamon)
"Daughter of Mitzvah" (Geela Rayzel Raphael and Simcha Paull Raphael)
"Mikvah Song" (Juliet Spitzer)
"Priestess Blessing" (Hanna Tiferet Siegel)
"Simchat Hochma" (Geela Rayzel Raphael)
"Weaning Song" (Margot Stein)
"Welcome Home" (Robbi Sherwin)
"To Ruth, Love Naomi" (Judy Kummer)
"Y'varechecha: Priestly Blessing" (Geela Rayzel Raphael)

Healing Songs

"Ana Ayl Na" (Hanna Tiferet Siegel)
"Ana El Na" (Geela Rayzel Raphael)
"Eyl Na R'fah Na La" (Nancy Abraham Talo)
"For Healing" (Robbi Sherwin and Steve Brodsky)
"Heal Me, Oh My God" (Andrea Beth Damsky)
"Help Us Heal" (Judy Kaplan Ginzberg)
"Lisabeth's Mi Shebeirach" (Lisabeth Kaplan)
"Misheberach" (Debbie Friedman)
"Or Hadash" (Hanna Tiferet Siegel)
"The Water in the Well" (Debbie Friedman and Tamara Ruth Cohen)
"Waters of Healing" (Shohama Harris Wiener)

Rosh Chodesh

"Birkat Halevana—Season of the Moon" (Debbie Friedman and Tamara Ruth Cohen)
"Blessing for the New Month" (Elaine Moise)
"Hachodesh Hazeh—Rosh Chodesh Song" (Hanna Tiferet Siegel)
"In the Dark Rays of the Moon" (Shefa Gold)
"Minyan of Women" (Margot Stein)
"Red Moon Magic" (Geela Rayzel Raphael)
"Rosh Hodesh Blessing" (Carol Boyd Leon)

"Rosh Chodesh Moon" (Geela Rayzel Raphael)
"Rosh Hodesh Song" (Orit Perlman)
"Women Gathering Round" (Linda Hirschhorn)

OTHER JEWISH LITURGICAL SONGS

(Songs promoting women's inclusion and gender equality in the Jewish liturgy, as might be appropriate for siddurim, machzorim, haggadot, and use in festivals and on holidays and new sacred days such as Yom HaShoah and Yom HaZikaron)

Shabbat
"Eishet Chayil mi Yimtza" (Fran Avni)
"Eyshet Chayil" (Rosalind Glazer)
"Gather In" (Juliet Spitzer)
"Hadlakat Neyrot Shabbat" (Marcia Falk and Linda Hirschhorn)
"Ilu Finu" (Linda Hirschhorn)
"L'cha Dodi" (Elaine Moise)
"L'khu, Reyot V'rey'im" (Fran Avni and Linda Hirschhorn)
"Mi Chamocha" (Hannah Spiro)
"Moving into Shabbos Time" (Geela Rayzel Raphael)
"Rock to the Rock" (Geela Rayzel Raphael)
"Shama Vatismach Tsiyon" (Linda Hirschhorn)
"Shama Vatismach Tsiyon" (Geela Rayzel Raphael)
"Sing Praises" (Marge Eisenman)
"Woman of Valor" (Juliet Spitzer)

Prayers, Blessings, and Jewish Holidays
"And You Shall Teach Your Children" (Hanna Tiferet Siegel)
"As We Bless" (Faith Rogow)
"Birkat HaChodesh" (Juliet Spitzer)
"Birkat Hagomel" (Aviva Rosenbloom)
"Blessing for Children" (Linda Hirschhorn)
"Dayenu" (Holy Taya Shere)
"Eden Once Again" (Margot Stein)
"Elohai Neshamah" (Naomi Less and Glenn Grossman)
"Etz Chayim" (Penina Adelman)
"Hameichina" (Ri J. Turner)

"Hochmot Nashim" (Juliet Spitzer)
"I Remember" (Shoshana Jedwab)
"Kosi Revaya" (Nancy Abraham Talo)
"Light and Dark" (Margot Stein)
"Ma'arivah" (Holy Taya Shere)
"Mah Tovu with Four Mothers" (Abbe Lyons)
"Nivarech" (Margot Stein)
"Sukkat Song" (Alan Scott Bachman)
"Welcome Home" (Robbi Sherwin)
"Winter Lights" (Elaine Moise)

Shechinah Songs and Songs Using Gender-Neutral God-Language
"Call to Her" (Juliet Spitzer)
"Elohim" (Yofiyah)
"Holy Mother, Shechinah Soul" (Geela Rayzel Raphael)
"Holy Shechinah: Ruach Hamidbar" (Alan Scott Bachman)
"In the Garden of Shechinah" (Hanna Tiferet Siegel)
"Invocation of Shechinah" (Elaine Moise)
"Jerusalem Dream Vision" (Geela Rayzel Raphael)
"The Majesty of Nurture" (Shefa Gold)
"My Light and My Salvation" (Geela Rayzel Raphael)
"Olamama" (Hanna Tiferet Siegel)
"Psalm 130" (Juliet Spitzer)
"Shechinah" (Yofiyah)
"Shechina Nigun" (Aviva Rosenbloom)
"Shechinah B'rucha At" (Alan Scott Bachman)
"Shechinah Coming" (Geela Rayzel Raphael)
"Shechinah, My Sister in the Wind" (Geela Rayzel Raphael)
"Shechinah Song" (Shayndl Kahn)
"Under the Wings" (Shefa Gold)
"Under the Wings of Shechinah" (Lisa Levine)
"Va'Anu Matzanu" (Penina Adelman)
"The Ways of a Woman" (Hanna Tiferet Siegel)

MISCELLANEOUS

(Songs reflecting issues of difference in Jewish life, such as race, ethnicity, class, and sexual orientation, and cultural groups such as Sephardi, Ashkenazi, Mizrachi, Beta Yisroel, and Jews from India)

"Aidel at Heart" (Leslie Ginsparg Klein)
"Ana" (Chana Rothman)
"Angels Carry You" (Geela Rayzel Raphael)
"Bat Adama—Kol She-re'ha" (Suri Levow Krieger)
"Battle of the Bulge" (Geela Rayzel Raphael)
"Damn Little Yiddish Folksong" (Batsheva Capek)
"Elohai, Netzor" (Leila Gal-Berner)
"Hear Our Voices" (Debbie Friedman)
"I Watched the Temple Fall" (The Shondes)
"Isaac and Ishmael" (Leila Gal-Berner)
"Jewish Lesbian" (Abbe Lyons)
"Kol Netivoteinu Shalom" (Aviva Rosenbloom)
"Meshuga'at—Crazy" (Glenn Grossman and Naomi Less)
"Mishkan" (Suri Levow Krieger)
"More Than One Way" (Chana Rothman)
"Rani V'Simchi" (Shefa Gold)
"She Is a Tree of Life" (MiRaJ)
"Shemesh Olah" (Leila Gal Berner)
"Sister" (Holy Taya Shere)
"Tefilah Atikah" (Sariel Beckenstein)
"V'Ahavta" (Hanna Tiferet Siegel)
"W'ana Feda D'al Umi: Song of Thanks from Daughter to Mother" (a Yemenite woman's song collected by Orit Perlman in 2002, as sung by Gila Bashari)

NOTES

INTRODUCTION

1. For further information about my fieldwork, see Appendix A. For information about the source materials used in this study, see Appendix B.

2. Scholars other than Koskoff who have considered the issue of gender in Jewish music scholarship include Judith Cohen, with her work on Judeo-Spanish wedding songs and women's role in Judeo-Spanish song traditions (1997). See also Heskes 1992; Shelemay 2009. In addition, some work has been done on Jewish women's songs in Kerala, India. See, for example, Johnson 2000.

3. The mainstream women's movement in America is usually divided into three waves. The first wave of feminism refers to a period of activity from the late nineteenth century to the early twentieth century in the United States and the United Kingdom. First-wave feminism was also linked to the abolitionist movement, but white women primarily focused on gaining political power, including the right to vote. The second wave of American feminism that arose out of the civil rights and antiwar movements of the twentieth century lasted from the mid-1960s through the 1980s. It addressed various primarily unofficial inequalities, such as women's second-class status in private and public contexts. Thus, the movement was split into different feminisms, including African American feminism, lesbian feminism, liberal feminism, and social feminism. Third-wave feminism is said to have begun in the early 1990s. Although it is mainly led and shaped by concerns of women ages 20–30, it can be understood as addressing the issues of the first and second waves as well as recent inequalities faced by women (see S. Ross 2009b, 43).

4. Activists in the Black Power Movement argued that integration was nearly impossible due to the impenetrable barriers of the American racial state and that true integration required cultural genocide (ibid.; see also Glanz 1977, 121).

5. The unofficial intellectual organ of the new Jewish counterculture became *Response* magazine, one of the most interesting alternative Jewish journals of the time (see Prell 2006, 165–66; Novak 2004, 284).

6. The Jewish Baby Boomers were middle-class Jews born between 1945 and 1965, who had been raised in relative affluence and with high expectations for themselves. They differed significantly from the members of their parents' generation because the experience of the Holocaust, the founding of the state of Israel, and anti-semitism played less of a role in their lives than in their parents' lives. Thus, the

younger generation of American Jews was not inclined to base its identity on those experiences.

7. A pioneer in developing and practicing havurah-style worship was the Havurat Shalom Community Seminary in Somerville, Massachusetts (see, for example, Sarna 2004, 319–22).

8. The revival turned political in the early 1960s with the rise of the New Left and the civil rights movement. For example, the Kingston Trio began to record satirical pieces and antiwar songs. Concurrently, a younger generation of songwriters armed themselves with guitars. What had originally been a southern tradition moved north, when singer-songwriters such as Bob Dylan and Phil Ochs started to learn folk musical traditions and created and performed songs protesting racism, the arms race, and middle-class conformity. With this development came a shift in both the meaning and the performance style and context of folk music (see, for example, Rodnitzky 1999, 56).

9. His first record album, released in 1959, was a mixture of traditional Hasidic and popular American folk music (see, for example, Sarna 2004, 346). These Hasidic-style songs soon became popular in the United States. Performed at Hasidic song festivals that came to America from Israel in the late 1960s and early 1970s, the songs were sung by well-known singers who, like the songs themselves, were not strictly Hasidic.

10. According to Jeff Klepper, as he stated in Ann Coppel's documentary (2003), American neo-Hasidic Orthodox folk music sounded Jewish. In the context of the havurah movement's evocation of previous times that were idealized and romanticized, and as a way to separate the movement from an increasingly secular American culture (see, for example, Prell 2006, 160 and 167), the turn to Hasidic music styles and remembering Eastern European musical aesthetics were considered as authentically Jewish, and consequently the best way to connect American Jews to their history and religion. Thus, the American folk music revival ended up influencing the Jewish music scene in what Alan Lomax referred to as the sense of rediscovering traditional music (2003; see also Sweers 2005, 25–29).

11. See the tractate on niddah in *Talmud Bavli*, *Talmud Yerushalmi*, and *Shulkhan Arukh*—the sixteenth-century codification of Jewish law written by Rabbi Yosef ben Karo—which include a number of laws and regulations concerning the behavior of a menstruating woman. What are known as the women's commandments are niddah and two other commandments: *challah* (separating a portion of dough), and *nerot* (candle lighting on Friday night, the Shabbat eve). Those mitzvahs are performed outside the synagogue, in the private sphere (see, for example, Koskoff 1987, 216).

12. Traditional Judaism teaches that God's message (the passing down of the Torah to Moses) was primarily addressed to men and can thus be conveyed only by men. At the moment when he received the Torah at Mount Sinai, Moses was talking only to the male members of the community ("And he said unto the people: Be ready against the third day; do not near a woman" [2 Moses 19:15]; see also Sered 1992, 16).

13. Arlene Agus's "This Month Is For You" (reprinted in an edited volume in 1976) is the first documentation of a feminist Rosh Hodesh ceremony. Since the publication of that article, Jewish women have become increasingly engaged in the rediscovery and study of the new moon festival. For a further discussion on Rosh Hodesh as a feminist Jewish ritual, see Adelman 1990; Agus 1996; Berrin 1996.

14. This dichotomy determined that the female, or the world of women, was associated with the *gashmiut* (the corporeal world) and is thus separated from the *ruhniut* (the spiritual world), which is for men only (see Alpert 1991, 67; Lefkovitz and Shapiro 2005, 104).

15. Starhawk, born in 1951 as Miriam Simos, was raised in a Jewish household. She is an internationally known American activist in the peace, women's, and environmental movements. She is also one of the foremost popular voices of ecofeminism and—as one of the most influential advocates of witchcraft as a goddess religion (Wicca)—is known for her writings on paganism and witchcraft as goddess religion (see, for example, Starhawk 1979). Starhawk describes herself as a witch (see, for example, Marini 2003, 170).

16. Other American scholars, from both Reform (R. Adler 1998) and Reconstructionist Judaism (Alpert 1998), and Israeli feminist scholars (see, for example, T. Ross 2004) followed Plaskow and provided further feminist and innovative approaches to Judaism and its theology (see D. Berman 2009, 12–13; Millen 2007, 27).

17. The issue of hierarchy—more precisely, of hierarchical dualism—is closely connected to the feminist reconceptualization of God. The traditional concept of God is seen as the paradigm of hierarchical dualism. Dichotomies like spiritual or material, sacred or profane, and mind or body are not only equated with the dichotomy of men or women but also define what in Jewish thought and religious praxis is considered sacred and what not. These associations point to a further fundamental tension between normative Judaism and feminism—namely, the traditional Jewish understanding of holiness as separation, in contrast to the feminist emphasis on relationships (see Plaskow 1994, 69, and 1996, 105).

18. In terms of the language of prayer, the poet and liturgist Marcia Falk made an important contribution to feminist Jewish liturgy. In *The Book of Blessings*

(1999)—a collection of reworked Jewish blessings for Shabbat, Rosh Hodesh, and daily life—Falk developed her notion of an immanent God and thus of an inclusive monotheism. In this book, Falk also offered original prayers as well as English translations of poems written by Jewish women in Hebrew or Yiddish that were intended to serve as alternatives to the patriarchal nature of traditional Jewish prayers and that were later set to music by feminist Jewish songwriters. Furthermore, Falk presents her commentaries on Jewish liturgy and explains how each prayer in her book is related to the traditional liturgy.

19. For a detailed description of her "new theology of sexuality," see Plaskow 1992, 234.

20. Interview with Elwell, March 2008.

21. This prohibition is not restricted to Judaism only. In Christianity Paul of Tarsus said that women should be silent during a liturgical ceremony (1 Corinthians 14:33–36). Referring to this prohibition, Irene Heskes states: "this parallel in religious practice proved highly significant in the developing rules governing gender and religious expression" (1994, 327).

22. For example, Michele Garner, who is known as the Rockin' Rebbetzin and who hosts "The Kol Isha Show" on WSIA, in Staten Island, New York, had to deal with the halakhic problem of men listening to women's music. Garner's radio show is the first (and so far the only) one to play Jewish female vocalists and musicians' spiritual songs. It is thus also where religious Jewish women's musical talent can be heard over the airwaves. Consequently, for Orthodox men, Garner's show poses a problem. Together with a local rabbi, Garner, who is a modern Orthodox woman, solved the problem by making an announcement at the beginning of her show, saying that she is going to play women's music now for the next two hours. That gives men the choice of listening or turning the radio off (the halakhic option). In addition, Garner argues that men do not see the women singing but only listen to them (interview with Garner, February 2007).

23. A passage in the Talmud can be used to support this: "The Rabbanan taught: anyone can be numbered among the seven [called to the Torah on Shabbat], even a minor, even a woman. But the Sages said that we do not call a woman to the Torah because of *Kevod HaTzibur* (the dignity of the congregation)" (Megillah 23a).

24. The following explanations of Rosh Hodesh are based on the research and fieldwork I conducted in 2003–4.

25. The Hebrew word *kavannah* describes the "conscious intention" when praying. According to Hasidic belief, prayers are not bound to a certain place but have to be spoken with kavannah to connect man and God. Some zaddikim and their

followers consider music and singing in this context more important than mere prayer (see, for example, Hajdu and Mazor 1971, 7:1421)

26. For detailed discussions of the role of popular culture and its relationship to third-wave feminism, which focuses on so-called girl culture, nonacademic and autobiographical texts, zines, and websites that emerged on the feminist scene from the mid-1990s on and which refashioned contemporary feminism, see, for example, Heywood (2006), Heywood and Drake (1997), and Munford (2004, 142).

1. WHO SINGS UNTO GOD? PIONEER FEMINIST JEWISH SINGER-SONGWRITERS IN THE UNITED STATES

1. Judah Cohen (2006a), Mark Kligman (2001b), and Jeffrey Summit (2000), demonstrate that there are differences in the musical conventions among the Jewish movements in the United States (Orthodox, Conservative, Reform, Reconstructionist, and Jewish Renewal), which can be manifested in their openness to musical innovations. Singing in synagogue worship marks who the members of a community are (for example, are they Reform or Orthodox Jews?) and what they believe as Jews. Each denomination developed its own rules and rationales for the incorporation of music into Jewish liturgy, determining what sounds were considered appropriate for Jewish worship (see, for example, Judah Cohen 2006a, 100–1; Summit 2000, 33).

2. In Reform Judaism, the cantorial repertoire that is taught at Reform cantorial schools is split between the traditional and Reform repertoire (Judah Cohen 2006a, 102).

3. The first Coalition for the Advancement of Jewish Education conference began on August 29, 1976 (Jewish Women's Archive 2015).

4. SWEJS is "Jews" spelled backward.

5. This song was recorded and released in 1984 under the title "Miriam." It is one of Raphael's most popular songs and probably set the stage for other songs on Miriam written by many other songwriters some years later (see G. Raphael 1998, 1).

6. Raphael is the mother of Yigdal and Hallel Raphael. Her husband, Simcha Raphael, is a psychotherapist, rabbinical pastor, spiritual director at the Reconstructionist Rabbinical College, and the author of *Jewish Views of the Afterlife* (2009).

7. According to my field notes, MiRaJ must have been founded in 1994.

8. For example, the song was interpreted and performed by the Or Hadash Makhaylah choir, directed by Barry W. Brian, at the Forty-Fourth Annual Delaware Valley Jewish Choral Festival at Gratz College, in Melrose Park, Pennsylvania, on June 5, 2008.

9. All three members of MiRaJ had a bat mitzvah, and in some cases their bat mitzvah was the first in the synagogues of their childhood. However, it is important to note that their bat mitzvahs took place on a Friday night, when the congregation does not read from the Torah. Boys usually have their bar mitzvahs on a Saturday morning, so that they can be called to read from the Torah (interview with MiRaJ March 2008).

10. The Arabic word *dhikr* means remembrance and describes the Sufi practice of repeating the name of God or any phrase from the Qur'an to become aware of God (Kamenetz 1997, 334, note 2).

11. I conducted this interview as part of my work as an online editor at the Jewish women's magazine *Aviva-Berlin*, which published the interview (S. Ross 2005).

12. At the age of forty-eight and after having served as a cantorial soloist at Kehilla Community Synagogue in Berkeley for over fifteen years, Linda Hirschhorn was officially invited to be a member of the cantor's assembly, the international association of Conservative cantors in the United States. Since 1988, she has been the cantor of Temple Beth Shalom in San Leandro, California (see Hirschhorn n.d.a).

2. THE FEMINIST JEWISH MUSIC SCENE

1. The percentages are problematic. Even though the American Jewish Data Bank has sponsored several nationwide population studies, the data about the size and character of the Jewish population in the United States remain controversial (Sarna 2004, 356). There are several reasons for this. First, there is no national Jewish census. Second, in demographical terms American Jews are considered to be a rare population, and one that is declining. Third, factors like intermarriage, conversion, and differing ways of self-identification (for example, does somebody consider him- or herself Jewish in terms of religion, ethnicity, or culture?) make an exact evaluation of the core Jewish population in the United States difficult (see ibid., 357; Sheskin and Dashefsky 2013).

2. Brier is an Israeli-born psychologist, an experienced spiritual facilitator, and an accomplished musician who has recorded a number of albums. She has taught at a variety of academic, holistic, and Jewish organizations, including Temple University; the Kripalu Center for Yoga, Health, and Wellness; and Gratz College. She is also a Reconstructionist rabbi with an MA in Jewish studies from the Reconstructionist Rabbinical College and an MA in psychology from West Chester University (Brier n.d.).

3. Zevit has experience in spiritual leadership, human relations training, interactive arts, and teaching. He has been a consultant for institutions and faith commu-

nities across North America and has taught on a variety of Jewish themes at Temple University. In addition he performs on tours original music from his recorded repertoire. Zevit is a senior consultant at and director of outreach and external affiliations for the Jewish Reconstructionist Federation (Mishkan Shalom n.d.).

4. Klotz is a spiritual director at the Reconstructionist Rabbinical College and a founding member of *Shabbat Unplugged*. She is also on the faculty of the Institute for Jewish Spirituality and a mentor with the Morei Derekh Program in Jewish Spiritual Direction. She codirects the Yoga and Jewish Spirituality Training Institute at Elat Chayyim Jewish Spiritual Retreat Center (Shechinah 2012b).

5. Becker-Klein is a graduate of the Reconstructionist Rabbinical College and has been performing and writing contemporary Jewish music since 1990. His music is influenced by bluegrass, folk, rock, klezmer, and other so-called world music. He is currently director of Jewish life and education at the Springfield Jewish Community Center in Springfield, Massachusetts. Among other things, he was assistant editor of the *High Holy Day Prayerbook*, published by the Reconstructionist Press. Becker-Klein's music and songwriting embrace the Jewish Reconstructionist spirit by bringing new melodies and contemporary meaning to ancient sentiments and Jewish life (Shechinah 2012b).

6. For further information on the band Shabbat Unplugged/Havdalah Live, see Shechinah 2012b.

7. Harmoniyah was founded as a grass-roots movement by musicians attending the Biennial Convention of the Jewish Reconstructionist Federation in 2004. It serves as a network for musicians throughout the Reconstructionist movement. Thus, the main goals of the organization are to create a list-serve and online music catalogue, to organize local and national music gatherings, and to provide continuing leadership to Jewish communities. In 2009, Stein and Zevit were members of the organization's Steering Committee (see Jewish Reconstructionist Communities n.d.).

8. For a further discussion of Ritualwell.org, see Lefkovitz and Shapiro 2005.

9. According to Raphael, in an unpublished manuscript in my possession (Raphael 1993).

10. Weissler lists three *kallot* (plural of kallah) at which the ritual took place: Berkeley, California; Bryn Mawr, Pennsylvania; and Fort Collins, Colorado (2006, 69).

11. At a time when very few women were ordained as rabbis, the title eshet hazon was thus understood as a woman's equivalent to rabbinic ordination (see Weissler 2006, 68).

12. As Tiferet Siegel's eshet hazon ceremony was held during Shavuot, the ketubah is meant to symbolize this feast, "in which the people of Israel are said to 'marry' the Torah at Sinai" (Weissler 2006, 67).

13. The Hebrew phrase quoted here refers to Genesis 31:35: "And she [Rachel] said to her father: 'Let not my lord be angry that I cannot rise up before thee; for the manner of women is upon me (ani b'derech nashim).' "

14. For a detailed description of the eshet hazon ceremony at the 2005 ALEPH kallah, see Weissler 2006.

15. The Jewish Feminist Center in Los Angeles was founded in 1991 and is now defunct.

16. In 1992, Yona Jacobovitz, Nancy Sigel, Mindy Sufski, Ann Lemor, and Riva Schertzman were members of this band (according to a letter from Raphael to Hirschhorn now in my possession).

17. The proposal written by Raphael and Mann is part of a loose-leaf-collection I received from Raphael during my fieldwork. It contains notions on how to teach and convey the idea of feminist Jewish music to an interested audience. No date is given on the proposal, but as it is part of the body of documents related to the original version of the songbook, presumably the workshop was meant to be hold in the early 1990s.

18. See the websites of Hirschhorn (n.d.b), G. Raphael (2012), and Gold (n.d.).

19. Raphael was honored for her song "Angels Carry You" at the Third Shalshelet International Festival in June 2008 (interview June 2008).

20. Hirschhorn and her ensemble Vocolot were finalists at the 2008 International Jewish Music Festival, in Amsterdam.

21. Cartun is a Reform- and Reconstructionist-trained rabbi and a performer in a local band.

22. The service took place at February 29, 2008 (Adar I 23, 5768), at the Congregation Etz Chayim.

23. Corrsin offered the Shirim service during her time at Temple Israel of West of Bloomfield, Michigan. She provided me with the documents used in this service.

24. To protect the privacy protection of people I did not interview, I have abbreviated some names here and below.

25. Sing Out! was founded in 1950 and grew out of the American folk music revival, in particular of a "legacy of social commitment and a tradition of singing both to effect change and to share the pure enjoyment of songs" (Deitz 2000). Leading figures of that time influencing the founding of Sing Out! were singer-songwriters and activists like Pete Seeger, Woody Guthrie, Lee Hays, Alan Lomax, Irwin Silber,

and Earl Robinson. *Sing Out!* publishes song collections, sound recordings, folk music books and directories, a quarterly magazine, and other publications and offers further multimedia resources.

26. The influence of globalization on the emergence of new musical genres has been widely discussed in the field ethnomusicology, as well as in studies on world music, such as Taylor 1997.

27. Only a few songwriters discussed in this study released some of their music in the category world music. An example is Hirschhorn, whose recording *Roots & Wings* is listed by CD Baby in the category "World" (CDBaby 2015d).

3. Feminist Voices in the Lyricists' Choice: A Content Analysis

1. "Ode to the Matriarchs" has been released on the album *Streams in the Desert* (2004).

2. Rachel eventually gave birth to Joseph and Benjamin, while Bilhah gave birth to Dan and Naphtali, who were raised by Rachel.

3. Leah gave birth to Reuben, Simeon, Levi, Judah, Issachar, Zebulun, and Dinah, while Zilpah gave birth to Gad and Asher.

4. The song was released by Vocolot on the album *Heart Beat* (2002).

5. Lilith was the ideal role model for the first generation of feminist Jews, as she embodies character traits such as being powerful, dangerous, and destructive that appealed to the women of the 1970s (see Prell 2007, 18).

6. Released on the album *Gather Round* (1989) by Hirschhorn and Vocolot.

7. The song is published on the album *Bible Babes A-Beltin'* (1997) and is sometimes also called "Miriam–By the Shores."

8. This song was released on the albums *And You Shall Be a Blessing* (1989), on *Live at the Dell* (1990), and *The Journey Continues* (1997).

9. The Hebrew words כֹּל("all") and קוֹל ("voice") are both pronounced and transliterated as *kol*.

10. The song has been released on the album *A Moon Note* (1995) by MiRaJ.

11. A video of a performance of this song to celebrate Raphael's sixtieth birthday can be seen online (G. Raphael 2013).

12. The song was released on Hanna Tiferet Siegel's album *Olamama* (1995).

13. This song was released on MiRaJ's *A Moon Note* (1995).

14. The song has been released on the album *Full Glory* (1998).

15. For further information on Jewish discourses on health and healing and the Jewish healing movement, see Prince 2009.

16. Another song titled "Ana El Na" was written by Juliet Spitzer. It was released on another recording by MiRaJ called *Healing Chants for the Soul* (2007). Raphael's song was arranged by MiRaJ and released on the album *A Moon Note* (1995).

17. To hear "Dayenu," see Shere n.d.

18. To listen to the song, see Newman n.d.

19. For further information on feminist Purim rituals, see Ritualwell 2015c.

20. For a performance of this song, see Rothman 2011.

21. The full Hallel (Psalms 113–18) is recited at joyous holidays such as Sukkoth, Pessach, Shavuot, and Hanukkah.

22. For more information about Shere's recordings, see Shere 2015.

23. This songwriter is unknown to me, and I could not identify the song mentioned here.

24. For a performance of this song, see Shondes 2010. For more information on the band, see Shondes n.d.

25. The building of a mishkan is mentioned in the Torah portion Vayakhel (and he assembled; Exodus 35:1–38:20), for example.

26. The song was released on the album *Selections from Marcia Falk's Blessings in Song* (1998) by Linda Hirschhorn and Fran Avni.

27. The Hebrew *lechu* is the feminine plural imperative form of the verb *lecha* (which comes from the root *lacha*, "to go").

4. THE MUSICAL CONCEPTION OF FEMINIST JEWISH SONGWRITING

1. Although there are no objective musical parameters that characterize a song as Jewish or not, during my fieldwork in several American Jewish communities, it became obvious to me that there is a common subliminal understanding of how Jewish music sounds.

2. "Hocket" is a musical term that means an interrupted rhythmic technique or effect in medieval and contemporary music in which a melody is divided between two parts, which alternate between singing and being silent.

3. The Torah says that God has no likeness and that no image can be made of him (see Exodus 20:2–4 and Deuteronomy 4.35). In addition, God is not even to be conceived as spirit; according to Jewish tradition, the term "spirit" is used to mean the energy of the divine (see Isaiah 31:3 and 40:13 and Zechariah 4:6).

4. In Sanhedrin 22a the Talmud says: "In his prayer a man should think that the Shekhinah is before him."

CONCLUSION

1. Critics may say that the term "discursive tradition" is redundant, as traditions are by nature discursive and in transition. Although this is true, I counter this argument with the following point: In the real world and in the imagination of our informants, traditions are also experienced as nondiscursive. For example, some tunes by the contemporary feminist songwriter Shefa Gold are considered as mi Sinai, which means "traditional" (in a metaphorical sense, "unchanged") with reference to the revelation at Mount Sinai (interview March 2008).

APPENDIX A: A NOTE ON FIELDWORK

1. Some music by Raphael, Hirschhorn, and Gold music is printed in Berrin 1996 and mentioned in Adelman 1990.

APPENDIX B: THE SOURCE MATERIALS

1. After Friedman's passing in 2011, the school was renamed the Debbie Friedman School of Sacred Music.

2. Among the tape recordings were some by Raphael that mainly feature her early, unpublished "Shechinah Songs," sung by her and B'not Levana, her Toronto-based women's group, and some liturgical songs she wrote in 1993 for the Reconstructionist Rabbinical College ApiChorus. The rest of the tape recordings feature unpublished works of the all-women's band Tofa'ah (whose members were Raphael, Rabbi Margot Stein, and Juliet Spitzer) and early works of Hirschhorn and Fran Avni, Hanna Tiferet Siegel, Laura Berkson, and other relatively unknown songwriters, such as Susan Rothbaum and the band Ashira. There was also Shefa Gold's recording *Heartfelt*, which she published under her former name Sherri Katz, together with Sky Schenkenberg.

GLOSSARY OF HEBREW TERMS

Aliyah (pl. *aliyot)*: literally, going up. The act of going up to the bimah, or being called to the Torah. Also the immigration of Jews from the Diaspora to the land of Israel.

Amidah: the "standing prayer"; also called the *Shmoneh Esreh* ("The Eighteen"). It is the central prayer in Jewish liturgy.

Bat kol: daughter of the voice.

B'racha (pl. *b'rachot*): blessing.

Gashmiut: corporeality, worldliness, materialism.

Havurah (pl. *havurot*): friendship, fellowship.

Imahot (sing. *ima*): mother.

Kabbalat Shabbat: Friday night prayer service receiving the Shabbat.

Kallah: convention or gathering.

Kavannah: conscious intention while praying.

Ketubah: a marriage contract.

Kol Isha: the woman's voice; also a Talmudic dictum, originally a rule that prohibited men from listening to women's voices.

Kotel: the Wailing Wall in Jerusalem.

Mekhitzah: partition or screen separating men's and women's areas, for example in a synagogue.

Mishna: codification of the oral Jewish law; this and the commentary on it (Gemara) constitute the Talmud.

Niddah: literally, someone who is excluded or expelled. The concept of niddah usually refers to a menstruating woman, or a woman who has menstruated and has not yet completed the required immersion in the mikvah. The term also refers to the laws of niddah, which are codified in the *Shulhan Arukh, Yoreh De'ah*, 183–200.

Niggun (pl. *niggunim*): Hasidic wordless song, tune.

Nusach: Jewish prayer modes.

Rosh Hodesh: a feminist new moon ritual.

Ruhniut: the spiritual world.

Shekhinah: the feminine aspect of God.

Simkhat Chokhmah: a ritual for celebrating wisdom as well as for reclaiming respect and honor for elders.

Taharat: purity. The *taharat hamishpaha* (laws of family purity) concern the sexual separation of husband and wife during the woman's menstrual period. They are based on the Torah (Leviticus 18:19 and 20:18).

Talmud: the codification of the oral Jewish law (*Mishna*) and the commentary on that law (*Gemara*); a compendium of Jewish teachings.

Tanach: the Hebrew Bible.

Tikkun olam: repairing the world.

Tisha B'Av: an annual fast day commemorating the destructions of the First and Second Temples in Jerusalem.

Tumah: ritual impurity. The notion of impurity has nothing to do with hygiene, but with the spiritual state that prevents a person from participating in communal worship. One becomes impure through a variety of means: illness, childbirth, physical discharges, or contact with a corpse.

Tum tum: a Talmudic term for androgyny.

REFERENCES

INTERVIEWS (IN PERSON UNLESS OTHERWISE INDICATED)

Alpert, Rebecca. Philadelphia, PA, March 2008.

Buchdahl, Cantor Angela. New York, February 2007.

Capek, Batsheva. Telephone and e-mail interviews June 2008.

Cartun, Rabbi Ari. Palo Alto, CA, February 2008.

Corrsin, Cantor Lori. New York, February 2007.

Elwell, Rabbi Sue Levi. Philadelphia, PA, March 2008.

Garner, Michele. Staten Island, NY, February 2007.

Gold, Rabbi Shefa. Jemez Springs, NM, March 2008; e-mail interview June 8, 2005.

Hirsch, Cantor Naomi. Philadelphia, PA, June 2008.

Hirschhorn, Linda. Email-interview in June and July 2005 and personal interview in San Francisco, CA, February 2008.

Katzew, Cantor Alane. New York, February 2007.

Levitt, Laura. Philadelphia, PA, March 2008; e-mail interview April 2009.

Milgram, Rabbi Goldie. Philadelphia, PA, March 2007 and March 2008.

MiRaJ. Philadelphia, PA, February 2007 and March 2008.

Raphael, Rabbi Geela Rayzel. Philadelphia, PA, February 2007 and March and June 2008; e-mail interviews between October 2003 and May 2009.

Raphael, Rabbi Simcha Paull. Philadelphia, PA, March 2008.

Rothman, Chana. Philadelphia, PA, June 2008; email-interviews September 1 and 2, 2008, and October 2008.

Shere, Holy Taya. Telephone interview February 2007; e-mail interviews February and March 2007 and February 2008.

Spitzer, Juliet I. Philadelphia, PA, February 2007 and March and June 2008.

Stein, Rabbi Margot. Philadelphia, PA, February 2007; March, June, and August–October 2008; e-mail interview October 2008.

Tiferet Siegel, Rabbi Hanna. Telephone interview February 2007.

Yofiyah (also known as Susan Deikam). Philadelphia, PA, March 2008.

PRIMARY SOURCES

Elwell, Sue, Linda Hirschhorn, Shelly Mann, Geela Rayzel Raphael, and Aviva Rosenbloom. 1992. "Jewish Feminist Songbook." Unpublished manuscript.

———. 1993. "Jewish Feminist Songbook." Revised and unpublished manuscript.

Raphael, Geela Rayzel. n.d. "Discussion Guide to Jewish Women's Music". Unpublished manuscript.

Talmud Bavli [Schottenstein Edition]. 1993. Brooklyn, NY: Mesorah.

Talmud Yerushalmi [Schottenstein Edition]. 2005. Brooklyn, NY: Mesorah.

SECONDARY SOURCES

Scholarly Books, Journal Articles, Theses, Dissertations, and Online Items

Ackelsberg, Martha. 1986. "Spirituality, Community, and Politics: B'not Esh and the Feminist Reconstruction of Judaism." *Journal of Feminist Studies in Religion* 2 (2): 109–20.

———. 1996. "Toward a Multicultural Politics: A Feminist Jewish Perspective." In *The Narrow Bridge: Jewish Views on Multiculturalism*, edited by Marla Brettschneider, 89–104. New Brunswick, NJ: Rutgers University Press.

Adams, Willi Paul. 2000. *Die USA im 20. Jahrhundert*. Munich: R. Oldenburg Verlag.

Adelstein, Rachel. 2013. "Braided Voices: Women Cantors in Non-Orthodox Judaism." PhD diss., University of Chicago.

Adler, Rachel. 1998. *Engendering Judaism: An Inclusive Theology and Ethics*. Boston: Beacon.

Adler, Samuel. 1992. "Sacred Music in a Secular Age." In *Sacred Sound and Social Change: Liturgical Music in Jewish and Christian Experience*, edited by Lawrence A. Hoffman and Janet R. Walton, 289–99. Notre Dame, IN: University of Notre Dame Press.

Adelman, Penina V. 1990. *Miriam's Well: Rituals for Jewish Women around the Year*. 2nd ed. New York: Biblio.

———. 1995. "A Drink from Miriam's Cup: Invention of Tradition among Jewish Women. In *Active Voices: Women in Jewish Culture*, edited by Maurie Sacks, 109–24. Urbana: University of Illinois Press.

Agus, Arlene. 1976. "This Month Is for You: Observing Rosh Hodesh as a Women's Holiday." In *The Jewish Women: New Perspectives*, edited by Elizabeth Koltun, 84–93. New York: Schocken.

———. 1996. "Examining Rosh Hodesh: An Analysis of the Holiday and Its Textual Sources." In *Celebrating the New Moon: A Rosh Chodesh Anthology*, edited by Susan Berrin, 3–12. Northvale, NJ: Jason Aronson.

Aleph. 2015. "Rabbi Zalman Schachter-Shalomi Dies at Age 89; Founder of Worldwide Jewish Renewal Movement." Accessed December 15, 2015. Aleph.org/reb-zalman.

Alfonso, Rita, and Jo Trigilio. 1997. "Surfing the Third Wave: A Dialogue between Two Third Wave Feminists." *Hypatia* 12 (3): 7–16.

Alpert, Rebecca T. 1991. "Our Lives Are the Text: Exploring Jewish Women's Rituals." *Bridges 2 (1)*: 66–80.

———. 1997. "Reconstructionist Judaism." In *Jewish Women in America: An Historical Encyclopedia,* edited by Paula E. Hyman and Deborah Dash Moore, 1132–35. New York: Routledge.

———. 1998. *Like Bread on the Seder Plate: Jewish Lesbians and the Transformation of Tradition*. New ed. New York: Columbia University Press.

Anderson, Benedict. 1991. *Imagined Communities: Reflections on the Origin and Spread of Nationalism*. Rev. ed. London: Verso.

Antler, Joyce. 1997. "American Feminism." In *Jewish Women in America: An Historical Encyclopedia*, edited by Paula E. Hyman and Deborah Dash Moore, 1:408–15. New York: Routledge.

Asad, Talal. 2009. "The Idea of an Anthropology of Islam." *Qui Parle* 17 (2): 1–30.

Bailey, Cathryn. 1997. "Making Waves and Drawing Lines: The Politics of Defining the Vicissitudes of Feminism." *Hypatia* 12 (3): 17–28.

Bartleet, Brydie-Leigh. 2004. "From Coffee Houses to Executive Suites: An Experimental Approach to Feminist Musicology." In *Music Research: New Directions for a New Century*, edited by Michael Ewans, Rosalind Halton, and John A. Phillips, 186–95. London: Cambridge Scholar.

Baskin, Judith R. 1995. "Silent Partners: Women as Wives in Rabbinic Literature." *In Active Voices: Women in Jewish Culture*, edited by Maurie Sacks, 19–37. Urbana: University of Illinois Press.

Baumgardner, Jennifer, and Amy Richards. 2000. *Manifesta: Young Women, Feminism, and the Future*. New York: Farrar, Straus and Giroux.

Benjamin, Beth Cooper, and Jodie Gordon. 2009. "*Koach Banot* (Girl Power): Talking Feminism with Jewish Teen Girls." In *New Jewish Feminism: Probing the Past, Forging the Future,* edited by Elyse Goldstein, 258–72. Woodstock, VT: Jewish Lights.

Berman, Donna. 2009. "Major Trends in Feminist Jewish Theology: The Work of Rachel Adler, Judith Plaskow, and Rebecca Alpert." In *New Jewish Feminism: Probing the Past, Forging the Future,* edited by Elyse Goldstein, 12–21. Woodstock, VT: Jewish Lights.

Berman, Saul J. 1980. "Kol Isha." In *Rabbi Joseph H. Lookstein Memorial Volume*, edited by Leo Landman, 45–66. New York: KTAV.

Bernstein, Ellen. 2009. "Creation Theology: Theology for the Rest of Us." *In New Jewish Feminism: Probing the Past, Forging the Future,* edited by Elyse Goldstein, 42–53. Woodstock, VT: Jewish Lights.

Berrin, Susan, ed. 1996. *Celebrating the New Moon: A Rosh Chodesh Anthology.* Northvale, NJ: Jason Aronson.

Biale, David. 1998. "The Melting Pot and Beyond: Jews and the Politics of American Identity." In *Insider/Outsider: American Jews and Multiculturalism*, edited by David Biale, Michael Galchinsky, and Susannah Heschel, 17–33. Berkeley: University of California Press.

———, Michael Galchinsky, and Susannah Heschel. 1998. "Introduction: The Dialectic of Jewish Enlightenment." In *Insider/Outsider: American Jews and Multiculturalism*, edited by David Biale, Michael Galchinsky, and Susannah Heschel, 1–13, Berkeley: University of California Press.

Biblio Press. n.d. Home page. Accessed May 2009. www.womenswork.org/biblio.

Blacking, John. 1973. *How Musical Is Man?* Seattle: University of Washington Press.

Bohlman, Philip V. 2002a. "Introduction: Jewish Music in Dialogue with Jewish Studies." In *The Oxford Handbook of Jewish Studies*, edited by Martin Goodman, 852–69. Oxford: Oxford University Press.

———. 2002b. "World Music at the 'End of History.'" *Ethnomusicology* 46 (1): 1–32.

———. 2008. *Jewish Music and Modernity.* New York: Oxford University Press.

Booth, Mark W. 1981. *The Experience of Song.* New Haven, CT: Yale University Press.

Braunstein, Peter, and Michael William Doyle, eds. 2002. *Imagine Nation: The American Counterculture of the 1960s and 70s.* New York: Routledge.

Brett, Philip, Elizabeth Wood, and Gary C. Thomas, eds. 1994. *Queering the Pitch: The New Gay and Lesbian Musicology.* New York: Routledge.

Brettschneider, Marla, ed. 1996. *The Narrow Bridge: Jewish Views on Multiculturalism.* New Brunswick, NJ: Rutgers University Press.

———and Dawn Robinson Rose. 2004. "Engaging Feminist Jewish Diversity Issues: Seven Concepts and Several Questions." *Nashim* 8 (fall): 180–88.

Brier, Sigal. n.d. "About Rabbi Sigal." Accessed December 16, 2015. http://rabbisigal.com/about/.

Brook, Vincent, ed. 2006. *You Should See Yourself: Jewish Identity in Postmodern American Culture.* New Brunswick, NJ: Rutgers University Press.

Burns, Kristine H., ed. 2002. *Women and Music in America since 1900.* 2 vols. Westport, CT: Greenwood.

Burns, Lori, and Mélisse Lafrance, 2002. *Disruptive Divas: Feminism, Identity & Popular Music*. New York: Routledge.

Capek, Batsheva. n.d. "I Am Batsheva. I Am Singer." Accessed June 2009. www.ibatshevasinger.com.

Caplan, Eric. 2002. *From Ideology to Liturgy: Reconstructionist Worship and American Liberal Judaism*. Cincinnati, OH: Hebrew Union College Press.

CDBaby.com. 2015a. "Bible Belts A Beltin.'" Accessed December 15, 2015. http://www.cdbaby.com/cd/rabbigrr2.

———. 2015b. "MiRaJ." Accessed December 15, 2015. http://www.cdbaby.com/cd/miraj1.

———2015c. "Olamama." Accessed December 16, 2015. https://www.cdbaby.com/cd/hannatiferet3.

———. 2015d. "Roots & Wings." Accessed December 16, 2015. http://www.cdbaby.com/cd/lhirschhorn2.

Christ, Carol P., and Judith Plaskow, 1992. "Introduction: Womanspirit Rising." In *Womanspirit Rising: A Feminist Reader in Religion*, edited by Carol P. Christ and Judith Plaskow, 1–18. San Francisco: Harper San Francisco.

Clayton, Martin. 2008. "Toward an Ethnomusicology of Sound Experience." In *The New (Ethno)musicologies*, edited by Henry Stobart, 135–69. Lanham, MD: Scarecrow.

Cohen, Debra Nussbaum. 2006. "Debbie Friedman: One People." CD booklet. Studio City, CA: Jewish Music Group.

Cohen, Judah M. 2006a. "Exploring the Postmodern Landscape of Jewish Music." In *You Should See Yourself: Jewish Identity in Postmodern American Culture*, edited by Vincent Brook, 97–118. New Brunswick, NJ: Rutgers University Press.

———. 2006b. "Singing Out for Judaism: A History of Song Leaders and Song Leading at Olin-Sang-Ruby Union Institute." In *A Place of Our Own: The Rise of Reform Jewish Camping*, edited by Michael M. Lorge and Gary P. Zola, 173–208. Tuscaloosa: University of Alabama Press.

———. 2008. "Whither Jewish Music? Jewish Studies, Music Scholarship, and the Tilt between Seminary and University." *AJS Review* 32 (1): 29–48.

Cohen, Judith R. 1997. "'Ya Salió de la Mar': Judeo-Spanish Wedding Songs among Moroccan Jews in Canada." In *Women and Music in Cross-Cultural Perspectives*, edited by Ellen Koskoff, 55–67. Urbana: University of Illinois Press.

Cohen, Norman J. 1984. "Miriam's Song: A Modern Midrashic Reading." *Judaism* 33 (2): 179–90.

Cohen, Tamara, Deborah Lynn Friedman, and Sue Levi Elwell. 1997. *The Journey Continues: The Ma'yan Passover Haggadah*. New York: Ma'yan Jewish Women's Project.

Cohen, Tamara, Jill Hammer, and Rona Shapiro. 2005. *Listen to Her Voice: Assessing the Experience of Women in the Jewish Community and Their Relationship to Feminism*. New York: Ma'yan.

Collins, Mary. 1993. "Principles of Feminist Liturgy." In *Women at Worship: Interpretations of North American Diversity*, edited by Marjorie Procter-Smith and Janet R. Walton, 9–25. Louisville, KY: Westminster.

Collins, Patricia Hill. 2000. *Black Feminist Thought: Knowledge, Consciousness, and the Politics of Empowerment*. 2nd ed. New York: Routledge.

Cook, Susan C., and Judy S. Tsou, eds. 1994. *Cecilia Reclaimed: Feminist Perspectives on Gender and Music*. Urbana: University of Illinois Press.

Cooley, Timothy J., and Gregory Barz. 2008. Introduction to *Shadows in the Field: New Perspectives for Fieldwork in Ethnomusicology*, edited by Gregory Barz and Timothy J. Cooley, 3–24. Oxford: Oxford University Press.

Coplan, David B. 1993. "Ethnomusicology and the Meaning of Tradition." In *Ethnomusicology and Modern Music History*, edited by Stephen Blum, Philip V. Bohlman, and David M. Neuman, 35–48. Urbana: University of Illinois Press.

Cormier, Holly. 1978. *Women and Folk Music: A Selected Bibliography*. Washington: Library of Congress.

Daly, Mary. 1968. *The Church and the Second Sex: With the Feminist Postchristian Introduction and New Archaic Afterwords by the Author*. Boston: Beacon.

———. 1973. *Beyond God the Father: Toward a Philosophy of Women's Liberation*. Boston: Beacon.

———. 1978. *Gyn/Ecology: The Metaethics of Radical Feminism*. Boston: Beacon.

Davidman, Lynn, and Shelly Tenenbaum, eds. 1994. *Feminist Perspectives on Jewish Studies*. New Haven, CT: Yale University Press.

Denisoff, Serge R. 1969. "Folk Music and the American Left: A Generational-Ideological Comparison." *British Journal of Sociology* 20 (4): 427–42.

Diamond, Beverly, and Pirkko Moisala, eds. 2000. *Music and Gender*. Foreword by Ellen Koskoff. Urbana: University of Illinois Press.

Dicker, Rory, and Alison Piepmeier. 2003. *Catching a Wave: Reclaiming Feminism for the 21st Century*. Boston: Northeastern University Press.

Dobkin, Alix. n.d. "Personal Statement." Accessed December 22, 2015. https://ladyslipper.org/rel/v2_home.php?storenr=53&deptnr=279.

Drake, Jennifer. 2006. "Music." In *The Women's Movement Today: An Encyclopedia of Third-Wave Feminism*, edited by Leslie Heywood, 1:225–31. Westport, CT: Greenwood.

Dreyfus, Benjamin W. 2001. "Hear the Echo of Miriam's Song: American Nusach in Concert." In *Studies in Jewish Musical Traditions: Insights from the Harvard Collection of Judaic Sound Recordings,* edited by Kay Kaufman Shelemay, 33–50. Cambridge, MA: Harvard University Press.

Dufour, Lynn Resnick. 2000. "Shifting through Tradition: The Creation of Feminist Jewish Identities." *Journal for the Scientific Study of Religion* 39 (1): 90–106.

Edelman, Marsha Bryan. 2006. "Continuity, Creativity, and Conflict: The Ongoing Search for 'Jewish' Music." In *You Should See Yourself: Jewish Identity in Postmodern American Culture*, edited by Vincent Brook, 119–34. New Brunswick, NJ: Rutgers University Press.

Eglash, Joel N., and Cheryl Friedman, eds. 2014. *New Jewish Tunes: Ruach 5773 Songbook*. Schaumburg, IL: Transcontinental.

Eilberg-Schwartz, Howard, ed. 1992. *People of the Body. Jews and Judaism from an Embodied Perspective*. Albany: State University of New York Press.

Ellenson, Ruth Andrew. 2006. *The Modern Jewish Girl's Guide to Guilt*. New York: Penguin.

———. 2009. "The Pink Ghetto." In *New Jewish Feminism: Probing the Past, Forging the Future,* edited by Elyse Goldstein, 277–81. Woodstock, VT: Jewish Lights.

Elwell, Sue Levi, comp. 1987. *The Jewish Women's Studies Guide*. 2nd ed. Lanham, MD: University Press of America.

———. 1993. "Reclaiming Jewish Women's Oral Tradition? An Analysis of Rosh Hodesh." In *Women at Worship: Interpretations of North American Diversity*, edited by Marjorie Procter-Smith and Janet R. Walton, 111–26. Louisville, KY: Westminster.

———, ed., 2002. *The Open Door: A Passover Haggadah*. New York, NY: Central Conference of American Rabbis.

———. 2009. "Feminism and the Transformation of the Synagogue." In *New Jewish Feminism: Probing the Past, Forging the Future,* edited by Elyse Goldstein, 155–64. Woodstock, VT: Jewish Lights.

Englander, Karen. 2004. "Bringing Practice to Theory: A Case Study of Language Use in Jewish Feminist Worship." *WILLA* 13: 4–29. Accessed December 17, 2015. https://scholar.lib.vt.edu/ejournals/WILLA/fall04/pdf/englander.pdf.

Epstein, Heidi. 2004. *Melting the Venusberg: A Feminist Theology of Music*. New York: Continuum.

Evans, Judith. 1995. *Feminist Theory Today: An Introduction to Second-Wave Feminism*. London: Sage.

Eyerman, Ron. 2002. "Music in Movement: Cultural Politics and Old and New Social Movements." *Qualitative Sociology* 25 (3): 443–58.

Falk, Marcia. 1999. *The Book of Blessings: New Jewish Prayers for Daily Life, the Sabbath, and the New Moon Festival*. Boston: Beacon.

Faludi, Susan. 1991. *Backlash: The Undeclared War against American Women*. New York: Anchor.

Firestone, Tirzah. 2009. "Transforming Our Stories through Midrash." In *New Jewish Feminism: Probing the Past, Forging the Future,* edited by Elyse Goldstein, 113–19. Woodstock, VT: Jewish Lights.

Fishman, Sylvia Barack. 1993. *A Breath of Life: Feminism in the American Jewish Community*. Hanover, NH: Brandeis University Press.

———. 2000. *Jewish Life and American Culture*. Albany: State University of New York Press.

Flick, Uwe. 2008. *Triangulation: Eine Einführung*. 2nd ed. Wiesbaden, Germany: Verlag für Sozialwissenschaften.

Fonrobert, Charlotte Elisheva. 2001. "Frauen im Judentum." In *Handbuch zur Geschichte der Juden in Europa*, edited by Elke-Vera Kotowski, Julius Schoeps, and Hiltrud Wallenborn, 2:79–89. Darmstadt, Germany: Primus Verlag.

Foucault, Michel. 1981. *Archäologie des Wissens*. Translated by Ulrich Köppen. Frankfurt: Suhrkamp.

Friedman, Deborah Lynn. 1987. *The Best of Debbie Friedman: A Modern Repertoire of Acclaimed Songs*. Owings Mills, MD: Tara.

Gair, Christopher. 2007. *The American Counterculture*. Edinburgh: Edinburgh University Press.

Garber, Marjorie, and Rebecca L. Walkowitz, eds. 1999. *One Nation under God? Religion and American Culture*. New York: Routledge.

Garofalo, Reebee, ed. 1992. *Rockin' the Boat: Mass Music and Mass Movements*. Cambridge, MA: South End.

Gibson, Pamela Church. 2004. "Introduction: Popular Culture." In *Third Wave Feminism: A Critical Exploration*, edited by Stacy Gillis, Gillian Howie, and Rebecca Munford, 137–41. New York: Palgrave Macmillan.

Gillis, Stacy, Gillian Howie, and Rebecca Munford. 2003. "Harvesting Our Strength: Third Wave Feminism and Women's Studies." *Journal of International Women's Studies* 4 (2): 1–6.

———, eds. 2004. *Third Wave Feminism: A Critical Exploration*. New York: Palgrave Macmillan.

Gillis, Stacy, and Rebecca Munford. 2006. "Genealogies and Generations: The Politics and Praxis of Third Wave Feminism." In *The Women's Movement Today: An Encyclopedia of Third-Wave Feminism*, edited by Leslie Heywood, 2:111–21. Westport, CT: Greenwood.

Girls' Night On. 2006. "About." Accessed November 4, 2015. http://www.girlsnighton.com/about.html.

Glanz, David. 1977. "An Interpretation of the Jewish Counterculture." *Jewish Social Studies* 39 (1–2): 117–28.

Glanzbeg-Krainin, Deborah, and Laura Levitt. 2009. "Feminist Theory and Jewish Studies." *Religion Compass* 3 (2): 241–52.

Goehr, Lydia. 1994. "Political Musics and the Politics of Music." *Journal of Aesthetics and Art Criticism* 52 (1): 99–112.

Gold, Shefa. n.d. "Rabbi Shefa Gold." Home page. Accessed October 31, 2015. www.rabbishefagold.com.

———. 1997. "*The Power of Chant.*" Accessed December 16, 2015. http://www.rabbishefagold.com/power-of-chant.

———. 2006. *Torah Journeys: The Inner Past to the Promised Land.* Teaneck, NJ: Ben Yehuda.

Goldman, Karla. 2007. "Women in Reform Judaism. Between Rhetoric and Reality." In *Women Remaking American Judaism*, edited by Riv-Ellen Prell with a foreword by David Weinberg, 109–33. Detroit, MI: Wayne State University Press.

Goldstein, Elyse, ed. 2009. *New Jewish Feminism: Probing the Past, Forging the Future*. Woodstock, VT: Jewish Lights.

Goodman, Martin. ed. 2002. *The Oxford Handbook of Jewish Studies*. Oxford: Oxford University Press.

Greenberg, Blu. 1998. *On Women and Judaism: A View from Tradition*. Philadelphia, PA: Jewish Publication Society of America.

Greenberg, Cheryl. 1998. "Pluralism and Its Discontents: The Case of Blacks and Jews." In *Insider/Outsider: American Jews and Multiculturalism*, edited by David Biale, Michael Galchinsky, and Susannah Heschel, 55–87. Berkeley: University of California Press.

Haddad, Yvonne Yazbeck, and John L. Esposito, eds. 2001. *Daughters of Abraham: Feminist Thought in Judaism, Christianity, and Islam.* Gainesville: University Press of Florida.

Hajdu, André, and Yaacov Mazor. 1971. "The Musical Tradition of Hasidism." In *Encyclopedia Judaica*, edited by Cecil Roth, 7:1421–32 Jerusalem: Keter.

Hammer, Jill. 2009. "To Her We Shall Return: Jews Turning to the Goddess, the Goddess Turning to Jews." In *New Jewish Feminism: Probing the Past, Forging the Future,* edited by Elyse Goldstein, 22–34. Woodstock, VT: Jewish Lights.

Hannatiferet. n.d. "Biography." Accessed December 16, 2015. http://hannatiferet.com/biography/.

Hauptman, Judith. 1994. "Feminist Perspectives on Rabbinic Texts." In *Feminist Perspectives on Jewish Studies*, edited by Lynn Davidman and Shelly Tenenbaum, 40–61. New Haven, CT: Yale University Press.

Heschel, Susannah, ed. 1983. *On Being a Jewish Feminist: A Reader.* New York: Schocken.

Heskes, Irene. 1992. "Miriam's Sisters: Jewish Women and Liturgical Music." *Notes* 2nd ser., 48 (4): 1193–1202.

———. 1994. *Passport to Jewish Music: Its History, Traditions, and Culture.* Westport, CT: Greenwood.

Heywood, Leslie, ed. 2006. *The Women's Movement Today: An Encyclopedia of Third-Wave Feminism*. 2 vols. Westport, CT: Greenwood Press.

———and Jennifer Drake. 1997. Introduction to *Third Wave Agenda: Being Feminist, Doing Feminism*, edited by Leslie Heywood and Jennifer Drake, 1–20. Minneapolis: University of Minneapolis Press.

Hirschhorn, Linda. n.d.a. "About Linda." Accessed December 16, 2015. http://www.lindahirschhorn.com/about.html.

———.n.d.b. "Music." Accessed December 16, 2015. http://www.lindahirschhorn.com/cds.

———. 1989. *Gather Round: New Hebrew Canons, Rounds, and Musical Settings.* Cedarhurst, NY: Tara.

Hyman, Paula E. 1997. "Jewish Feminism." In *Jewish Women in America: An Historical Encyclopedia*, edited by Paula E. Hyman and Deborah Dash Moore, 1:694–98. New York: Routledge.

Ihde, Don. 1976. *Listening and Voice: A Phenomenology of Sound*. Athens: Ohio University Press.

Irwin, John. 1977. *Scenes*. Beverly Hills, CA: Sage.

Jacobs, Jill. 2007. "The History of 'Tikkun Olam.'" Accessed October 25, 2015. www.zeek.net/706tohu.

Jewish Feminist Resources. 2009. Home page. Accessed May 2009. www.jew-feminist-resources.com.

Jewish Reconstructionist Communities. n.d. "Harmoniyah-Reconstructionist Music Network." Accessed December 16, 2015. https://jewishrecon.org/harmoniyah.

Jewish Women's Archive. n.d. "Debbie Friedman." Accessed December 15, 2015. http://jwa.org/feminism/friedman-debbie.

———. 2015. "First CAJE Conference." Accessed October 29, 2015. http://jwa.org/thisweek/aug/29/1976/caje.

Johnson, Barbara C. 2000. "'Hen noseot et mahberoteihen itan'—shirei nashim Yehudiot mi-Kochin be-sfat ha-makom." *Pe'amim* 82:64–80.

Kabbalah Kirtan. 2015. "About Yofiyah." Accessed December 16, 2016. http://www.kabbalahkirtan.com/bio.html.

Kamenetz, Rodger. 1997. *Stalking Elijah: Adventures with Today's Jewish Mystical Masters*. San Francisco: HarperSanFrancisco.

Kaplan, Mordecai. 1994. *Judaism as Civilization: Toward a Reconstruction of American-Jewish Life*. Philadelphia: Jewish Publication Society.

Kent, Stephen A. 2001. *From Slogans to Mantras: Social Protest and the Religious Conversion in the Late Vietnam War Era*. Syracuse, NY: Syracuse University Press.

Kinser, Amber. 2004. "Negotiating Space for/through Third-Wave Feminism." *NWSA Journal* 16 (3): 124–53.

Kirschenblatt-Gimblett, Barbara. 1994. "Spaces of Dispersal." *Cultural Anthropology* 9 (3): 339–44.

Klein, Melissa. 1997. "Duality and Redefinition: Young Feminism and the Alternative Music Community." In *Third Wave Agenda: Being Feminist, Doing Feminism*, edited by Leslie Heywood and Jennifer Drake, 207–25. Minneapolis: University of Minneapolis Press.

Kligman, Mark. 2001a. "The Bible, Prayer, and Maqām: Extra-Musical Associations of Syrian Jews." *Ethnomusicology* 45 (3): 443–79.

———. 2001b. "Contemporary Jewish Music in America." In *American Jewish Yearbook,* edited by David Singer and Lawrence Grossman, 101:88–141. New York: American Jewish Committee.

———. 2005. "Recent Trends in New American Jewish Music." In *The Cambridge Companion to American Judaism*, edited by Dana Evan Kaplan, 363–79. Cambridge: Cambridge University Press.

Koenig, Leah. 2007. "The New, Hip Music Mavens." *Lilith* 32 (4): 4–5.

Kok, Roe-Min. 2002. "Women-Identified Music." In *Women and Music in America Since 1900: An Encyclopedia*, edited by Kristine H. Burns, 2:674–76. Westport, CT: Greenwood.

KolAlpeh. 2013. Home page. Accessed December 16, 2015. http://kolaleph.org/category/aleph-kallah-aleph-retreats.

Kolot: Center for Jewish Women's and Gender Studies. 2015. Home page. Accessed November 1, 2015. http://www.rrc.edu/kolot.

Koltun, Elizabeth. 1976. *The Jewish Women: New Perspectives*. New York: Schocken.

Koskoff, Ellen, 1987. "The Sound of a Woman's Voice: Gender and Music in a New York Hasidic Community." In *Women and Music in Cross-Cultural Perspective*, edited by Ellen Koskoff, 213–224. Urbana: University of Illinois Press.

———. 1993. "Miriam Sings Her Song: The Self and the Other in Anthropological Discourse." In *Musicology and Difference: Gender and Sexuality in Music Scholarship*, edited by Ruth A. Solie, 149–63. Berkeley: University of California Press.

———. 2001. *Music in Lubavitcher Life*. Urbana: University of Illinois Press.

———. 2002. "Is Female to Male as Modern Is to Postmodern? Implications for a New Ethno/Musicology." In *Encomium Musicae: Essays in Memory of Robert J. Snow*, edited by David Crawford, 733–44. Hillsdale, NY: Pendragon.

———. 2005a. "(Left out in) Left (the Field): The Effects of Post-Postmodern Scholarship on Feminist and Gender Studies in Musicology and Ethnomusicology, 1990–2000." *Women and Music* 9:90–98.

———. 2005b. *Music Cultures in the United States: An Introduction*. New York: Routledge.

———2014. *A Feminist Ethnomusicology: Writings on Music and Gender.* Urbana: University of Illinois Press.

Ladyslipper Music. n.d. Home page. Accessed November 1, 2015. www.ladyslipper.org.

Laing, David. 2001. "Folk Music Revival." In *The New Grove Dictionary of Music and Musicians*, edited by Stanley Sadie, 9:67–68. 2nd ed. Oxford: Oxford University Press.

Lefkovitz, Lori Hope. 1995. "Eavesdropping on Angels and Laughing at God: Theorizing a Subversive Matriarchy." In *Gender and Judaism: The Transformation of Tradition*, edited by Tamar M. Rudavsky, 157–67. New York: New York University Press.

———. 2009. "'Does It Hurt Shirley to Learn to Speak Up?' Tevye's New World Legacy in the Jewish Daughter's Father." *Bridges* 14 (1): 97–103.

———and Rona Shapiro. 2005. "Ritualwell.Org—Loading the Virtual Canon, Or: The Politics and Aesthetics of Jewish Women's Spirituality." *Nashim* 9 (spring): 101–25.

———. 2009. "The Politics and Aesthetics of Jewish Women's Spirituality." In *New Jewish Feminism: Probing the Past, Forging the Future,* edited by Elyse Goldstein, 66–80. Woodstock, VT: Jewish Lights.

Levitt, Laura. 1997. *Jews and Feminism: The Ambivalent Search for Home*. New York: Routledge.

———. 2001. "Judaism and Gender." In *International Encyclopedia of the Social & Behavioral Sciences,* edited by Neil J. Smelser and Paul B. Baltes, 8011–14. Oxford: Elsevier Science.

Lipstadt, Deborah E. 2001. "Feminism and American Judaism: Looking back at the Turn of the Century." In *Women and American Judaism: Historical Perspectives,* edited by Pamela S. Nadell and Jonathan D. Sarna, 291–308. Hanover, NH: University Press of New England.

Litman, Jane Rachel. 2009. "If the Shoe Doesn't Fit, Examine the Soul: Jewish Feminism and Gender Expression." In *New Jewish Feminism: Probing the Past, Forging the Future,* edited by Elyse Goldstein, 250–57. Woodstock, VT: Jewish Lights.

Lomax, Alan. 2003. *Alan Lomax: Selected Writings 1934–1997*. Edited by Ronald D. Cohen. New York: Routledge.

Lont, Cynthia M. 1992. "Women's Music: No Longer a Small Private Party." In *Rockin' the Boat: Mass Music and Mass Movements,* edited by Reebee Garofalo, 241–53. Cambridge, MA: South End.

Lorge, Michael M., and Gary P. Zola, eds. 2006. *A Place of Our Own: The Rise of Reform Jewish Camping.* Tuscaloosa: University of Alabama Press.

Love, Nancy Sue. 2002. "'Singing for Our Lives': Women's Music and Democratic Politics." *Hypatia* 17 (14): 71–94.

Lund, Jens, and R. Serge Denisoff. 1971. "The Folk Music Revival and the Counter Culture: Contributions and Contradictions." *Journal of American Folklore* 84 (334): 394–405.

Magnus, Shulamit. 1992. "Reinventing Miriam's Well: Feminist Jewish Ceremonials." In *The Uses of Tradition: Jewish Continuity in the Modern Era,* edited by Jack Wertheimer, 331–47. New York: Jewish Theological Seminary.

Marini, Stephen A. 2003. *Sacred Song in America: Religion, Music, and Public Culture*. Urbana: University of Illinois Press.

McClary, Susan. 1991. *Feminine Endings: Music, Gender and Sexuality*. Minneapolis: University of Minnesota Press.

McLean, Jaime. 2006. "Religion and Spirituality." In *The Women's Movement Today: An Encyclopedia of Third-Wave Feminism*, edited by Leslie Heywood, 1:272–76. Westport, CT: Greenwood.

Michals, Debra. 2002. "From 'Consciousness Expansion' to 'Consciousness Raising': Feminism and the Countercultural Politics of the Self." In *Imagine Nation: The American Counterculture of the 1960s and 70s*, edited by Peter Braunstein and Michael William Doyle, 41–68. New York: Routledge.

Millen, Rochelle L. 2007. " 'Her Mouth Is Full of Wisdom': Reflections on Feminist Jewish Theology." In *Women Remaking American Judaism,* edited by Riv-Ellen Prell with a foreword by David Weinberg, 27–50. Detroit, MI: Wayne State University Press.

Mishkan Shalom. n.d. "Rabbi Shawn Zevit: Liturgist, Musician, Writer, Teacher, Activitst, Congregational Consultant, Community Leader." Accessed December 16, 2015. https://mishkan.org/rabbi-shawn-zevit-liturgist-singer-writer-teacher-advisor-to-jewish-communities.

Moisala, Pirkko, and Beverly Diamond, eds. 2000. *Music and Gender*. Urbana: University of Illinois Press.

Moise, Elaine, and Rebecca Schwartz. 2002. *The Dancing with Miriam Haggadah: A Jewish Women's Celebration of Passover*. 3rd ed. Palo Alto, CA: Rikudei Miriam.

Morris, Bonnie J. 1999. *Eden Built by Eves: The Culture of Women's Music Festivals*. Los Angeles, CA: Alyson.

Munford, Rebecca. 2004. " 'Wake Up and Smell the Lipgloss': Gender, Generation and the (A)Politics of Girl Power." In *Third Wave Feminism: A Critical Exploration*, edited by Stacy Gillis, Gillian Howie, and Rebecca Munford, 142–53. New York: Palgrave Macmillan.

Musleah, Rahel. 1995. "An Explosion of Jewish Women's Popular Music." *Lilith* 20 (4): 18–29.

MyJewSpot. n.d. "Interview with Chana Rothman". Accessed June 2009. www.myjewspot.blogspot.com/2008/02/chana-rothman.html.

National Havurah Committee. n.d.a "About the NHC." Accessed November 1, 2015. http://havurah.org/institute/the-nhc/about-the-nhc/.

———. n.d.b. “Artists in Residence 2009.” Accessed December 16, 2015. http://havurah.dreamhosters.com/institute2009/artists-in-residence.

Nettl, Bruno. 2005. *The Study of Ethnomusicology: Thirty-One Issues and Concepts.* Urbana: University of Illinois Press.

Neuls-Bates, Carol, ed. 1996. *Women in Music: An Anthology of Source Readings from the Middle Ages to the Present.* 2nd ed. Boston: Northeastern University Press.

Nidel, Richard. 2005. *World Music: The Basics.* New York: Routledge.

Novak, Bill. 2004. “The Making of a Jewish Counter Culture.” In *The Jewish 1960s: An American Sourcebook*, edited by Michael Staub, 282–86. Waltham, MA: Brandeis University Press.

Ochs, Vanessa L. 2007a. *Inventing Jewish Ritual.* Philadelphia: Jewish Publication Society.

———. 2007b. “Miriam’s Object Lesson: Ritualizing the Presence of Miriam.” In *Women Remaking American Judaism*, edited by Riv-Ellen Prell with a foreword by David Weinberg, 257–77. Detroit, MI: Wayne State University Press.

Oppenheimer, Mark. 2003. *Knocking on Heaven’s Door: American Religion in the Age of Counterculture.* New Haven, CT: Yale University Press.

Orr, Catherine M. 1997. “Charting the Currents of the Third Wave.” *Hypatia* 12 (3): 29–45.

Pegg, Carole. 2001. “Folk Music.” In *The New Grove Dictionary of Music and Musicians*, edited by Stanley Sadie, 9:63–67. 2nd ed. Oxford: Oxford University Press.

Perone, James E. 2004. *Music of the Counterculture Era.* Westport, CT: Greenwood.

Petersen, Karen E. 1987. “An Investigation into Woman-Identified Music in the United States.” In *Women and Music in Cross-Cultural Perspective*, edited by Ellen Koskoff, 203–12. Urbana: University of Illinois Press.

Peterson, Richard A., and Andy Bennett. 2004. “Introducing Music Scenes.” In *Music Scenes: Local, Translocal, and Virtual*, edited by Andy Bennett and Richard A. Peterson, 1–16. Nashville, TN: Vanderbilt University Press.

Picard, Jacques. 2004. “Transition Spots: Über das Verhandeln auf beiden Seiten des Bindestrichs und das Beispiel amerikanisch-jüdischer Pluralisierung.” In *Integration des Widerläufigen*, edited by Nicole Wachter and Elke Huwiler, 257–72. Hamburg, Germany: LIT Verlag.

———. 2007. “Homeland America: Der amerikanisch-jüdische Diasporabegriff zwischen säkularer Pluralisierung und mythischer Überhöhung.” In *Exil als*

Krisenerfahrung: Jüdische Bilanzen und Perspektiven, edited by Armin Eidherr, Gerhard Langer, and Armin Müller, 67–82. Vienna: Klagenfurt.

Pickow, Peter, and Amy Appleby. 1988. *The Billboard Book of Songwriting*. New York: Billboard.

Plaskow, Judith. 1983. "The Right Question Is Theological." In *On Being a Jewish Feminist: A Reader*, edited and with introductions by Susannah Heschel, 223–33. New York: Schocken.

———. 1990. *Standing Again at Sinai: Judaism from a Feminist Perspective*. San Francisco: Harper and Row.

———. 1992. *Und wieder stehen wir am Sinai: Eine jüdisch-feministische Theologie*. Translated by Veronika Merz. Lucerne, Switzerland: Edition Exodus.

———. 1994. "Jewish Theology in Feminist Perspective." In *Feminist Perspectives on Jewish Studies*, edited by Lynn Davidman and Shelly Tenenbaum, 62–83. New Haven, CT: Yale University Press.

———. 1996. "Feminist Jewish Theologies." In *Dictionary of Feminist Theology*, edited by Letty M. Russell and J. Shannon Clarkson, 104–6. Louisville, KY: Westminster.

———. 2003. "Dealing with Difference Without and Within." *Journal of Feminist Studies in Religion* 19 (1): 91–95.

———. 2007. "Gender Theory and Gendered Realities: An Exchange between Tamar Ross and Judith Plaskow." *Nashim* 13 (spring): 207–51.

———. 2009. "Calling All Theologians." In *New Jewish Feminism: Probing the Past, Forging the Future*, edited by Elyse Goldstein, 3–11. Woodstock, VT: Jewish Lights.

Porath, Yehoshua. 1972. "Historical Survey of Israel (1948–1970)." In *Encyclopedia Judaica*, edited by Cecil Roth. CD-ROM ed. Jerusalem: Keter.

Porterfield, Amanda. 2001. *The Transformation of American Religion: The Story of a Late-Twentieth-Century Awakening*. Oxford: Oxford University Press.

Post, Jennifer C. 1994. "Erasing the Boundaries between Public and Private in Women's Performance Traditions." In *Cecilia Reclaimed: Feminist Perspectives on Gender and Music*, edited by Susan Cook and Judy S. Tsou, 35–51. Urbana: University of Illinois Press.

Prell, Riv-Ellen. 1989. *Prayer and Community: The Havurah in American Judaism*. Detroit, MI: Wayne State University Press.

———. 2006. "America, Mordecai Kaplan, and the Postwar Jewish Youth Revolt." *Jewish Social Studies* 12 (2): 158–71.

———. 2007. "Introduction: Feminism and the Remaking of American Judaism." In *Women Remaking American Judaism*, edited by Riv-Ellen Prell, with a foreword by David Weinberg, 1–26, Detroit, MI: Wayne State University Press.

Prince, Michelle F. 2009. "Judaism, Health, and Healing: How a Jewish Communal Field Took Root and Where It Might Grow." *Journal of Jewish Communal Service* 84 (3–4): 280–91.

Raimist, Rachel. 2006. "Hip-Hop Feminism." In *The Women's Movement Today: An Encyclopedia of Third-Wave Feminism*, edited by Leslie Heywood, 1:173–75. Westport, CT: Greenwood.

Ramon, Einat. 2005. "The Matriarchs and the Torah of Hesed (Loving-Kindness)." *Nashim* 10 (2): 154–77.

Raphael, Geela Rayzel. 1993. "Criteria for Jewish Feminist Songbook." Unpublished manuscript.

———. 1998. "Study Guide to Bible Babes A-Beltin.'" Unpublished manuscript.

———. 2001. "Still Dancing with Miriam." In *All the Women Followed Her: A Collection of Writings on Miriam the Prophet & the Women of Exodus*, edited by Rebecca Schwartz, 83–92. Mountain View, CA: Rikudei Miriam.

———. 2005. *Friday Night Revived.* CD booklet. Philadelphia, PA: Rayzel Raphael/Radio Active Productions.

———. 2009. "Father-Daughter Placenta Planting Ritual." *Bridges* 14 (1): 23–24.

———. 2012. "Rabbi Geela Rayzel Raphael." Accessed November 1, 2015. http://www.shechinah.com/.

———, Sarah Ross, and Goldie Milgram. Forthcoming. *Adding Our Voices: The Torah of Jewish Women in Song.* New Rochelle, NY: Reclaiming Judaism.

Raphael, Simcha Paull. 2009. *Jewish Views of the Afterlife. 2nd ed. Lanham, MD:* Rowman and Littlefield.

———. 2010. "'Miriam Took Her Timbrel out and All the Women Danced': A Midrashic Motif of Contemporary Jewish Feminism." *Women in Judaism* 7 (2): 1–12.

Regev, Motti. 2000. "Global Pop: World Music, World Markets by Timothy D. Taylor." *Popular Music* 19 (2): 259–60.

———and Edwin Seroussi. 2004. *Popular Music and National Culture in Israel.* Berkeley: University of California Press.

Reynolds, Simon, and Joy Press. 1995. *The Sex Revolts: Gender, Rebellion, and Rock and Roll.* London: Serpent's Tail.

Rischar, Richard. 2002. "Women's Sphere." *In Women and Music in America Since 1900: An Encyclopedia*, edited by Kristine H. Burns, 2:678–79. Westport, CT: Greenwood.

Ritualwell. n.d. "Simhat Bat for Baby Girl Greene." Accessed December 16, 2105. www.ritualwell.org/sites/default/files/Baby%20Naming.pdf.

———. 2015a. Home page. Accessed November 1, 2015. ritualwell.org.

———. 2015b. "Lifecycles." Accessed November 3, 2015. http://www.ritualwell.org/lifecycles.

———. 2015c. "Purim." Accessed November 3, 2015. http://www.ritualwell.org/categories/22.

Rodnitzky, Jerry L. 1999. *Feminist Phoenix: The Rise and Fall of a Feminist Counterculture*. Westport, CT: Praeger.

Rogow, Faith. 1990. "Why Is This Decade Different from All Other Decades? A Look at the Rise of Jewish Lesbian Feminism." *Bridges* 1 (1): 67–79.

Rosenthal, Gilbert S. 2005. " 'Tikkun ha-Olam': The Metamorphosis of a Concept." *Journal of Religion* 85 (2): 214–40.

Rosenzweig, Rosie. 2009. "Post-Triumphalism and the New Haskalah." In *New Jewish Feminism: Probing the Past, Forging the Future,* edited by Elyse Goldstein, 397–403. Woodstock, VT: Jewish Lights.

Ross, Sarah. 2004. "Zum Gesang jüdischer Frauen im Kontext des Rosh Chodesh–Rituals." MA thesis, University of Cologne.

———. 2005. "Interview with Linda Hirschhorn." *Aviva-Berlin*, July 19. Accessed December 16, 2015. http://www.aviva-berlin.de/aviva/content_Women%20+%20Work.php?id=5726.

———. 2009a. "Musik für Frauen." In *Lexikon Musik und Gender*, edited by Annette Kreuziger-Herr and Melanie Unseld, 227–28. Kassel, Germany: Bärenreiter Verlag.

———. 2009b. "Performing the Political in American Jewish-Feminist Music." PhD diss., University of Music and Theatre Rostock.

———. 2010. "Die sinnliche Erfahrbarkeit Gottes. Zur Ästhetik jüdisch-feministischer Musik in den USA." In *Pop: Aesthetiken: Beiträge zum Schönen in der populären Musik*, edited by Anja Brunner and Michael Parzer, 113–38. Innsbruck, Austria: Studienverlag.

———. 2011. " 'What Would Miriam Sing?' Die Prophetin Miriam als Vorbild und Inspiration Jüdisch-Feministischer Ritualmusik." In *Musik | Kultur | Wissenschaft*, edited by Hartmut Möller and Martin Schneider, 19–42. Essen, Germany: Blaue Eule Verlag.

Ross, Tamar. 2004. *Expanding the Palace of Torah: Orthodoxy and Feminism.* Hanover, NH : Brandeis University Press.

Roszak, Theodore. 1995. *The Making of a Counter Culture: Reflections on the Technocratic Society and Its Youthful Opposition.* With a new introduction. Berkeley: University of California Press.

Ruttenberg, Danya, ed. 2001. *Yentl's Revenge: The Next Wave of Jewish Feminism.* Foreword by Susannah Heschel. Seattle, WA: Seal.

Sacks, Maurie. 1995. "An Anthropological and Postmodern Critique of Feminist Jewish Theory." In *Gender and Judaism. The Transformation of Tradition*, edited by Tamar M. Rudavsky, 295–305. New York: New York University Press.

———, ed. 1997. *Active Voices: Women in Jewish Culture.* Urbana: University of Illinois Press.

Sager, Rebecca. 2006. *Creating a Musical Space for Experiencing the Other-Self within the Musical Human: Rethinking John Blacking's Ethnomusicology in the Twenty-First Century.* Aldershot, UK: Ashgate.

Sarna, Jonathan. 2003. "The Question of Music in American Judaism: Reflections at 350 Years." *American Jewish History* 91 (2): 195–203.

———. 2004. *American Judaism: A History.* New Haven, CT: Yale University Press.

Schachter-Shalomi, Zalman. 2003. *First Steps to a New Jewish Spirit: Reb Zalman's Guide to Recapturing the Intimacy & Ecstasy in Your Relationship with God.* Woodstock, VT: Jewish Lights.

Schiller, Benjie-Ellen. 1992. "The Hymnal as an Index of Musical Change in Reform Synagogues." In *Sacred Sound and Social Change: Liturgical Music in Jewish and Christian Experience*, edited by Lawrence A. Hoffman and Janet R. Walton, 187–212. Notre Dame, IN: University of Notre Dame Press.

———. 2005. "The Cantor's Spiritual Challenge: Defining 'Agency' in Prayer." *Journal of Synagogue Music* 30 (1): 59–62.

Schoeps, Julius H., ed. 2000. *Neues Lexikon des Judentums.* Gütersloh, Germany: Gütersloher Verlagshaus.

Schreiber, Baruch David. 1984–85. "The Woman's Voice in the Synagogue." *Journal of Jewish Music and Liturgy* 7:27–32.

Schroeder, Joy A. 2014. *Deborah's Daughters: Gender, Politics and Biblical Interpretation.* Oxford: Oxford University Press.

Schütze, Fritz. 1977. *Die Technik des narrative Interviews in Interaktionsfeldstudien—dargestellt an einem Projekt zur Erforschung von kommunalen Machtstrukturen*. Bielefeld, Germany: Fakultät für Soziologie, University of Bielefeld.

Schwarz, Sidney. 2003. *Finding a Spiritual Home: How a New Generation of Jews Can Transform the American Synagogue*. Woodstock, VT: Jewish Lights.

Schwer, Silvia. 1995. "Auf dem Weg zu einer feministischen Rekonstruktion der Geschichte Israels." In *Feministische Exegese: Forschungsbeiträge zur Bibel aus der Perspektive von Frauen*, edited by Luise Schottroff, Silvia Schroer, and Marie-Therese Wacker, 83–174. Darmstadt, Germany: Primus Verlag.

Sered, Susan. 1992. *Women as Ritual Experts: The Religious Lives of Elderly Jewish Women in Jerusalem*. New York: Oxford University Press.

Setel, Drorah. 1986. "Feminist Reflections on Separation and Unity in Jewish Theology." *Journal of Feminist Studies in Religion* 2 (spring): 113–18.

Shahar, Nathan. 2009. "Hebrew Song, 1880–2000." *Jewish Women: A Comprehensive Historical Encyclopedia*. Jewish Women's Archive. Accessed December 16, 2015. http://jwa.org/encyclopedia/article/hebrew-song-1880-2000.

Shannon, Jonathan H. 2004. "The Aesthetic of Spiritual Practice and the Creation of Moral and Musical Subjectivities in Aleppo, Syria." *Ethnology* 43 (4): 381–91.

Shechinah. 2009. "The Women of MiRaJ." Accessed May 2009. www.shechinah.com/miraj/women.html.

———. 2012a. "MiRaJ." Accessed December 15, 2015.

———. 2012b. "Shabbat Unplugged". Accessed December 16, 2015. http://www.shechinah.com/shabbat-unplugged.html.

———. 2012c. "Tof B'Yada". Accessed December 16, 2015. http://www.shechinah.com/tof-byada.html.

Shelemay, Kay Kaufman. 2009. "The Power of Silent Voices: Women in the Syrian Musical Tradition." In *Music and the Play of Power in the Middle East, North Africa and Central Asia*, edited by Laudan Nooshin, 269–88. Farnham, UK: Ashgate.

Shere, Holy Taya. n.d. "Dayenu / More Than Enough." Accessed December 16, 2015. https://holytaya.bandcamp.com/track/dayenu-more-than-enough.

———. 2015. "Albums." Accessed November 5, 2015. www.holytaya.com/#!music/c46c.

Sheskin, Ira M. and Arnold Dashefsky. 2013. "Jewish Population in the United States, 2013." *American Jewish Yearbook, 2013*. Accessed December 16, 2015. http://www.jewishdatabank.org/Studies/downloadFile.cfm?FileID=3111.

Shondes, The. n.d. Home page. Accessed December 16, 2015. http://www.shondes.com/the-band/.

Siegel, Richard, Michael Strassfield, and Sharon Strassfield, eds. 1973. *The First Jewish Catalogue: A Do-It-Yourself Kit.* 3 vols. Philadelphia: Jewish Publication Society of America.

Sing Out! n.d. "Sing Out! History." Accessed November 1, 2015. http://singout.org/sohistry.html.

Slawek, Stephen M. 1988. "Popular Kirtan in Benares: Some 'Great' Aspects of a Little Tradition." *Ethnomusicology* 32 (2): 77–92.

Slobin, Mark. 1982. *Tenement Songs: The Popular Music of the Jewish Immigrants.* Urbana: University of Illinois Press.

———.1993. *Subcultural Sounds: Micromusics of the West.* Hanover, NH: University Press of New England.

———. 2002. *Chosen Voices: The Story of the American Cantorate.* 1st paperback ed. Urbana: University of Illinois Press.

Smith, Sara. 2012. "The Imahot in the Amidah: A History." *Contemporary Jewry* 32 (3): 309–27.

Solie, Ruth A., ed. 1993. *Musicology and Difference: Gender and Sexuality in Music Scholarship.* Berkeley: University of California Press.

Spencer, Jane. 2004. "Introduction: Genealogies." In *Third Wave Feminism: A Critical Exploration*, edited by Stacy Gillis, Gillian Howie, and Rebecca Munford, 9–12. New York: Palgrave Macmillan.

Spiro, Hannah. 2015. "Bio." Accessed August 28, 2014. www.hannahspiro.com/bio.

Spitzer, Juliet I. n.d. "Juliet I. Spitzer." Accessed October 30, 2015. http://www.julietspitzer.com/.

Starhawk. 1979. *The Spiral Dance: A Rebirth of the Ancient Religion of the Goddess.* San Francisco: Harper and Row.

Staub, Michael E. 2004. Introduction to *The Jewish 1960s: An American Sourcebook,* edited by Michael E. Staub, xv–xxiii. Waltham, MA: Brandeis University Press.

Steinsaltz, Adin. 2000. *Guide to Jewish Prayer.* New York: Schocken.

Summit, Jeffrey. 1993. "'I'm a Yankee Doodle Dandy?' Identity and Melody at an American Simhat Torah Celebration." *Ethnomusicology* 37 (1): 41–62.

———. 2000. *The Lord's Song in Strange Land: Music and Identity in Contemporary Worship.* New York: Oxford University Press.

Suskin, Alana. 2003. "Hearing the Daughter Voice: The *Bat Kol* as Rrrabbi Grrrl." In *Catching a Wave: Reclaiming Feminism for the 21st Century*, edited by Rory Dicker and Alison Piepmeier, 263–78. Boston: Northeastern University Press.

Sweers, Britta. 2005. *Electric Folk: Changing Face of English Traditional Music*. Oxford: Oxford University Press.

Taylor, Timothy D. 1993. "The Gendered Construction of the Musical Self: The Music of Pauline Oliveros." *Musical Quarterly* 77 (3): 385–96.

———. 1997. *Global Pop: World Music, World Markets*. New York: Routledge.

———. 2000. "World Music in Television Ads." *American Music* 18 (2): 162–92.

Tiferet Siegel, Hanna. n.d. "*Eshet Hazon Goes Public as a Model of Empowerment: 25 years later at the ALEPH Kallah.*" Accessed July 2009. http://aleph.dss-demo.com/documents/EshetHazon.pdf.

Umansky, Ellen M., and Dianne Ashton. 1992. "Piety, Persuasion, and Friendship: A History of Jewish Women's Spirituality." In *Four Centuries of Jewish Women's Spirituality: A Sourcebook*, edited by Ellen M. Umansky and Dianne Ashton, 1–36. Boston: Beacon.

URJ Books and Music. n.d. "Sounds Write Production History." Accessed December 16, 2015. https://www.urjbooksandmusic.com/pages.php?pageid=23.

Vallee, Mickey. 2006. "Book Review: 'Music Scenes: Local, Translocal, and Virtual,' ed. by Andy Bennett and Richard A. Peterson (2004), Nashville, TN: Vanderbilt University Press." In *Space and Culture* 9 (4): 468–70.

Walker, Rebecca. 2001. *Black White and Jewish: Autobiography of a Shifting Self.* New York: Riverhead.

———2006. "Becoming the Third Wave." In *The Women's Movement Today: An Encyclopedia of Third-Wave Feminism*, edited by Leslie Heywood, 2:3–5. Westport, CT: Greenwood.

Walton, Janet R. "North American Culture and Its Challenges to Sacred Sound." In *Sacred Sound and Social Change: Liturgical Music in Jewish and Christian Experience*, edited by Lawrence A. Hoffman and Janet R. Walton, 1–8. Notre Dame, IN: University of Notre Dame Press.

Waskow, Arthur. 1982. *Seasons of Our Joy: A Celebration of Modern Jewish Renewal*. New York: Bantam.

Wasserfall, Rahel. 1992. "Menstruation and Identity: The Meaning of Niddah for Moroccan Women Immigrants to Israel." In *People of the Body: Jews and Judaism from an Embodied Perspective*, edited by Howard Eilberg-Schwartz, 309–27. Albany: State University of New York Press.

Wegener, Judith Romney. 1988. *Chattel or Person? The Status of Women in the Mishnah*. Oxford: Oxford University Press.

Weissler, Chava. 2006. "'Women of Vision' in the Jewish Renewal Movement: The Eshet Hazon Ceremony." *Jewish Culture and History* 8 (3): 62–86.

———. 2007. "Meanings of Shekhinah in the 'Jewish Renewal' Movement." In *Women Remaking American Judaism,* edited by Riv-Ellen Prell with a foreword by David Weinberg, 51–82. Detroit, MI: Wayne State University Press.

———. 2013. "Shifting Feminisms in the Jewish Renewal Movement." Paper presented at the 2013 Center for Studies on New Religions conference in Falun, Sweden. Accessed December 15, 2015. http://www.cesnur.org/2013/swe-weissler.doc.

Yofiyah. 2004. "Hebrew Kirtan: Calling to the Divine." Accessed December 16, 2015. http://www.kabbalahkirtan.com/hebkirtanfull.html.

———. 2006. "Kabbalah Kirtan." CD booklet. Boulder, CO: Yofiyah, Sounds True.

Zaidman, Nurit. 1996. "Variations of Jewish Feminism: The Traditional, Modern, and Postmodern Approaches." *Modern Judaism* 16 (1): 47–65.

Zeigler, Robin. 1996. "My Body, My Self and Rosh Chodesh." In *Celebrating the New Moon: A Rosh Chodesh Anthology*, edited by Susan Berrin, 33–39. Northvale, NJ: Jason Aronson.

Zimmermann, Heidy. 2000. *Tora und Shira: Untersuchungen zur Musikauffassung des rabbinischen Judentums*. Bern: Peter Lang.

Zinn, Maxine Baca, and Bonnie Thornton Dill. 1996. "Theorizing Difference from Multiracial Feminism." *Feminist Studies* 22 (2): 321–31.

Zola, Gary P. 2006, "Jewish Camping and Its Relationship to the Organized Camping Movement in America." In *A Place of Our Own: The Rise of Reform Jewish Camping*, edited by Michael M. Lorge and Gary P. Zola, 1–26. Tuscaloosa: University of Alabama Press.

ZoomInfo, 2015. "Hanna Tiferet." Accessed December 16, 2015. http://www.zoominfo.com/p/Hanna-Tiferet/314728080.

Magazine and Newspaper Articles:

Cabot, Vicki. 2000. "Spiritual Chords: Ancient, Modern Melodies Elevate Synagogue Worship." *Jewish News of Greater Phoenix,* May 12.

Cohen, Debra Nussbaum. 1996. "Crossover Dreams: Does Folksinger Debbie Friedman Have the Cure for Our Spiritual Blues?" *Moment*, June 1996, 50–71.

Drusin, Joanna. 2005. "Girl's Night On! & Girls on Film: Catering to the Young Jewish Women." *Blueprint*, July–August 2005, 7.

Josephs, Susan. 1996. "From Shul to Carnegie Hall." *Hadassah,* August–September 1996, 46–47.

Rogat, Janna. 1998. "Journeying with Jewish Music: Debbie Friedman Gives Judaism a New, More Accessible, Melody." *Cleveland Jewish News*, July 17.

Targan, Lynnda Lewis. 1995. "A Woman's World: Miraj Is No Mirage—It Gives Voice to Jewish Feminism." *Jewish Exponent*, December 22, 1995. Accessed December 22, 2015. https://www.highbeam.com/doc/1P1-2379433.html.

Theiner, Manny. 2008. "Jewish Folk-Singer Debbie Friedman Performs at Temple Sinai." *Pittsburgh City Paper*, May 1. Accessed October 28, 2015. www.pittsburghcitypaper.ws/gyrobase/Content?oid=oid%3A45977.

RECORDINGS:

Video

Coppel, Ann, dir. 2003. *A Journey of Spirit: A New Documentary from Ann Coppel*. Seattle, WA: Ann Coppel Productions.

Friedman, Deborah Lynn. n.d.a. "Devorah's Song." Accessed June 2009. www.ruachcd.com/music/5763/devorahs_song.htm.

———. n.d.b. "My Music My Story Part 1." Accessed December 21, 2015. https://www.youtube.com/watch?v=M_G9vFzrU6Q.

Raphael, Geela Rayzel. 2013. "Minyan of Women." Accessed December 16, 2015. www.youtube.com/watch?v=hPwoeoSjHt4.

Rothman, Chana, 2011. "Chana Rothman—World Cafe Live Songwriters Circle - Philadelphia—Ana w/C Lanzbom." Accessed December 16, 2015. https://www.youtube.com/watch?v=1fizBeXrLMo.

Shondes, The. 2010. "The Shondes—I Watched the Temple Fall." Accessed December 16, 2015. https://www.youtube.com/watch?v=woZINwloL6Q.

Yofiyah. 2008. "Hamakom—Kabbalah Kirtan with Yofiyah." Accessed December 16, 2016. https://www.youtube.com/watch?v=TpPyq7ZBphM.

Audio

Alberstein, Chava. 1969. *Yiddish Greatest Hits Volume 1*. Vinyl LP. N.p.: CBS Records 64842.

Azen, Margot Stein. 1991. *Create Out of Nothing*. Compact disc. Philadelphia, PA: Oznaiim Communications OF591CD.

———. 1993. *Guarding the Garden: A Journey from Eden to the Edge*. N.p.: Cassette Tape. New Legends OF 593.

Bikel, Theodore. 1958. *Theodore Bikel Sings Jewish Folk Songs*. Vinyl LP. Israel: Elektra–EKS 7141, Elektra–U-5010.

Friedman, Debbie. 1989. *And You Shall Be a Blessing*. Compact disc. San Diego, CA: Sounds Write Productions SWP 601.

———. 1990. *Live at the Dell: Extended Play Concert Performance*. Compact Disc. San Diego, CA: Sounds Write Productions SWP 607.

———. 1994. *In the Beginning*. Compact disc. San Diego, CA: Sounds Write Productions SWP 600.

———.1997. *The Journey Continues: Ma'yan Passover Haggadah in Song*. Compact disc. San Diego, CA: Sounds Write Productions SWP 614.

———. 1998. *It's You*. Compact disc. San Diego, CA: Sounds Write Productions.

———. 2001. *The Water in the Well*. Compact disc. SISU Home Entertainment, 7417.

———. 2005. *Songs of the Spirit: The Debbie Friedman Anthology*. 2 compact discs. Jewish Music Group.

———. 2006. *One People*. Compact disc. Studio City, CA: Jewish Music Group JMG 18032-2.

Gold, Shefa. 1993. *Tzuri: My Rock*. Cassette tape. Shefa Gold.

———. 1994. *Chants Encounter*. Accessed December 22, 2015. http://www.oysongs.com/products/albums.cfm?artist_id=200&album_id=5441.

———. 1997. *Chanscendence*. Compact disc. Shefa Gold.

———. 2008. *The Majesty of Nurture*. Compact Disc. Shefa Gold WRA8-3065.

Hirschhorn, Linda. 1992. *Roots & Wings*. Compact disc. Berkeley, CA: Oyster Albums, Kehila Productions (BMI).

———. 1998. *Selections of Marcia Falk's Blessings in Song*. Compact disc. Berkeley, CA: Oyster Albums, Kehila Productions (BMI).

———. 2007. *Becoming*. Compact disc. Berkeley, CA: Oyster Albums, Kehila Productions (BMI), OA11110.

———and Fran Avni. 1998. *Selections from Marcia Falk's Blessings in Song*. Compact disc. Berkeley, CA: Oyster Albums, Kehila Productions (BMI).

Hirschhorn, Linda, and Vocolot. 1989. *Gather Round: Songs of Celebration and Renewal*. Compact disc. Berkeley, CA: Oyster Albums, Kehila Productions (BMI).

Klein, Leslie Ginsparg. 2006. *Girls' Night On: Live at the Makor*. Compact Disc. Girls' Night On!

MiRaJ. 1995. *A Moon Note*. Compact disc. Philadelphia, PA: Red Thread Records 608 W.

———. 1999. *Counting Angels in the Wilderness.* Compact disc. Philadelphia, PA: Red Thread Records.
———. 2007. *Healing Chants for the Soul.* Compact disc. Philadelphia, PA: MiRaJ/Radio Active Productions.
Newman, Benjamin. n.d. "Masquerade." MP3 Sound File. Accessed December 16, 2015. www.sccs.swarthmore.edu/users/01/bnewman/songs/music/Masquerade.mp3.
Raphael, Geela Rayzel. c. 1987. *Shechinah Songs.* Undistributed tape recording.
———. 1997. *Bible Babes 'A-Beltin.'* Compact disc. Philadelphia, PA: Rayzel Raphael/Radio Active Productions.
———. 2005. *Friday Night Revived.* Compact disc. Philadelphia, PA: Rayzel Raphael/Radio Active Productions RR6039.
Rosenbloom, Aviva. 2004. *Streams in the Desert.* Compact disc. Independent.
Rothman, Chana. 2007. *We Can Rise.* Compact disc. Oyhoo Records.
Shere, Holy Taya. 2009. *Wild Earth Shebrew.* Compact disc. Portland, OR: CDBaby 700261273143.
Shondes, The. 2007. *The Red Sea.* Compact disc. Portland, OR: CDBaby 616892942627.
Spiro, Hannah. 2010. *Aliyah.* Compact disc. Hannah Spiro 884501324533.
———. 2012. *It Is upon Us.* Compact disc. Hannah Spiro 884501684361.
Spitzer, Juliet I. 1998. *Full Glory: Songs of Hope, Consolation, and Joy.* Compact disc. Bala Cynwyd, PA: Hakol Music.
———. 2005. *Shifting Edge.* Compact disc. Bala Cynwyd, PA: Juliet I. Spitzer.
Tiferet Siegel, Hanna. 1990. *Shir Hadash; Or Shalom–Songs of the Heart.* Cassette tape. Hanna Tiferet.
———. 1995. *Olamama.* Compact disc. Hanna Tiferet Siegel 888295113632.
———. 1998. *A Voice Calls.* Compact disc. Hanna Tiferet Siegel.
Vocolot. 2002. *Heart Beat.* Compact Disc. Berkeley, CA: Oyster Albums, Kehila Productions (BMI) OA 1119.
Yofiyah. 2006. *Kabbalah Kirtan.* Compact disc. Boulder, CO: Yofiyah, Sounds True M1078D.
———. 2010. *OPEN—Kabbalah Kirtan II.* Compact disc. Yofiyah.

INDEX

NOTE: Page references in *italics* refer to photos and musical notation.